# Dwelling places

MANCHESTER
UNIVERSITY PRESS

# Dwelling places

## Postwar black British writing

James Procter

Manchester University Press

Manchester and New York

distributed exclusively in the USA by Palgrave

The right of James Procter to be identified as the author of this work has been asserted by him in accordance with the Copyright, Designs and Patents Act 1988.

*Published by* Manchester University Press
Oxford Road, Manchester M13 9NR, UK
*and* Room 400, 175 Fifth Avenue, New York, NY 10010, USA
www.manchesteruniversitypress.co.uk

*Distributed exclusively in the USA by*
Palgrave, 175 Fifth Avenue, New York,
NY 10010, USA

*Distributed exclusively in Canada by*
UBC Press, University of British Columbia, 2029 West Mall,
Vancouver, BC, Canada V6T 1Z2

*British Library Cataloguing-in-Publication Data*
A catalogue record for this book is available from the British Library

*Library of Congress Cataloging-in-Publication Data applied for*

ISBN 0 7190 6053 2 *hardback*
       0 7190 6054 0 *paperback*

First published 2003

11 10 09 08 07 06 05 04 03      10 9 8 7 6 5 4 3 2 1

Typeset in Minion and Rotis display
by Koinonia, Manchester
Printed in Great Britain
by Biddles Ltd, Guildford and King's Lynn

# Contents

List of illustrations                *page* vi

Acknowledgements                viii

1   Introduction                1

2   Dwelling places                21

3   The street                69

4   Suburbia                125

5   The north                160

6   Conclusion: train stations and travel bags          202

Select bibliography                211

Index                220

# Illustrations

1 'The shebeen' (E. Huxley, *Back Street New Worlds,* London: Chatto, 1964). © Rogers, Coleridge and White  *page* 29

2 *Race Today* cartoon, February 1973 (*Race Today* Publications)  70

3 Horace Ove, *Pressure,* 1974 (*Black Film/British Cinema,* ICA Document 7, London: ICA, 1988) (Institute of Contemporary Arts)  71

4 *Race Today* carnival drawings, July/August 1978 (*Race Today* Publications)  73

5 'The village in the sky', *Race Today,* July 1971 (*Race Today* Publications)  83

6 C. Laird, 'Song treads one and two' (*Savacou,* 9/10, 'Writing away from home', 1974)  89

7 'The Mangrove protest' (*Savacou,* 9/10, 'Writing away from home', 1974)  90

8 Amrit and Rabindra Singh, 'The Last Supper', 1994/5 (The Singh Twins: Amrit and Rabindra Kaur Singh, twinstudio@hotmail.com)  131

9 Amrit and Rabindra Singh, 'Indian summer at Dhigpal Nivas', 1994/5 (The Singh Twins: Amrit and Rabindra Kaur Singh, twinstudio@ hotmail. com)  132

10 Bradford, 'Living in the past', 1994 (National Museum of Photography Film and Television, Bradford Council, Simon Warner Photography, Camera Crew)  173

11 Bradford, 'We've got the lot', 1994 (National Museum of Photography Film and Television, Bradford Council, Simon Warner Photography, Camera Crew)  177

12 *Bradford Travel Manual, 1995* (National Museum of Photography Film and Television, Bradford Council, Simon Warner Photography, Camera Crew)  178

13 Ingrid Pollard, 'Pastoral interludes', 1984 (Ingrid Pollard)  182

14 Ingrid Pollard, 'Pastoral interludes', 1984 (Ingrid Pollard)  183

15 Ingrid Pollard, 'Pastoral interludes', 1984 (Ingrid Pollard)  184

16 Ingrid Pollard, 'Pastoral interludes', 1984 (Ingrid Pollard)  185

17 Ingrid Pollard, 'Pastoral interludes', 1984 (Ingrid Pollard)  186

18 Bradford, 'A surprising place', 1990s (National Museum of Photography Film and Television, Bradford Council, Simon Warner Photography, Camera Crew)  196

19  'New arrivals at Victoria Station', 1956 (Hulton Getty)                    203
20  'New arrivals at Victoria Station', 1956 (Hulton Getty)                    204
21  'Travel bags: "Rooms to let"' (Hulton Getty)                              206
22  'Travel bags: unpacking suitcases at Clapham Shelter' (Hulton Getty)      207
23  'Travel bags: in search of accommodation'                                 208

# Acknowledgements

This book began life as a Ph.D. thesis at the University of Leeds (1994–98). I am grateful to the School of English for their support (both financial and intellectual) during those years. I'd like to thank my examiners, John McLeod and Paul Gilroy, for their time, their questions and suggestions, which were a great help when I came to revise and rethink the text. My supervisor David Richards was an enthusiastic and stimulating presence throughout the writing of the thesis and I'm extremely grateful for his support. Marcus Wood, Alison Donnell and Alex Tickell have all offered insightful criticism on this project at various stages. Matthew Frost at Manchester University Press has made the practical aspects of producing this book a pleasure and I thank him for his help, humour and patience. My new friends, colleagues and students in the Department of English Studies at the University of Stirling have been a vital support over the last three years. Thanks most of all to Kathryn, my parents and my brother, who have had to share my anxieties concerning this project for the last seven years.

Finally, in a book about the politics of location, I must also acknowledge the influence of a particular place, my birthplace: Bradford. I 'arrived' in this city at the start of the 1970s, after South Asian settlement had transformed its geography for good. It was a growing sense of the differences between this local, familiar landscape and the metropolitan migrant literature, criticism and theory I encountered 'away' at university that provided the single most important context for this study.

# 1

# Introduction

## Devolving black Britain

You have to live in London. If you come from the sticks, the colonial sticks, where you really want to live is right on Eros Statue in Piccadilly Circus. You don't want to go and live in someone else's metropolitan sticks. You want to go right to the centre of the hub of the world. You might as well. You have been hearing about that ever since you were one month old. (Stuart Hall)[1]

I suppose at the end of the day I want to say that some of us were born here, some of us are struggling to come to terms with our ambiguous, incomplete and subordinate experience of Englishness – at the same time as we connect ourselves to black histories elsewhere and yet also recognise the emptiness of national identities as such. None of us has a monopoly on black authenticity. (Paul Gilroy)[2]

This book explores some of the key dwelling places of black British writing and culture across the postwar period. Basements and bedsits, streets and cafés, the suburbs and the city are recurrent locations within black literary discourse of the past fifty years. Yet at stake in what follows is more than an imaginative geography. *Dwelling Places* offers an analysis of black cultural production in which literary locations are themselves historically and geographically *located* in relation to the shifting postwar British landscape.

The four chapters below seek to extend existing work within black British literary and cultural studies on identity politics to consider the politics of location. Despite the increasingly sophisticated debates over the category 'black' (as an ontological sign of both difference and *différance*) in recent accounts of black British culture, 'Britain', the material site at which these identities are played out, has tended to remain a stable bland monolith, a singularly undifferentiated setting.[3] The proliferation of difference that has seen black re-energised and rendered multiple has left Britain a homogeneous unified flatland, as if it is somehow the same to be black in London as it is in Llandudno.

*New ethnicities* `(handwritten in left margin)`

Despite revelations concerning the constructedness of black subjectivity in the 1980s, there is still a sense of a genuine *place* of black expression, a sense that certain venues are more authentic than others. Part of the project of this book is to consider the role place plays in black British cultural production. If, as Stuart Hall convincingly argues, the 'originality' of cultural formations since the mid 1980s 'is precisely that they tell the black experience as an *English* experience', then what, for example, is black *Englishness?* What differences does it contain, and how does it differ from black Welshness, Scottishness, Irishness or Britishness?[4]

In the epigraphs above both Stuart Hall and Paul Gilroy make it clear they are speaking as black Englanders, and, more specifically, black Londoners. This particular geographical focus testifies to the hegemonic status of these locations within black cultural debate more generally. Yet the ease with which the precise positions of these two commentators gets incorporated into accounts of black *British* culture speaks of a broader series of elisions and blurrings. At a one-day conference on black British writing held at Dundee in November 2001, several of the participants expressed concern about the repeated slippage in papers and plenary sessions between 'English' and 'British'.[5] Given the post-devolution context in which the conference took place and from which many of the contemporary writings being discussed there emerged, the need to account for such slippages becomes increasingly important. In *Devolving English Literature* Robert Crawford argues that such gaps in post-colonial criticism

> reached the point of absurdity in 1997 when, only two months before the election which brought to power a British government committed to devolution ... Homi Bhabha with the British Council presented a major conference-cum-festival called *Re-Inventing Britain* ...
>
> Incredibly, the project contained nothing whatsoever about the devolution debate, or how the changing relationships between Scotland, England, and Wales, not to mention Ireland, might contribute to 're-inventing Britain'. Such an omission seems to me highly significant, and suggests much about the blind-spots in postcolonial criticism as well as a continuing institutional awkwardness about the treatment of 'British culture' or sometimes, more honestly, 'British cultures.'[6]

Although Crawford does not himself attend to the blind-spots he identifies, focusing entirely on white English, Scots and Irish literature, the point he makes is a significant one. Such debates about the politics of location and nationality, it will be argued below, have been neglected because of the deterritorialising tendencies of diaspora discourse, in which issues of dislocation and transnationalism have dominated the agenda. The growing calls for political autonomy across the United Kingdom's different national communities, the rise of Welsh and Scottish nationalism and escalating violence in Northern Ireland serve to highlight widening discrepancies across Britain's supposedly homogeneous national landscape in the late twentieth and early twenty-first centuries. Even within England the notion of 'two nations – the affluent, silicon South and the once-Industrial North where the impact of structural unemployment has been greatest' remains a key imagined geography.[7] While these discrepancies rarely feature in accounts of black cultural production, events such as the so-called 'northern riots' in Bradford, Burnley and Oldham in 2001 or the murder of the Kurdish asylum-seeker in Glasgow's Sighthill in the same year signal the need to attend to local and regional differences. Meanwhile, Home Secretary David Blunkett's drive to instil a sense of *national* citizenship across Britain's diverse ethnic communities speaks of desire to silence these regional differences through what is beginning to look like a nostalgic, Thatcherite appeal to 'one nation'.[8]

By dwelling on a range of territories across the national landscape from the rooms occupied by the early pioneer settlers in London to the landscapes of northern England and, finally, Scotland, this book examines the limits of a dislocated diaspora poetics and the possibilities of a situated reading of postwar black British writing. In doing so, it pursues an increasingly differentiated, *devolved* cultural geography of black Britain over the past fifty years. Black literary and cultural narratives of the 1950s and 1960s ritually focus on a central, 'tourist' London that includes Piccadilly Circus, Hyde Park and Trafalgar Square. Writing of the 1970s and early 1980s on the other hand, announces a tangible shift outward, away from the monumental landscape of the metropolis to the surrounding inner-city venues of Southall, Brixton, Notting Hill. It was around such black enclaves that a highly territorial, politicised black identity came to be structured in the 1970s and early 1980s. From the mid-1980s an increasingly non-metropolitan literature, outside the capital of London, becomes available, opening up a range of 'provincial', suburban and rural geographies. Of course this is in no sense a template for black literary and cultural production since 1945, which could never be neatly, or schematically confined to the temporal and spatial boundaries set here. Nevertheless the general movement it outlines is a significant one, announcing increasingly diverse, contradictory articulations of black *Britain*. Black British writing has not been satisfactorily 'placed' in relation to the landscapes and discourses within and alongside which it has been produced, disseminated and consumed. Part of the reason for this prolonged critical neglect of place has to do with the 'placelessness' of those post-national, post-colonial diasporic vocabularies and frameworks currently being used to 'describe' black cultural production.

Postwar post-colonial migration to England in the 1950s and 1960s amounted to more than the abandonment of 'home', or to an ontological condition of 'homelessness'. It also involved a desperate territorial struggle *for* home within the context of housing shortages and the overtly racialised 'colour bar' surrounding domestic space. Chapter 2 charts in detail the white imagination of black housing over the early postwar period, before exploring it as a recurring figure within 'pioneer' West Indian fictions. The basements and bedsits of these early narratives, it is argued, constitute a pre-eminent dwelling place in postwar writing at which the struggle over and for local territory is articulated.

Chapter 3 focuses on an unlikely site of dwelling: the street. Tracing the emergence and transformation of black pedestrian rhetorics across the postwar period, it moves from the 1950s *flâneur* to the postmodern 'nomad' of late twentieth-century writing. The chapter concentrates on the 1970s when black Britons found themselves increasingly criminalised on and policed off the street. To 'loiter' or hang about in this context became a subversive mode of occupying pedestrian space.

Chapter 4 considers the possibilities of suburbia as a symbolic venue within contemporary writing. It reads the suburbs not as a diasporic border of itinerant crossings but as a stubbornly isolated locale, distinct from the multicultural spaces of the city. Focusing on the work of Meera Syal and Hanif Kureishi, it considers the implications of suburbia for a 'provincial' black British experience, self-consciously detached from the sophisticated cosmopolitanism of the city.

Chapter 5 pursues the move away from the metropolis to consider the place of the north and a regional black British discourse. The focal point of this exploration will be Bradford, a city that has become a key symbolic site within racial discourse since the 1990s.[9] Following an account of Bradford's re-imagination of itself as a heritage site and tourist venue in the aftermath of the 'Rushdie Affair', this chapter closes with a consideration of recent black British travel writing. The focus here is not on the transatlantic travels of Caryl Phillips, Salman Rushdie and V.S. Naipaul, but a more kitsch, working-class tourism that takes in Butlin's, Blackpool and the Lake District.

## 'Black': a brief British history

To use Britain as the sustaining site for an exploration of black culture is not to exhaust what it means to be 'black'. As Gilroy's epigraph suggests, the nation does not provide the borders of black experience.[10] However, since the late 1980s there has been an increasing recognition among black British intellectuals and artists of the need to engage with what it means to be 'born here' as Gilroy puts it. Of course this kind of recognition, what Jim Pines identifies in terms of filmic discourse over the 1980s as a shift from being '"black in Britain" to being "black" and "British"' cannot be reduced to an intellectual or artistic 'moment' in the late twentieth century. It involves a much more radical deconstruction of the idea that 'blacks are an external problem, an alien presence visited on Britain from the outside'.[11] 'Britain' is constituted by a black experience that supposedly lies beyond its shores, as the following autobiographical aside by Stuart Hall makes clear:

> People like me who came to England in the 1950s have been there for centuries; symbolically, we have been there for centuries. I was coming home. I am the sugar at the bottom of the English cup of tea. I am the sweet tooth, the sugar plantation that rotted generations of English children's teeth. There are thousands of others beside me that are, you know, the cup of tea itself. Because they don't grow it in Lancashire, you know. Not a single tea plantation exists within the United Kingdom. This is the symbolisation of English identity – I mean, what does everybody know about an English person, except that they can't get through the day without a cup of tea? Where does it come from? Ceylon – Sri Lanka, India. That is the outside history that is inside the history of the English. There is no English history without that other history.[12]

Empire brought Britain and its black communities together long before the Nationality Act of 1948 prompted mass migration to Britain from its colonies and former colonies.[13] Within this context any analysis of postwar Britain needs to give careful consideration, not just to the terms 'black' and 'British' but to the complex relationship between them.

As a positive label of racial pride, 'black' did not emerge as a category internal to the British nation, but was imported from America during the new social movements of the 1960s and 1970s. However, if 'black' is increasingly recognised as a dispersed, diasporic signifier, then it does also have a locally accented history, peculiar to Britain. There are crucial differences in the etymologies of 'black' in the United States and the United Kingdom. 'Black' in the US has conventionally referred to a particular 'racial' community (African-American). However in the UK,

Kobena Mercer argues, 'the racializing code of "color" is put *under erasure*'. In the British context 'black' has been translated as a 'political, rather than racial, category', an 'achievement' that is 'specific and unique to British conditions':[14]

> Throughout the seventies and eighties, the rearticulation of this term [black] as an inclusive political identity based on alliances among Asian, African and Caribbean peoples, brought together in shared struggles against racism in Britain, has helped to challenge and displace common assumptions about 'blackness' as a fixed or essential identity. (81)

Within the racially hostile context of the 1970s and early 1980s 'black' was a label adopted by settlers of African and Asian descent in order to articulate an alliance, a collective stand against racism in Britain. As Gilroy puts it, 'despite their differences' the 'Afro-Caribbean ancillary in a hospital and the hip-hopping Asian youth of West London may all discover within that colour a medium through which to articulate their own experiences and make sense of their common exclusion from Britain and Britishness'.[15]

While the inclusive nature of 'black' in the 1970s offered a way of overcoming cultural 'differences', it also led to the suppression of difference in presenting a united front against racism. 'Black' was forced to conceal and perpetuate a range of inequalities and tensions internal to the imagined community it drew together. If the label was politically successful in bringing about an alliance and exchange between Britain's different migrant communities, then this conversation was often uneven and one-sided. Cultural and political expression by a diverse range of ethnicities tended to get subsumed beneath a hegemonic male (and masculine) African-Caribbean discourse in this period. The result was that feminist, South Asian and queer discourses were frequently marginalised in the 1970s and early 1980s.[16]

## Blackness and the 'burden of representation'

These shifts in the signification and value of 'black' are crucial to an understanding of black artistic production over the same period because they are bound up with the politics of *representation*. The late 1980s witnessed a radical re-interrogation of notions of a 'unified' black community as a new set of theoretical agendas began to accumulate towards the end of what became termed a 'critical decade'.[17] The 1980s were critical both in the sense that they were crucial to shifts in black modes of representation, as well as critically self-consciousness about those shifts.

In January 1987 the conflicting responses of three of Britain's most influential cultural commentators, Salman Rushdie, Stuart Hall and Darcus Howe, were published in *The Guardian*. Their divided opinion, part of a wider ongoing debate, was centred on two films: the Black Audio Film Collective's *Handsworth Songs* (1987) and Sankofa's *The Passion of Remembrance* (1986). However, at stake in these debates were larger issues concerning the politics of representation and interpretation. In his attack on Rushdie's review of *Handsworth Songs*, Hall takes issue with Rushdie's claim that documentary film represents "'the wrong language" in a way which seems to assume that his songs are not only different but better, presumably because they don't deal with all that dreary stuff about riots and the police etc.'.[18]

This debate is not significant only because it points to a critical disagreement from within the black community and the destabilisation of 'black' as a singular or consensual category. It is significant also because it prompted a much larger inquiry into that very process of destabilisation which was initiated in Hall's seminal essay, 'New ethnicities'. Returning to the *Guardian* debate in this essay, Hall reiterates his concern with the 'critical innocence' that allowed Rushdie to suggest that 'we all know what good films are': 'I no longer believe we can resolve the questions of aesthetic value by the use of these transcendental, canonical cultural categories.'[19] In turn Hall advocates a politics of representation which refuses 'to represent the black experience in Britain as monolithic, self-contained, sexually stabilised, and always "right on" – in a word, always and only positive or what Hanif Kureishi has called "cheering fictions"'.[20]

It is significant, given the hegemonic African Caribbean blackness of the 1970s and early 1980s, that Hall enlists Kureishi in support of his notion of a decentred, destabilised black Britishness. A British-born writer whose mother is white, whose father is Pakistani, and whose work regularly deals with queer sexualities, Kureishi is used by Hall to exemplify a shift away from earlier, monolithic notions of blackness towards the new ethnicities of the late 1980s and 1990s.

While 'black' was placed under critical scrutiny in the late 1980s, it has not been abandoned as a cultural and political category in black British cultural studies. As Hall has argued:

> despite the fact that efforts are being made to give this 'black' identity a single or unified content, it continues to exist as an identity alongside a range of differences. Afro-Caribbean and Indian people continue to maintain different cultural traditions. 'Black' is thus an example, not only of the *political* character of new identities – i.e. their *positional* and conjunctural

character (their formation in and for specific times and places) – but also of
the way identity and difference are inextricably articulated or knitted
together in different identities, the one never wholly obliterating the other.[21]

The term 'black' as it is used in this text is not intended to replace or
subsume the ethnicities 'Caribbean' and 'South Asian'. Rather it is used as
an additional term 'alongside' them both in order to signal points of
linkage or articulation, 'their positional and conjunctural character'.
Since the late 1980s 'black' has been evoked less as a 'racial' or biological
sign then as an imagined community and ethnicity. It is called upon to
draw attention to its own constructedness, its potential as a *constitutive*,
rather than a reflexive formation. 'Black' is forced to register difference in
this context as it becomes what Paul Gilroy, via Volosinov, calls 'a
necessarily multi-accentual sign'.[22]

At stake in the debates above is an internalisation of those points of
conflict and contestation traditionally defining black Britishness. This
does not signal a retreat from the politics of racism 'out there', rather it
recognises that any offensive or 'front' needs to be accompanied by a
critical self-referentiality if 'black' is to survive as a viable political formation. Within this context there has been an increasing emphasis on those
internal differences – gender, generation, sexuality, ethnicity, religion –
that 'black' *articulates*. (Significantly, and surprisingly, location and class
have been neglected as sites of internal difference within these debates, a
fact which *Dwelling Places* seeks to redress.) Black cultural production of
the late twentieth and early twenty-first century sees a shift away from an
oppositional politics polarising 'black minorities' and white mainstream
culture. One of the most dramatic, if critically unspoken, consequences
of this shift is that the difference between inside and outside, black and
white, become unstable as the boundary conditions of the black imagined
community are recognised as porous and hazy. If 'black' in the 1970s and
early 1980s was typically defined in opposition to a white, Anglo-Saxon
Britishness that existed outside it, then since the late 1980s, at least, this
has been recognised as an untenable position.

Hall's 'New ethnicities' argues that 'black' does not refer to a given,
authentic subjectivity, but to a discursively constructed category, which
challenges the essentialist identifications of the 1970s. In doing so Hall
articulates, for the first time, a crucial transformation in the 'burden of
representation' over the postwar period.[23] His analysis focuses on what he
tentatively identifies as a shift in black cultural politics emerging in the
mid- to late 1980s. Hall is keen to stress that this 'moment' does not
constitute a break, or watershed, but the point at which an earlier black

politics is displaced as opposed to replaced. At the same time, the essay does go on to make a number of significant distinctions between the two. The first phase, which we might take to characterise the period covered in Chapter 3 (the 1970s and early 1980s), saw an appropriation of 'black' as 'the organising category of a new politics of resistance' (27). The second, which emerged in the late 1980s, saw 'the end of the innocent notion of the essential black subject' and a 'recognition that "black" is essentially a politically and culturally constructed category, which cannot be grounded in a set of fixed transcultural or transcendental categories and which therefore has no guarantees in Nature' (28).

Building on these debates, critics such as Isaac Julien and Kobena Mercer have worked to elaborate on the implications of new ethnicities for black artistic production more generally. Particularly useful is their attention to the fraught relationship between representation as a mode of narrative depiction and representation as a process of political or institutional delegation:

> Where access and opportunities are rationed, so that black films tend to be made only one-at-a-time, each film text is burdened with an inordinate pressure to be 'representative' and to act, as a delegate does, as a statement that 'speaks' for black communities as a whole ...
>
> Marginality circumscribes the enunciative modalities of black film as cinematic discourse and imposes a double bind on black subjects who speak in the public sphere.[24]

Julien and Mercer note that, within black cultural production, delegation has traditionally been the central problematic. However, they suggest that those factors constraining representation (as delegation) in the 1970s and early 1980s have been gradually dismantled in recent years: '... as various "marginal" practices (black British film, for instance) are becoming demarginalized at a time when "centred" discourses of cultural authority ... are becoming increasingly decentred and destabilized.'[25]

The discursive shift outlined by Mercer and Julien has clear ramifications for the dominant aesthetics of black British literary production over the same period. As Chapter 3 argues, realism was the prevailing mode of artistic representation in the 1970s and early 1980s owing to larger political pressures which required black art to be 'representative' in order to 'correct' dominant stereotypes and to 'inform, agitate and mobilise political action'. The 'modernism' (as Mercer and Julien call it) emerging in artistic production since the mid-1980s freed up the 'enunciative modalities' of black representation as the burden of delegation from the previous decade lifted.[26]

## Literary into cultural studies, or from realism to modernism

This book considers the implications of these shifting politics of black representation for an understanding of literary production. The debates outlined above have taken place not within studies of black British culture generally but within black British *cultural studies* in particular. Moreover black British cultural studies has (for what were at the time good reasons) neglected the role of literature within black cultural politics, privileging instead, a wide range of popular black cultural production (including film, photography, music and style) instead.[27] As John Frow has argued:

> The exclusion of the literary from cultural studies in favour of devalued practices of popular culture was a strategic delimitation of the field against an older and more prestigious discipline which was perceived to be deeply committed to a fetishized object of study. But there is no reason of principle why this exclusion should continue to be sustained, and the time has now perhaps come for a rapprochement in which literary studies would learn to attend in a more routine manner to the social relations of signification, and cultural studies would in its turn be reminded of the constitution of its major explanatory categories in practices of reading.[28]

Where black British cultural studies has tended to exclude literary discourse, literary studies has failed to properly register black British writing's 'social relations'. For example, the implications of the political character of blackness identified above by Mercer, Hall and Gilroy have not been properly pursued in relation to literature.[29] References to black British writing within English studies are still generally restricted to African and Caribbean writing, while South Asian cultural production tends to be viewed as a discrete cultural category. This compartmentalisation of cultural production perhaps signals the influence of African-American literary studies, in relation to which black British writing has tended to be seen as subordinate.[30] Of course such divisions also allow for a more nuanced consideration of Britain's different ethnic communities and a consideration of what Hall calls 'the internal frontlines which cut through and bisect so-called black British identity',[31] and are not in themselves necessarily problematic. However, the absence of similar attempts to consider Asian and African-Caribbean literature collectively as a *community* of black writings also speaks of a critical reluctance to engage with the *political, positional* history of that cultural production as well as its rhetorical and intertextual relations. This book works toward the kind of rapprochement identified by Frow above. It explores what

*Not that I will be talking about 1970 →*
*Lit → political Shift in Lit.*
Introduction                                                                        11

cultural studies' attention to the wider social relations of discourse has to offer a study of black British writing and what literature contributes to the existing debates on popular cultural forms within black British cultural studies.

*Dwelling Places* locates a range of African-Caribbean and South Asian writing within the broader political context of postwar black British history in order to consider the possibilities of these social relations. Chapter 2 focuses on the 1950s and 1960s and the years before 'black' had emerged as communal signifier. Chapter 3 explores the 1970s and early 1980s when 'black' began to articulate African-Caribbean and South Asian experience for the first time. It considers how the burden of representation impacted on literary production of the period to produce a realist aesthetics privileging 'transparency', 'immediacy' and 'authenticity'. Chapters 4 and 5 on the other hand, concentrate on contemporary cultural production since late 1980s, as the essential, 'right-on' black subject of the 1970s was destabilised and realism was displaced by increasingly experimental self-consciousness.

While tracing the general shifts in black politics and black representation across the postwar period, each chapter offers sustained readings of individual writers and texts, from George Lamming and Sam Selvon in the 1950s to the more recent work of Hanif Kureishi and Meera Syal in the 1990s. This means that none of the chapters in this book can claim to be 'representative'. The first half of the book privileges cultural production by male Caribbean writers in Britain, an artistic community central to the constitution of 'black' as a political signifier. The second half concentrates on British South Asian literature which, it will be argued, has been central to the destabilisation of blackness since the late 1980s. While this framework arguably reproduces some of the silences and inequalities of the signifier 'black' across the postwar period, it also allows a consideration of what the 'imagined community' black Britain might offer to an understanding of these writings as a collective body of cultural production. This comparative approach seeks to disrupt the 'canonical' status accorded many of the literary figures associated with this field of writing – Salman Rushdie, Ben Okri, V.S. Naipaul – which encourages a fetishisation of the individual author and a move from the specific to the universal. It argues for example that a reading of an 'exemplary' novel like *The Satanic Verses* benefits from a knowledge of local black politics in the 1980s, even as it appears to 'transcend' those politics.

## Dwelling and diaspora

*Where do you come from?*
'Here,' I said, 'Here. These parts.' (Jackie Kay)[32]

Once travelling is foregrounded as a cultural practice then dwelling, too, needs to be reconceived. (James Clifford)[33]

To read black Britain in terms of a series of territories or dwelling places is straight away to contradict the logic of diaspora discourse, which has tended to foreground the deterriorialised, itinerant nature of migrant cultures. It is this tension between dwelling and diaspora that *Dwelling Places* seeks to elaborate upon. Part of the project of this book is to take stock of the rhetoric employed by diaspora critics at a time when it risks becoming naturalised and non-negotiable.[34] The aim here is *not* to dispute the very real contributions of diaspora discourse but rather to extend research in the area by thinking more critically about the conditions and vocabularies that that discourse embraces at a time when it risks becoming 'common sense'. On one level the four chapters that follow are attempts to intervene in, and interrupt, the logic of diaspora thinking: reintroducing and supplementing its 'travelling theories' with an investigation into the cultural politics of 'dwelling'.

These issues demand careful consideration when considering a specific diaspora community such as black Britain.[35] Black Britain has been at the forefront of many of the recent debates in diaspora discourse and is (or has been) 'home' to some of the subject's leading commentators: Avtar Brah, Paul Gilroy, Stuart Hall, Kobena Mercer, Homi Bhabha. Moreover, the extent to which an international community of diaspora scholars have been informed by black British cultural production is notable.[36] The concept of diaspora was central to the destabilisation of 'black' as an essentialist category outlined above. As Stuart Hall notes in 'New ethnicities', a 'process of cultural diaspora-ization' has become increasingly prevalent within black British artistic production since the mid-1980s, producing a diaspora aesthetic that privileges 'unsettling, recombination, hybridisation and 'cut-and-mix'.[37] Yet this aesthetic has often entailed a forgetting of Stuart Hall's crucial point, made within his influential essay 'Cultural identity and diaspora': 'If this paper seems preoccupied with the diaspora experience and its narratives of displacement, it is worth remembering that all discourse is "placed", and the heart has its reasons.'[38]

One of the crucial contributions of diaspora discourse, is its recognition of black Britain's condition as a 'hybrid' (as Bhabha would call it) or 'syncretic' (as Gilroy would call it) formation that 'necessitate[s] a twofold approach, both intranational and outernational'.[39] At the same time, if, as I will suggest, diaspora communities have been largely seen as detached from the local, material landscapes in which they have 'settled', then staying with such landscapes might be important. The regional and national landscapes of Britain have not simply been eroded or deterritorialised within black British cultural production during the post-war period. On the contrary, the chapters that follow reveal locale as an increasingly prominent and nuanced signifier.

The word 'diaspora' can be traced back to the Greek *diaspeiran* (disperse), from *dia* (over, through) and *speiren* (sow, scatter). Its etymology privileges a rhetoric of journeying in which '*movement* can provide an alternative to the sedentary poetics of either blood or soil'.[40] As Avtar Brah observes in *Cartographies of Diaspora*: 'At the heart of the notion of diaspora is the image of the journey'.[41] Once referring specifically to the dispersal of the Jews, the rapid acceleration in mass movements, migrations and in global technologies over the late twentieth and early twenty-first centuries has seen the geographical and conceptual horizons of the term pushed back. Diaspora is becoming an increasingly *diasporic* concept, the buzzword for a whole range of cultural formations in which it has come to be seen as 'the exemplary condition of late modernity'.[42] The proliferation of a diverse body of new journals, survey studies, monographs and articles since the late 1980s and 1990s confirms something of the ambitious new terrain of the term.[43] Today 'diaspora' evokes a plethora of global migrations: not just Jewish, but Romanian, Indian, African, 'black', Sikh, Irish, Lebanese, Palestinian, Vietnamese, Korean and so on. A corresponding expansion in the conceptual horizons of the term has also taken place, with a growing interest in the vocabularies of liminality, border, itinerancy, dislocation, hybridity. This at a time when, within cultural analysis more generally, 'metaphors of travel … home, displacement, of borders and crossings, have become exceptionally widespread'.[44] Deleuze and Guattari's influential concepts 'deterritorialisation', 'rhizome' and 'nomadology' are instructive here.[45] Such concepts, themselves dislocated from their precise philosophical contexts, have been used to draw attention to the 'diasporicity' not only of migrant culture but of 'culture' more generally. This new terminology, particularly within academic fields such as English studies and cultural studies, has contributed to a wider sense of subjectivity as decentred, uprooted, dispersed, mobile. Significant here is the extent to which diaspora has become an increasingly *figurative* concept associated as much with a multiplying series of travelling metaphors and tropes as with any particular, referential community or geography.[46] As Krishna-swamy has noted, 'The metaphorization of postcolonial migrancy is becoming so overblown, overdetermined and amorphous as to repudiate any meaningful specificity of historical location or interpretation.'[47]

Dwelling, which is used in this book as both a noun (a house, a home, a territory) and a verb (to linger, to settle, to stay), would appear an inappropriate figure to evoke within the context of an epistemological framework that singles out movement and migration. Diaspora discourse, as the quotation from James Clifford suggests, has prioritised travel over, and at the expense of, dwelling.[48] The implication here is that dwelling is somehow 'outside' travel; it is travel's Other. In contrast, this book argues that dwelling constitutes a kind of para-site, *within* travel.[49] As Clifford goes on to argue, dwelling should 'no longer [be conceived as] the ground from which traveling departs, and to which it returns'.[50] The two terms are mutually constitutive.

Diaspora, as Avtar Brah has pointed out, signifies not simply dispersal but dispersal *from*.[51] The term paradoxically retains the sense of a 'centre', nation, locality, territory (that is homogeneous, indigenous, 'settled') *from* which communities migrate. Returning to the etymology of diaspora: 'sowing' and 'scattering' cannot be said to be uncontaminated by a 'sedentary poetics'. To sow is not simply to disperse, it is also to deposit, it involves an act of plantation and presumes a ground, land, soil, territory or 'field'. To put it another way, the etymology of diaspora suggests both routes (scattering) and roots (sowing). Diaspora in this sense is inseparable from, and dependant upon, dwelling.[52] A deconstruction of the concept 'diaspora' provides a means of returning to the politics of place, location and territory within diaspora literature – a politics that too often gets endlessly deferred within its journeying metaphors.

Travelling rhetorics tend to underplay the extent to which diaspora is also an issue of *settlement* and a constant battle over territories: over housing and accommodation, over the right to occupy a neighbourhood, over the right to 'stay put'. Movement, dislocation and dispersal are not the only, or even the dominant, experiences or strategies of diasporas. To be part of a diaspora community you do not have to have *travelled somewhere*. *Dwelling Places* works to raise questions over the deterritorialising tendencies of diaspora discourse and the ways in which it has tended to evoke a 'non-place-based solidarity' that situates migrant subjectivities outside locality, region and nation.[53]

While diasporas certainly represent a challenge to the nation-state, this book remains sceptical of the ability of diaspora communities to transcend national or territorial frameworks, however desirable that possibility might be. The collective commitment to the creation of a homeland within the Sikh (Khalistan) and Zionist (Israel) diasporas, or the etymology of *muhajir* within Islamic culture, are telling within this context.[54] Indeed there is evidence to suggest that the diasporisation of culture has seen a resurgence of national and territorial sentiments. To equate the rise of transnational movements with the erasure of locality, regionality and nationality seems to me to be premature in this context. Diaspora has not seen a straightforward recession of the nation-state. On the contrary, the rise in diasporic formations has witnessed a sustained reinvestment in such categories.[55] Equally, the national landscape of Britain is more than simply a nodal location within a global matrix of travel; it is also a dwelling place that has been home to a 'sedentary' black British experience. The perhaps unfashionable notion of Britain as, on one level, the *terminus* of a black diaspora, becomes increasingly difficult to ignore as that youthful community of post-1948 settlers moves towards old age and black Britain enters the museum (a 'point of entry' that will be taken up in the conclusion to this book).[56]

By focusing on dwelling, this text is not calling for a return to the privileged 'organic' units of community and culture, themselves, as Vijay Mishra points out, 'imaginary'.[57] Nor does it propose a xenophobic return to some mythic notion of a watertight nation-state. Within this text, dwelling and dwelling places are not fixed, monolithic, rooted or absolute acts or locations, but are themselves conditional and contingent. The focus on a range of dwelling places across the chapters of this book, from the basements of central London to the suburbs and beyond, also puts into operation a particular *journey*, suggesting that the imagination of black British settlement is itself by no means 'settled' across the postwar period. Moreover, *Dwelling Places* argues that specific modes of travel within these settings – walking in the street, commuting in the suburbs, travelling in the country – are in themselves markers of dwelling. For example to commute, Chapter 4 argues, is not just to criss-cross the city; it is also a geographically specific mode of transport, particular to the suburbs. To travel in this context is also to dwell, to be grounded in a particular landscape. Equally, to dwell is not necessarily to arrive or 'settle': dwelling is a spatial and temporal *process*, rather than a signifier of closure or resolution.

## Notes

1  S. Hall, 'The local and the global: globalization and ethnicity', in A.D. King (ed.), *Culture, Globalisation and the Third World System: Contemporary Conditions for the Representation of Identity*, Basingstoke: Macmillan, 1991, p. 24.

2  Paul Gilroy, 'Nothing but sweat inside my hand: diaspora aesthetics and black arts in Britain', in *Black Film/British Cinema*, ICA Document 7, London: ICA, 1988, p. 46.

3  Stuart Hall considers the implications of difference and Derridean *différance* for identity politics in his essay 'New ethnicities', in *Black Film/British Cinema*, ICA Docement 7, London: ICA, 1988.

4  Stuart Hall, 'Song of Handsworth praise', in *Black Film/British Cinema*, p. 17.

5  The conference, organised by Gail Low, was entitled 'A Black British Canon?'.

6  Robert Crawford, *Devolving English Literature*, Edinburgh: Edinburgh University Press, [1992] 2000, p. 309. I am extremely grateful to Alasdair Pettinger for drawing my attention to this text.

7  See Rob Shields, *Places at the Margin: Alternative Geographies of Modernity*, London: Routledge, 1991, pp. 207–51, for a persuasive account of this imagined geography.

8  Speaking in December 2001, in the aftermath of the 'northern riots' in Oldham, Burnley and Bradford, David Blunkett called for ethnic minorities to develop a sense of national 'belonging' and 'citizenship' in order to aid 'social cohesion'. See David Blunkett, 'It's not about the cricket tests', *The Guardian*, 14 December 2001.

9  Evidence of this fact can be seen in recent black British writing. In Zadie Smith's *White Teeth* (2000), Millat and his gang go to King's Cross to buy tickets to Bradford in order to lend their support. The date is 14 January 1989. Kureishi's *The Black Album* (1995) and *My Son the Fanatic* (1999) also draw obliquely on events in Bradford in the aftermath of the Rushdie affair.

10  Paul Gilroy has argued convincingly that to recognise the black British community as a diaspora community is to provide an important 'alternative to the different varieties of absolutism which would confine culture in "racial", ethnic or national essences' (*There Ain't no Black in the Union Jack*, London: Routledge, 1987, p. 155).

11  Jim Pines, 'Representations of black Britishness', in D. Morley and K. Robins (eds) *British Cultural Studies: Geography, Nationality, Identity*, Oxford: Oxford University Press, 2001, p. 61; Gilroy, 'Nothing but sweat', p. 11.

12  Hall, 'The local and the global', pp. 48–9.

13  As Catherine Hall notes in Morley and Robins (eds) *British Cultural Studies*, the 'British population itself is shaped by imperial history: the African-Caribbean and South Asian presence' (p. 27).

14  Kobena Mercer, *Welcome to the Jungle*, London: Routledge, 1994, p. 28.

15  Gilroy, *There Ain't no Black in the Union Jack*, p. 236. These alliances were not just played out in the political arena, but are to be witnessed in the cultural

production of the period (see Chapter 3). Linton Kwesi Johnson, writing within the context of protest in Bradford, spoke of how 'rite now, / African / Asian / West Indian / an' Black British / stan firm'. Similarly, Asian writers such as Farrukh Dhondy and Salman Rushdie interpellated themselves as black in this period, while foregrounding a dialogue between African-Caribbean and Asian culture in their writing.

16  It is significant in this context that the work of women writers such as Moniza Alvi, Jackie Kay, Meera Syal, Ravinder Randhawa, the Asian Women Writers' Collective and gay cultural critics such as Kobena Mercer and Isaac Julien have played an instrumental role in the destabilisation of 'black' as a singular, containing category in the 1980s and 1990s.

17  A term first used in the photographic journal *Ten 8* by David A. Bailey and Stuart Hall in 1992. This issue explores black photography of the 1980s.

18  First published in *The Guardian*, Hall's letter (along with Rushdie's and Howe's) is also reproduced in J. Procter (ed.) *Writing Black Britain*, Manchester: Manchester University Press, 2000, p. 264.

19  Hall, 'New ethnicities', p. 30.

20  Hall, 'New ethnicities', p. 30.

21  Hall 'The question of cultural identity', in S. Hall and B. Gieben (eds) *Modernity and its Futures*, Cambridge: Polity Press, 1992, p. 309.

22  Paul Gilroy, 'Cruciality and the frog's perspective', in *Small Acts: Thoughts on the Politics of Black Cultures*, London: Serpent's Tail, 1993, p. 112.

23  Stuart Hall and Paul Gilroy both discuss the politics (and burden) of representation in *Black Film/British Cinema*. The phrase was first used by Mercer and Julien in their essay 'Introduction: de margin and de centre', *Screen*, 29:4 (1988), pp. 2–11.

24  Julien and Mercer, 'Introduction', p. 5.

25  Julien and Mercer, 'Introduction', p. 2.

26  In order to illustrate their argument, Julien and Mercer have cited Channel 4 and the Labour-administered Greater London Council, whose funding was to influence both the British Film Institute and the Arts Council of Great Britain in the early 1980s. It was institutional support of this kind that played a direct role in freeing the 'enunciative modalities' of black cultural production at this time, they argue.

27  Gilroy's provocative question in 'Cruciality and the frog's perspective', p. 101 – 'is there *any* black audience for some of the most highly prized products of the black arts movement?' – informs and I think legitimises this neglect. I return in Chapter 3 to the issue of avant-garde aesthetic forms in relation to Salman Rushdie.

28  John Frow, 'Literature as regime (meditations on an emergence)', in E. Bissell (ed.) *The Question of Literature*, Manchester: Manchester University Press, 2001.

29  Indeed some critics have expressed open hostility to the term. See Fred D'Aguiar 'Against black British literature', in M. Butcher (ed.) *Tibisiri: Caribbean Writers and Critics*, Sydney: Dangeroo Press, 1989.

30  Speaking on black British writing, Moya Petithomme's claim that 'there is no
     real tradition of "immigrant literature" in Britain the way there is in the
     United States' articulates a more pervasive sense of African-American pre-
     eminence in terms of cultural production.
31  Stuart Hall, 'Aspiration and attitude … reflections on black Britain in the
     nineties', New Formations, 33 (spring 1998), pp. 38–47 (p. 39).
32  Jackie Kay, 'In my country', in Other Lovers, Newcastle-upon-Tyne: Bloodaxe
     Books, 1993.
33  James Clifford, 'Traveling cultures', in Lawrence Grossberg, Gary Nelson,
     Paula Treichler (eds) Cultural Studies, London: Routledge, 1992, p. 115.
34  It is fair to say that since I first made this observation in 1994, diaspora critics
     have become much more critical in their use of 'diaspora'. For more sustained,
     penetrating critiques of diaspora than I am capable of here, see C. Kaplan,
     Questions of Travel, Durham: Duke University Press, 1996; R. Krishnaswamy,
     'Mythologies of migrancy: postcolonialism, postmodernism and the politics
     of (dis)location' Ariel 26:1 (1995), pp. 125-46; A. Brah, Cartographies of Dias-
     pora, London: Routledge, 1996; J. Braziel, and A. Mannur (eds), Theorizing
     Diaspora, Oxford: Blackwell Publishers, 2002, p. 21.
35  Diaspora discourse, as it is evoked within this text, includes a broad range of
     narratives and vocabularies that are themselves by no means internally
     consistent. These include Salman Rushdie's poetics of 'translation'; Paul
     Gilroy's work on the 'black Atlantic', Avtar Brah's concept of 'diaspora space'
     and Homi Bhabha's 'third space' as well as Stuart Hall's and Kobena Mercer's
     broader work on migrant identities and aesthetics.
36  See for example the work of Vijay Mishra, James Clifford and Carol Boyce
     Davies.
37  Hall 'New ethnicities', p. 30.
38  Stuart Hall, 'Cultural identity and diaspora', in P. Williams and L. Chrisman
     (eds) Colonial Discourse and Post-colonial Theory: A Reader, London:
     Harvester, 1993, pp. 392–403 (p. 392).
39  Mercer, Welcome to the Jungle, p. 25.
40  Paul Gilroy 'Diaspora and the detours of identity', in Kathryn Woodward
     (ed.) Identity and Difference, London: Sage Publications, 1997, p. 317. The
     etymology of 'diaspora' has recently been seen as a 'mixed blessing' by certain
     critics working in the field who have recognised the concept's androcentrism
     (diaspora and semen share the same Greek root: speirein). And yet it is
     perhaps worth keeping in mind this etymology, precisely because it draws
     attention to the ways in which the discourses of diaspora and travel have been
     historically male-centred. Diaspora's etymology reveals other silences.
41  Brah, Cartographies of Diaspora, p. 182.
42  Vijay Mishra, 'The diasporic imaginary', Textual Practice, 10:3 (1996), p. 426.
     Bryan Cheyette describes diaspora in slightly different terms as being 'at the
     heart of the new gospel of postmodernity' (Textual Practice, 10:2 (1996), p.
     295). The term diaspora is being used increasingly widely across a range of

subject boundaries, from cultural anthropology to queer studies. See, for example, Alan Sinfield, 'Diaspora and hybridity: queer identities and the ethnicity model', *Textual Practice*, 10:2 (1996), pp. 271–93.

43  As Robin Cohen notes in *Global Diasporas*, Seattle: University of Washington Press, 1997: 'Migration scholars – normally a rather conservative breed of sociologists, historians and geographers – have recently been bemused to find their subject matter assailed by a bevy of postmodernists, novelists and scholars of cultural studies' (p. 127). Cohen makes this comment in relation to the birth of the influential US journal *Diaspora* in 1991.

44  Chris Rojek and John Urry (eds) *Touring Cultures: Transformations of Travel and Theory*, London: Routledge, 1997, p. 10.

45  Gilles Deleuze and Felix Guattari, trans. B. Massumi, *A Thousand Plateaus: Capitalism and Schizophrenia*, London: The Athlone Press, 1988. The work of several diaspora critics (for example Kobena Mercer) has been influenced by this rhetoric. Others (James Clifford; Avtar Brah; Paul Gilroy) have adopted their vocabulary while appearing more sceptical about 'abstract nomadologies' (Clifford, *Routes*, Cambridge, Mass.: Harvard University Press, 1997, p. 259).

46  Homi Bhabha has spoken illuminatingly on this significance of metaphor within the context of diaspora thinking: 'Metaphor, as the etymology of the word suggests, transfers the meaning of home and belonging, across the 'middle passage', or central European steppes, across those distances, and cultural differences, that span the imagined community of the nation-people' (Bhabha, *The Location of Culture*, London: Routledge, 1994, pp. 139–40).

47  Krishnaswamy, 'Mythologies of migrancy', p. 128.

48  Although Clifford *does* speak of 'traveling-in-dwelling, dwelling-in-traveling' in 'Traveling cultures' (p. 108), 'dwelling' is not defined. It remains unclear what Clifford means by the term. In contrast to the hollow, transparent signifier 'dwelling', travel is rendered complex and pluri-signifying.

49  I borrow the term para-site from Rey Chow, *Writing Diaspora: Tactics of Intervention in Contemporary Cultural Studies*, Bloomington: Indiana University Press 1993, pp. 16–17.

50  Clifford, 'Traveling cultures', p. 115.

51  Brah, *Cartographies of Diaspora*, p. 181.

52  As Jon Stratton argues within a different context: 'The modern discourse of diaspora evolved out of the association of the idea that a national population is homogeneous and the idea that it is distributed over a particular territorial space.' Jon Stratton, '(Dis)placing the Jews: historicizing the idea of diaspora', *Diaspora*, 6:3 (1997), p. 310.

53  Gilroy, 'Diaspora and the detours of identity', p. 328.

54  In Urdu the 'term for migrant, *muhajir*, is from the same Arabic root which gives us the word for *hijra*, the migration of the Prophet Muhammad from Mecca to Medina in AD 622' (P. Lewis, *Islamic Britain: Religion, Politics and Identity among British Muslims*, London: I.B. Tauris, 1994, p. 50). In Muslim ideology notions of migration stand in stark opposition to Rushdie's secular

translation of the term. Islam associates migrancy with a 'physical movement towards self definition' (ibid., p. 50) and the territorial possession of space. For Rushdie, on the other hand, *muhajir* signals the destabilisation and dispersal of subjectivity and detachment from territory.

55  Khachig Tölöyan makes this point in his preface to the first issue of *Diaspora* (1991): 'To affirm that diasporas are the exemplary communities of the transnational moment is not to write the premature obitury of the nation-state, which remains a privileged form of polity' (p. 5). Tölöyan goes on to explore how cyberspace and the internet have paradoxically become key channels through which diasporas have reasserted claims on territory.

56  Caryl Phillips has remarked that the decision to produce a screenplay of *The Final Passage* was 'triggered' by the fact that 'It became clear to me that the generation of people who came over in the fifties was dying ... There are old people's homes in Yorkshire full of West Indians who are veterans of that period' (*The Guardian*, 16 December 1995).

57  Vijay Mishra, 'The diasporic imaginary'.

# 2

# Dwelling places

## Introduction: the 'open door' and the domestic threshold

> My landlady's too rude,
> In my affairs she likes to intrude.
> This is how she start
> A lot of restrictions to break your heart.
> After ten o'clock
> Tenants must know my front door lock,
> And on the wall she stick up a notice
> 'No lady friends not even a Princess'. (Lord Kitchener)[1]

> When a West Indian buys a house, it means more to the neighbours than the fact that another family is moving into the street. For them it is a nation, a race and a world. (Donald Hinds)[2]

'The faces of the buildings tell whether they are the ones in which the migrants are concentrated' observes Ruth Glass in her influential socio-logical study of black settlement in the 1950s, *Newcomers: The West Indians in London* (1960):

> The tall houses, structurally similar to those of the south [of Kensington], are badly in need of repair: the woodwork is unpainted; window frames are rotten; plaster has fallen away from the outside walls, showing patches of bare brick. Occasionally, there is a gap in a long parade of terrace houses: the missing house seems to have fallen down. These are the streets of transi-tion where a considerable number of West Indians have found rooms.[3]

Here Glass describes an area of North Kensington in the late 1950s, a landscape she compares with earlier accounts of that locality dating back to the late nineteenth century.[4] This postwar residential setting, Glass tells us, has deteriorated in recent years. However, the extent of the dilapidation is not simply a reminder of the Blitz. The 'faces' of these dwelling places 'tell' us something about communities gathered within them. Privileging the domestic façade as the site at which to diagnose and make sense of the new immigrant communities, Glass's account is indicative of a much larger body of writing to appear in the 1950s and early 1960s to evoke a black presence *through* the dwelling place.

What follows is an account of some of these writings and the shifting representation of black accommodation during the 1950s and 1960s. Focusing on narratives of housing across a range of non-literary discourses (sociological, journalistic, political), this introduction will locate the literary chronotope of the dwelling place pursued in later sections. While I am interested here in tracing some of the shared *tropes* of housing across both literary and non-literary discourse, a key function of this chapter is also to remind us that the figure of the house is not merely figurative. Housing did not emerge out of the blue as a primary signifier in early postwar black British writing, but during a period of acute housing shortages in which the dwelling had established itself as a key arena of racial contestation. To read the 'face' of Glass's dwelling, with its unpainted, peeling and rotting surfaces, is not simply to encounter a metaphor of black housing. It is also to gain a sense of the very real discomfort and dispossession encountered by the early postwar settlers.

The dwelling place was, perhaps more than the official point of entry, the site at which the regulation, policing and deferral of black settlement were most effectively played out. It was around housing that the national panic surrounding black immigration tended to accumulate and stage itself in this period. Housing was, more than any other aspect of life in the early postwar period, subject to a 'colour bar'. Its fortification is recorded in a range of different narratives and practices. In the signs of racial exclusion displayed in the windows of shops, guest houses and hotels: 'Rooms to Let. Sorry, No Dogs and No Coloureds'.[5] In the 'scattered' reception centres, hostels, and temporary shelters designed to stop 'the creation of a single "coloured quarter"'.[6] In the historically specific vocabularies of the early postwar years – 'Rachmanism', the 'colour-tax', 'black-listing' – that indicates something of the fraught, highly racialised conditions of the dwelling place at that time.[7]

The threshold of the British homestead took on the significance of a national frontier in this context. Indeed the latter was repeatedly figured as the former in this *laissez-faire* phase of postwar black settlement otherwise known as the period of the 'open door'.[8] As the nation opened its doors to its colonies and former colonies through the Nationality Act of 1948, those thresholds guarding the nation's residential hinterlands were being closed. It was at this domestic frontier that the spectacle and trauma of a black/white encounter was most sensationally staged in accounts left over from this period. 'One lady actually fainted when she opened the door and saw us!' recalls one West Indian in Anthony Richmond's sociological study of black workers in Liverpool.[9] Similarly, an article published in *Picture Post* on 30 October 1954 claims that 'there are still landladies who scream and shut the door, and some who faint, at the sight of a Negro on the doorstep after dark' (23).[10] The domestic entrance constituted a fraught contact-zone within racial discourse of the period. If the 'open door' had been 'lubricated by the economic boom', and the need to replenish a depleted labour force in the early postwar years, then the racialisation of domestic property, aggravated by the acute housing shortages of the 1950s, was to quickly slam it shut again.[11]

Those properties whose thresholds were crossed by the black settler quickly came to display the symptoms being diagnosed more generally by the white national community. The following extract comes from another highly influential sociological text of this early period, Sheila Patterson's *Dark Strangers* (1963):

> The houses in these roads are large, ugly, dilapidated, Victorian structures, semi-detached, with neglected and rubbish-strewn gardens ... The exteriors are for the most part dingy, unpainted, and crumbling. Front steps and windows are grimy and most windows are hung with sleazy, unlined rayon curtains that are drawn across day and night. Dustbins and junk stand in front of most houses. Many front doors have lost their knockers and bells, and their wooden or glass panels are broken or cracked. Inside the front door of such houses one may expect to find a number of unclaimed letters, pools coupons, and circulars, and several large, new, gleaming prams. There is also a vague, all-pervading smell of ancient dirt, of inefficient and over-worked plumbing, unaired rooms, cooking, paraffin stoves, sometimes of mice, and always of many people congregated together.[12]

The housing portrayed here is presented as emblematic, or *representative*, of the black dwelling place more generally. Patterson begins her account by pointing out that 'the majority of houses owned by West Indians in Brixton conform to the following composite picture of an average West Indian-owned house in the Somerleyton-Geneva Road area'.[13] What the reader is being presented with is not a single house but a kind of collage (a 'composite image'), a series of accounts pulled together and combined to produce a 'definitive' black British dwelling place. Even as the dwelling appears as an empirical, transparent, indisputable site of investigation within the sociological text, it is being actively *composed* by it. What is momentarily revealed here is the constructedness of the dwelling place, the extent to which it has become mythologised by the early 1960s.

On the one hand, this account is indicative of the very real conditions of squalor that black settlers were subjected to in the early postwar years. The housing shortage and overtly racist practices associated with the property market in this period meant that black settlers were often forced to share cramped, derelict housing in the worst areas of the city. At the same time these conditions are presented in white accounts of the time as symptoms of black settlement rather than pre-existing problems inherited by the immigrants.[14] Patterson's composition is ultimately less notable for its faithfulness to the contemporary conditions of black housing 'proper' (what ever that might be) than for its faithfulness to and consistency with other racial narratives of housing from this period and earlier. The dwelling place described above also needs to be seen as a discursively produced, intertextual formation, composed and 'concretised', not in bricks and mortar but via a specific range of narratives, sign systems, mythologies that were circulating in this period. The shared vocabularies of dilapidation, decay and squalor within the extracts from Glass and Patterson above (themselves indicative of a larger body of early postwar sociological discourse), tell us less about the similarities of the black British homestead in the 1950s than about the consistency of the language being used to evoke it.

In this context the prams in the entrance of Patterson's 'model' house are typical of the rich dwelling-place semiotics in circulation during this period. Gleaming against a backdrop of Victorian decay and dereliction, they signal primary panics surrounding black hyper-sexuality, hedonism and miscegenation in the 1950s and 1960s, via contemporary myths of dwelling. Left in the hallway, 'unclaimed' like the letters scattered around them, the prams suggest a black sexuality that is out of control.

'Always', Patterson tells us in the quotation above, the black dwelling place reveals 'many people congregated together'. The very *density* of this occupancy – a major area of concern among the white national community of this period – is inextricably linked to pseudo-scientific notions of 'higher fertility among the recent immigrants'.[15] It is no coincidence that the most decrepit sections of Patterson's house are those in which evidence of miscegenation is to be discovered: 'The worst-kept rooms are usually those in which live single men, or men with transient white girls. In such houses the individual rooms tend to be almost as dirty as the shared parts, and tenants add little of their own, whether linoleum, wallpaper, pictures, or radiograms.'[16] It is difficult to ignore the suggestive equation between shared parts (halls, passageways, stairwells) and the *sharing of parts* (miscegenation) in this passage. The failure of Patterson's miscegenating couples to regulate and discipline their bodies and bodily thresholds is reproduced in the architecture of the house(s) she describes. Not only are the doorways blocked by abandoned prams, letters and dustbins, but the doors themselves 'have lost their knockers and bells, and their wooden or glass panels are broken or cracked'. Outside, the front steps and windows are grimy. The 'sleazy' curtains appear on the one hand to expose too much (they are unlined, transparent) and conceal too much (they are drawn day and night). Inside, the plumbing is 'overworked' and the rooms 'unaired'. The broken, dirty, unregulated passages of the house (doorways, windows, letterboxes, pipes) constitute amplified locations at which to read the spreading contagion associated with miscegenation in this period.

In Patterson's account the dwelling place is invested with the same kind of fragile boundary conditions as the white female body. Both harbour and embody a national culture threatened with penetration and pollution by the transgressive black settler. At once permeable and impervious, they are sites at which cultural differences are reproduced and regulated.[17] The creation of a temporarily porous nation-space between 1948 and 1962 (when the first Immigration Act came into effect) facilitated migration from the Commonwealth to Britain across previously 'impervious' boundaries. This placed an emphasis on the need to police (like the landlady of Kitchener's calypso) and fortify the thresholds of the body and the dwelling place, defining and refining their relations to inside and outside, inclusion and exclusion, membership and non-membership.

Although the Immigration Act of 1962 was designed to stem immigration and secure these national and domestic thresholds, housing persisted as a key signifier in racial discourse. In 1964 Conservative MP Peter Griffiths won a seat in the Labour stronghold of Smethwick with the unofficial slogan, 'If you want a Nigger for a Neighbour, vote Labour'. A year later, in a series of articles published on Britain's 'Dark million' in *The Times*, the racialised dwelling place became the lowest common denominator in the indexing of postwar national decline: 'the British have been in retreat ever since they won the last war … the debris of a falling Empire has crashed into their own back yards'.[18] Perhaps most notable of all, Enoch Powell's 'Rivers of blood' speech (1968), so often read as the high tide mark of popular political racism, imagines the threat posed to the nation by immigration in terms of the invasion and desecration of a seven-roomed house in the Midlands.

Powell's narrative is presented in the form of a letter, 'one of … hundreds' he tells us he has received from his constituents.[19] Forming the centrepiece of his speech, it tells of how 'Eight years ago in Wolver-hampton a house was sold to a negro. Now only one white (an old-age pensioner) lives there' (166). This 'defenceless' pensioner, whose husband and children died in the war, turns her only asset, her home, into a boarding house. She did well until 'the immigrants moved in':

> With growing fear, she saw one house after another taken over. The quiet street became a place of noise and confusion. Regretfully, her white tenants moved out.
> The day after the last one left, she was awakened at 7 a.m. by two negroes who wanted to use her phone to contact their employer. When she refused, as she would have refused any stranger at such an hour, she was abused and feared she would have been attacked but for the chain on her door. (167)

Once more we have a gendered doorstep encounter in which the vulnerable thresholds of the house and the female body are threatened with violation by the black male 'intruder'. Only the chain on the door prevents the men gaining access. These men are not simply figured outside (the house), but as *outsiders*: both a domestic and national theshold are under seige here. Although the old lady does her best to defend herself from this invasion, refusing to take black tenants and turning down their offers to buy the property ('at a price which the prospective landlord would recover from his tenants in weeks'), she soon becomes a prisoner in her own home. Ultimately the passages of the boarding house are breached by the black neighbours: 'windows are broken. She finds excreta pushed through her letterbox' (167). The similarities with the broken limits of Patterson's house are striking here. However, Powell's is ultimately a much more hostile narrative of the housing problem. What appears in *Dark Strangers* to be a 'failure' on the part of the black settlers to regulate domestic and corporeal boundaries becomes in Powell's letter part of a much more assertive, wilful and menacing plot to penetrate the national and domestic borders housing white British culture.

Powell's account was part of a broader shift in the way the dwelling place was evoked in the 1960s. Griffiths's Smethwick slogan of 1964, like Powell's speech four years later show the extent to which the housing question had entered into popular government politics. In the 1950s the fortification of the domestic threshold was played out at an unofficial level: it tended to involve an 'anonymous' system of exclusions by landlords, estate agents and other property owners that went unchecked by the law. By the mid-1960s, however, black housing was being con-structed increasingly in terms of its existence outside the law. Invoking the Public Health Act in his racist manifesto *A Question of Colour?* (1966), Peter Griffiths states that 98 per cent of legal proceedings for lack of hygiene were brought against Indians and Pakistanis.[20] Hygiene (or lack of it) is also a subtext in Powell's speech, where he uses the house in Wolverhampton to point to the law's betrayal of the white national community. It is ironic, states Powell, that new laws being considered by the government will mean it is the pensioner who will be arrested for refusing black tenants, while the aggressive and intimidating behaviour of the black neighbours goes unchecked. 'When the new Race Relations Bill is passed, this woman is convinced she will go to prison. And is she so wrong? I begin to wonder' (167).

However, and as Paul Gilroy illustrates convincingly in *There Ain't no Black in the Union Jack* (1987), it is in terms of shebeen that black dwellings were most consistently criminalised from the mid-1960s onwards. Sheila Patterson noted that the 'rapid increase of basement drinking and dancing clubs with a West Indian management and clientele in residential areas had provided a new source of friction since 1958'.[21] At this stage, however, the shebeen is not classified in terms of its lawlessness: Patterson observes people drinking in 'moderation' and 'no overt evidence of gambling or ganja-smoking' (365). By the mid-1960s however, the illegality of the shebeen was gaining currency in racial discourse, as Peter Griffiths's anecdote of a West Indian house party indicates: 'A police raid on ... a party in Smethwick found 250 West Indians crammed into a tiny terraced house. It was so crowded that the police could not get in to turn them out!'[22]

The shebeen was a particularly effective environment in which to narrate West Indian everyday life because it imagined black settlement outside the workplace and in leisure time. It captured the community in acts of consumption as opposed to production and could therefore stage the tensions between black pleasure and 'moral panic' that Gilroy has argued were central to the criminalisation of black British culture in this period.[23] A major area of confrontation between black and white neighbours, these late-night parties were one of the earliest sites at which forms of black pleasure were policed. The two different accounts of the shebeen below are typical of this period. The first is from the series of newspaper articles on Britain's 'Dark million' mentioned earlier:

> wherever there are West Indians – the police have learnt to be tactful. They come respectfully, saying: 'Would you mind turning the radiogram down a bit, please. The neighbours want some sleep.' These late night parties ... are a monster-sized projection of the West Indian's extrovert personality.

... I looked for sin. There was drink – ... Once I caught a man going upstairs ... A bit later he beckoned me down to follow ... 'Can you give us some advice? We want to get our daughters over, and cannot get a passport.'[24]

The second account, along with the image that follows it (see figure 1), first appeared in a series of articles published in *Punch* in 1964; they were subsequently reproduced in a book by their author, Elspeth Huxley:

down in the dirty basements are whiffs of Kingston, Nassau, Port-of-Spain. You squeeze past a smelly lavatory ... into a low-ceilinged, tightly sealed-off place as dark and private as the womb. The centre is bare for dancing, there's a bench all round, a small soft-drink bar. (No licence.) ... The men wear hats at saucy angles, the women stiletto heels and tight cottons ... There's a thick fog of cigarette smoke with a ganga undertone. On Saturdays, jiving and twisting don't get under way before midnight and go on till winter dawn ... here's a corner of a foreign field that is temporarily, if not forever, Caribbean.[25]

Huxley squeezes into a cramped basement, while *The Times* reports that the sheer weight of packed black bodies threatens to demolish the very house in which it takes place: 'the floor began to sag. A West Indian announced: "We have to stop. We shall all tumble into de cellar. De house is about to crash down upon our poor heads." '[26] As the cooker in figure 1 suggests, these rooms are subject to multiple usage, they represent, like the dwellings considered earlier, 'crammed' space, noteworthy for their acute density. Again this density is suggestive of a black hyper-sexuality. Within the context of the shebeen it is the dancefloor, a deeply threatening territory in racial discourse of the 1950s and early 1960s, that promotes unauthorised permissiveness, intimacy and tactility between young black and white, male and female bodies. The music emanating from these confined spaces, like the saucy hats, stiletto heels and tight cottons of Huxley's dancers, project a threatening sexuality: 'it sounded like an orgy' remarks the correspondent for *The Times*. These shebeens act symbolically in this sense as sites of fecundity: they are, in the words of Huxley, 'as dark and private as the womb'.

However there is an emergent criminality within these two shebeens that distinguishes them from similar accounts of the 1950s like Glass's and Patterson's. Together they dramatise many of the issues at stake in the imagination of shebeen culture that would gain momentum in the 1970s. Both are structured as explorations or searches for a black lawlessness which is ultimately confirmed: whether in terms of unlicensed bars, noise pollution, drug consumption or illegal immigration. A ganga tone, absent in Patterson's shebeen, forms a thick fog in Huxley's.

Despite the preoccupation across all of the accounts in this section

1  'The shebeen'

with an essentially 'interior' black everyday life, there is (as in the earlier accounts) a significant convergence and disturbance of the boundaries between private, domestic space and the public/political realm beyond them. In figure 1 the pavement of the street also forms the roof of the room: any easy division of indoors and outdoors is refused through the elison of the interior (private) space of the house and the exterior (public) domain of the city streets. As with Patterson's composite house and the pensioner's home in Powell's speech, the West Indians in these accounts seem to be 'disturbing' because they fail to regulate and maintain such boundaries, not just between inside and outside but between day and night, legality and illegality. The pen-and-ink drawing indicates a narrative running from the notice board, advertising accommodation, to the unhoused black figures on the street, to the indoor venue of the shebeen. Yet the narrative is not linear or sequential: does the woman on the far right of the image stand outdoors, in front of the notice board, or indoors with partygoers? Similarly, the 'time' of this image is anachronistic. Beneath an evening sky, we have daylight and daytime activities: children playing, mothers walking babies, men loitering. The image collapses different spaces, times and locations within a single space. The room structurally occupies a subterranean space, while its 'contents' appear projected at street-level: the pavement, which 'houses' the basement, comes to stage the hedonism and fecundity it conceals: the pram (also a key signifier in Patterson's account), unemployed adults, unattended youth. What emerges across these different depictions of housing in the 1950s and 1960s is a concern with the thresholds of the dwelling (windows, façades, doorways), and in turn the thresholds of the body and the law. These are thresholds which black settlers are depicted either being excluded from or in various ways 'breaking'.

It is tempting, when considering the racialisation of the domestic threshold in early postwar discourse, to translate the black British dwelling as an *unhomely* venue. What the accounts above neglect, however, is the cultural investment in *making* home and domesticating space as well as the political struggle *for* dwelling. In what is too often narrated as a prepolitical phase of black British history, it tends to be overlooked that it was in relation to the dwelling place that some of the first instances of a black communal politics were to take shape. The South Asian 'mortgage clubs', Jamaican 'pardner' and Trinidadian 'sou sou' systems were unprecedented in this sense, working as collectives to facilitate property purchase, long before the mobilising forces of Black Power got under way. Such struggles to become *housed* need accommodating alongside the itinerant agendas of diasporic discourse if the 'tenacity' of the pioneer settlers and their potential to *dwell* is to be properly addressed. What follows is an attempt to pursue this potential in relation to some of the dominant venues of early postwar black British writing: basements and bedsits.

## Descending the stairwell: basements and bedsits

If, as Helen Tiffin argues, the house is a 'motif of indigenization' within nationalist literatures, then the dislocated, transnational subject of diaspora discourse would appear essentially homeless.[27] Yet within black British literature of the early postwar years the house is not simply a point of departure but a conspicuous locus of return and recollection. Writers such as James Berry, Wole Soyinka, E.R. Braithwaite and G.R. Fazakerley elaborate on the struggle to find and sustain accommodation. Shiva and V.S. Naipaul return to dwell on their early experiences of boarding houses and bedsits in a series of autobiographical and semi-autobiographical accounts published across the postwar period. Mean-while, Ralph Singh of V.S. Naipaul's *The Mimic Men* (1967) recollects the narrative of *his* fictional autobiography from a respectable London hotel.[28] O.R. Dathorne's *Dumplings with Soup* (1963) focuses on the various goings-on at Number 30, a cramped lodging house for black immi-grants.[29] Sam Selvon's fiction is largely organised around basement and bedsit life, and his so-called 'Moses trilogy' follows Moses Aloetta as he moves from basement to attic and back again. It is within the rich body of (mostly) prose fiction remaining from this early postwar period that some of the most extended accounts of the dwelling place were to appear. To read these writings collectively, is to encounter the dwelling place as a repetitious referent.

The privileging of 'homelessness' and 'home as everywhere' within recent diaspora theory and fiction, neglects the kind of personal and social investment in dwelling highlighted within the work of these early writers.[30] What the various narratives enlisted above expose is the emo-tional and cultural preocccupation in home and housing, an investment that was heightened rather than displaced by the fear of homelessness. To leave 'home' for Britain was not simply an issue of departure or travel: it also involved a fraught territorial struggle over local space. In this context the ontological or metaphysical experience of homelessness that has tended to preoccupy post-colonial diaspora theory (with its accent on identity politics) needs to be distinguished carefully from the physical geography of 'home' and the search for residency explored below.

This chapter focuses on two novels notable for their treatment of the geography of the dwelling place: George Lamming's *The Emigrants* (1954) and Sam Selvon's *The Lonely Londoners* (1956). Travelling from the Caribbean to England on the same boat, these two men have not only come to represent key figures within the canon of black British literary production in the 1950s: it is within their work that the figure of the dwelling place arguably emerges at its most concentrated and contra-dictory. Lamming's London is almost entirely confined to an interior (under)world of basements, barber shops and living rooms. Similarly, *The Lonely Londoners* sees Moses's basement room become an unofficial shelter and sanctuary for the city's West Indian 'boys'. Unlike *The Emigrants*, Selvon's novel also explores the metropolitan centre beyond the dwelling place. The final section of this chapter considers *The Lonely Londoners'* broader habitation of London and the possibilities it creates for dwelling beyond the domestic interior.

George Lamming's second novel, *The Emigrants*, was also the first to record the experience of postwar Caribbean settlement in England. It describes the journey of a wide cross-section of West Indians: the Governor and Tornado, Trinidadians who both served in the RAF; the Jamaican, Collis, a writer; Phillip, an aspiring law student; Dickson, a school teacher from Barbados. The novel is structured in three sections. 'A voyage' charts the emigrants' two-week journey by ship to Plymouth; 'Rooms and residents' records their early experiences of settling in London; 'Another time' picks up the story of the emigrants some two years after their arrival. This chapter will focus on 'Rooms and residents', in which London appears through a series of (mostly basement) interiors.[31]

The opening section of *The Emigrants*, 'A voyage', comprises a series of horizontal journeys across space, firstly between the islands of Trinidad and Tobago, Barbados, Jamaica, Grenada, Martinique and Guadeloupe as the emigrants gather on the *Golden Image*; followed by their voyage to England and culminating in a train journey to the interior, from Plymouth to Paddington. In contrast, the second section, 'Rooms and residents', opens with a detailed account of a downward journey into the basement room of a barber's shop, typifying a section of repeated descents. This shift from horizontal to vertical trajectories, from movement across to movement down, indicates a new direction in the novel.

'Rooms and residents', as the title suggests, is overwhelmingly situated indoors. The narrative shifts back and forth between basement, house and hostel. The basement locations – Fred Hill's barber shop, Miss Dorking's flat and hair salon, Tornado and Lilian's bedsit – are exclusively West Indian territories. These rooms are interwoven, almost consecu-tively, with the homes of the novel's English and anglophile characters: the Pearsons, the Wardens, the Redheads. Transaction between these domestic worlds (the black world below and the white world above) is an infrequent and always negative experience. In terms of this substantial interior geography, I want to concentrate primarily on two basement dwellings: Fred Hill's barber shop and Miss Dorking's flat and hair salon. The barber shop and hair salon is a key urban locus in this and other black British fictions of the early postwar period.[32] If on the one hand these locations imply a self-conscious refashioning of black subjectivity through the straightening and trimming of black hair, they are also spaces in which a black British communal identity and politics are consolidated early on.[33]

At the same time the act of entering these basements is at once more difficult and disorienting than we might expect:

> The men couldn't see each other in the dark, but they took it for granted that they were not in the wrong place. When the door closed, blocking the light, the street disappeared like a thief, and the steps led them feebly in a crooked angle along the walls down towards the basement. The change was too obvious for comment, and their silence suggested that the atmosphere had produced a similar sensation in each. The stairs descended uncertainly like raindrops trickling down the wounded face of a rock. The angle sharpened here, the next step was missing, and suddenly like a blow on the head, the foot made a final drop, and the body fought for its balance before preparing to move on. They drew closer now, waiting without a word for someone to explore the dark. It was dingy and damp, a hole which had lost its way in the earth; and they put their hands out along the wall and over the floor like crabs clawing for security.[34]

In this quotation from the opening paragraph of 'Rooms and residents' the narrator dwells on the crooked, convoluted stairwell. The passageway marks a significant threshold between the white metropolis (above/ outside) that the emigrants have just left, and the black world (below/ inside) of the basement they are about to enter. The journey it describes appears to be a negative one. The winding descent is characterised by uncertainty, instability, danger and discomfort, as the men navigate a route downward through darkness, missing steps and unexpected twists and turns. The discontinuous staircase, with its gaps and angles, is difficult to traverse and the group's footsteps describe a hesitant, jerky pathway of stops and starts concluding in a jarring, destabilizing 'final drop'. During this tentative descent the men remain totally silent: not one word is exchanged between them. This communicative fracture is reiterated not only in the narrator's refusal to elaborate ('the change was too obvious for comment'), but in the disjointed journey down the stairwell itself. Together, the absence of steps and speech recompose this interstitial location as one of fissures, faults and gaps. This tricky, tense (sub)terrain, is more fraught with danger, more difficult to transgress than diaspora discourse has suggested.

In the introduction to his collection of essays *The Location of Culture* Homi Bhabha uses the African-American artist Renée Green and her imaginative evocation of the stairwell to foreground his thesis on migrant culture:

> The stairwell as liminal space, in-between the designations of identity, becomes the process of symbolic interaction, the connective tissue that constructs the difference between upper and lower, black and white. The hither and thither of the stairwell, the temporal movement and passage that it allows, prevents identities at either end of it from settling into primordial polarities. This interstitial passage between fixed identifications opens up the possibility of a cultural hybridity that entertains difference without an assumed or imposed hierarchy.[35]

Although the liminal staircases of Bhabha and Lamming offer a passage between worlds, the nature of this passage is constructed in alternative ways: they take us in very different directions. If for Bhabha the 'symbolic interaction' allowed by the staircase offers 'cultural hybridity' then for Lamming the staircase is an emblem of 'imposed hierarchy'. The 'hither and thither' of Bhabha's stairwell is a groping and stumbling in *The Emigrants*. The enlightenment and continuity that the stairway's 'connective tissue' offers Bhabha is darkness, insecurity and discontinuity for Lamming's emigrants, who find themselves clawing blindly 'like crabs"' in a 'dingy damp ... hole which had lost its way in the earth'. The gloomy underworld that Lamming evokes at the base of his stairwell is more like a space of imprisonment where the 'movement and passage' of Bhabha's staircase is brought to an abrupt halt.

A comparison of these two very different stairwells may at first appear opportunistic. Bhabha's is an essentially *metaphorical* passageway that we are not encouraged to situate within any particular historical or geographical context. And yet this is why the divergent trajectories of these stairwells illustrate something of the limits of contemporary diasporic discourse. Despite a rich, highly sophisticated spatial vocabulary, Bhabha's liminal passageway appears without co-ordinates in *any* physical, 'referential' geography. His is an essentially imaginative conceptualisation of space that appears simultaneously 'no-place' within the material landscapes of, say, 1950s London.[36] It is worth grounding (as opposed to fixing) the discrepant poetics of Lamming and Bhabha in terms of the racialised architecture of the stairwell in early postwar discourse at this point.

The stairwell constituted a key symbolic location within accounts of the black dwelling place during the 1950s and early 1960s: not as a site of cultural hybridity but as a racially fraught contact-zone at which blacks and whites came into confrontation. The stairwell was regularly an index of the squalor and cramped conditions to be found in black housing of this period. Often a site of multiple usage, the competition for space within the lodgings of the early black communities meant that the stairwell was regularly reconfigured as the kitchen. Its function as passageway was compromised in this context, as it became a congested, contestatory site of dwelling and a marker of black degradation: 'we were obliged to pay £3 and £3.50 for one room. And at that, you had to cook outside. In the passageway they would have this stove, and maybe three, four people are to use one stove. It was a rat race really.'[37]

In terms of the shared, multiracial household, it was at the stairwell that the dangers of admitting the black lodger were to be frequently witnessed, and at which the white tenant was perceived as at greatest risk from a squalid, socially deviant black presence. Although, as one sociologist put it at the time, 'Who should clean and maintain shared facilities, such as stairs and passageways, is often a subject of dispute in multi-occupied premises – irrespective of the tenants' race', the (lack of) cleanliness and maintenance in these public/private sections of the house was in fact deeply racialised.[38]

In Sheila Patterson's composite house discussed earlier, the debris of the black tenant, 'an assortment of unwashed utensils and crockery, and one or more grease-splashed cookers' accumulates 'on the landings' of the stairwell. It is here that black sanitation is drawn into question.[39] More worryingly, the stairwells and passageways of the multiracial household appear as sites at which a physically intimidating, hyper-sexual black presence lurks: '"The elderly women often think they are likely to be raped or attacked. The worst cases occur when the statutory tenant has a flat on an upper floor. Those in a basement flat usually have a separate entrance and facilities so that contact is not so frequent."'[40] In support of her argument, Patterson records 'A case involving an elderly statutory tenant [that] was heard before Judge Clothier at Lambeth County Court on 6 December 1954':

Miss M. [a white woman] said she had been a tenant in the house since 1914. F. [a black man] bought the house last year. Whenever she entered, F. barred her way. When visitors called, he and his lodgers told them that she did not live there or that she was not in when she was. Coloured men came upstairs to her flat and onto her landing at night.[41]

The consistency across descriptions of the stairwell encounter in this period is striking. In an article published in *Picture Post* on 30 October, 1954 – 'Would you let your daughter marry a Negro?' – the reporter records 'A friend of mine, who is small, tolerant and blonde described to me a few days ago the inexplicable terror which swept through her as a Negro walked behind her up the stairs of a boarding house. The man was only going up stairs. She was terrified.'[42] By 1968 Enoch Powell was referring to the similar, if more sinister, experience of an old-aged white woman who rented from a black landlord, and how 'In the darkness when going upstairs she would receive a thump on the back'.[43] To ground Bhabha's abstract spatial metaphor of the stairwell in terms of the specific cultural history of 1950s Britain is to encounter a very different kind of symbolic venue. The stairwell of that period was a haunting, contestatory contact zone at which the terror of black settlement was encountered face to face, as opposed to an emancipatory space of cross-cultural negotiation. Such historical accounts render contingent the kind of celebratory hybridity of Bhabha's symbolic stairwell, exposing certain discrepancies that tend to remain concealed within current conceptions of diaspora culture. If Bhabha's stairwell is exceptional for its ability to entertain difference, it is clearly much less capable of accommodating the kind of historical and geographical differences that appear across alternative diasporic landscapes. Demarcating, while crucially disturbing, the passage between 'indoors' and 'outdoors', Lamming's passageway is informed by a rhetoric of black settlement prevalent in the 1950s and early 1960s that is absent in Bhabha's of the 1990s.

As we saw in the opening section, the thresholds of the dwelling place – doors and doorways, walls and windows – are repetitious referents within racial discourse. A similar preoccupation with thresholds permeates *The Emigrants*, a novel in which the borders of the dwelling are meticulously, even obsessively, narrated. It is perhaps not surprising that Lamming's stairwell is bounded at both ends by a doorway. It is a threshold framed by thresholds. At the top of the stairs we are told a door shuts, shrouding the men in darkness: 'the door closed, blocking the light, the street disappeared like a thief' (129).[44] At the bottom, the men are confronted with another door, which leads to the barber's basement. The geography of this basement is described from the perspective of a Jamaican customer whose eyes slowly follow the 'hard, rigid nakedness' (135) of the walls:

> He passed on to the wall opposite which claimed the only window in the basement, a long narrow window, railed perpendicularly with bars of iron

which made sombre shadows against the thick green glass. The glass looked surprisingly irrelevant behind bars of iron and gave the whole window an accidental, almost absurd appearance. It had steadied the Jamaican's glance; indeed, centred it. He watched the window as though it were the only thing of importance in the room, trying all the time to reclaim the feelings which the window had aroused. (136)

This passage is typical of the lingering, enigmatic threshold narratives of the novel. Such prolonged descriptions don't offer verisimilitude or clarity. Their primary function is not to 'describe'. Paradoxically, the sustained, repetitive references to the window serve only to make it unfamiliar. This is a window that draws into question its own definition as such. It is a window without a view; a window so heavily barred that it does not require glass, that no longer operates as a threshold. Like the basement door which is 'shut tight', 'pushed too far into the space for which it was made' (137), the window is a border that has become a barrier, a marker of confinement and incarceration.[45]

Nevertheless, this basement room is more than a prison. Its thresholds also facilitate passage. In contrast to the staggered and discontinuous descent of the men down the stairwell, the threshold that takes the emigrants into the barber's shop is distinguished by an unimpeded reciprocity: 'Tornado had found a knob which began to turn slowly in his hand. He withdrew his hand and stepped aside, and the door slid back, gradually making a crease of light through which he could see the back of a head' (129). The basement's threshold performs an uncanny act of self-regulation as the room *itself* admits the men, sliding open to draw the emigrants inside. The 'crease of light' revealed behind the door appears to signify salvation: 'The men who were standing returned the barber's look with a pleasure which showed surprise and rescue' (127). A Jamaican customer rises to meet Tornado: 'they greeted each other with a violent shaking of hands ... an act of loyalty'. The barber, Fred Hill, moves easily between his work and banter with the customers gathered around him: 'These men were his immediate community, and any word, attitude, gesture, was an occasion for thinking' (128). This atmosphere of exchange and dialogue is reiterated through the symbolic layout of the room and the reflexive quality of the mirrors and photographs that run around it:

They turned to admire the photographs that were stuck on the walls, photographs of an American jazz band whose members had given their autographs to the barber. These faces smiling and expansive betrayed a curious, reciprocal intimacy between them and the instruments that were held so lovingly to their mouths. The barber felt their admiration, and turned to give information about the different players. (133)

These pictures, housed on the walls of the basement room, demarcate a new territory in London. The dispersed representatives of the African diaspora symbolically unsettle the foundations of the metropolis. The 'reciprocal intimacy' that flows between the players and their instruments exceeds the frames of these photographs, emerging in the gaze of the customers, whose admiration for the pictures is returned by the barber's histories of them. As the Jamaican surveys the room, listening to the babble of voices within it, he feels 'impressed by this new intimacy' that he has found in London and with which the scene closes: 'The cigarette smoke drifted about their heads, and the voices rose and fell in talk which had rambled, easily and naturally, from the mystery of Azi to the trouble of the times' (135).

It is here, beneath the streets of London, that the emigrants argue over and refine their sense of communal identity: 'The main historical point o' dis age is dis ... It is de age of colonial concern.' ... 'Dat's why we in all the colonies will fight' (132), says Fred Hill. Although it would be wrong to suggest that the basement is a utopian space of black solidarity and resistance (Fred Hill's argument here is repeatedly challenged by an African customer), the room is much more than a simple site of incarceration: it accommodates the possibilities of an emergent black consciousness.[46] This is certainly how the white community beyond the basement perceives things: '"they think there is some black underground connecting every one of us"' (159) says the Jamaican, after a visit from the police.

The boundary conditions of the basement are equivalent to frontiers, metaphorically demarcating an imagined black community. These frontiers are not simply exclusionary, they are policed by the pioneering black settlers: despite a wider sense of urban apartheid around them, this group of emigrants practise their own exclusions, border definitions and controls. This becomes apparent during the policeman's visit following the arrest of Higgins at Marble Arch as a suspected drugs dealer. At this point the threshold of the basement becomes an exclusionary barrier:

> 'Come in,' the barber shouted. The men who were squatting against the door had got up to make room, but no one entered. The barber jerked his head round again and shouted his invitation.
>     'I doan' think you can hear from outside,' Tornado said ... The men who stood nearest the door agreed.
>     'Open up there,' the barber said, pointing the scissors from one man to the brass knob that turned the lock. The man turned the knob testily and brought the door towards him as he retreated. (161)

Again the threshold of the basement room appears to be a self-regulating passage. This time though, the emphasis is on a deferred entry. The door that earlier yielded to Tornado's touch, inviting the West Indians to enter, is now locked: the threshold becomes a barrier. The barber's 'shouted' invitations go unheard on the other side of the door, emphasising the segregation of black and white worlds and the difficulty of transaction or negotiation between them. Even when inside, the policeman, 'remained in the doorway' (157), hesitating on the boundary between stairwell and basement, his passage arrested. Although it is the policeman who appears to be subjecting the basement to surveillance, his movements are also policed, subject to the control of those inside who have let him in. The policeman's survey of the basement is checked by the collective gaze that falls on him: 'Tornado moved across to the window to get a better view of the policeman' (157), regarding him with an increasingly 'deep suspicion' (160). It is the policeman, more than the emigrants, who is subject to interrogation: the gathering's increasingly aggressive barrage of questions (far outnumbering those of the officer), insist that he account for his assumptions about London's black communities. In the subterranean world of Fred Hill's basement, the racial discourses of the dwelling place are turned upside-down. It is the emigrants here who become the insiders in an underworld whose sanctity is threatened by the white policeman, an outsider in this new Caribbean enclave within and beneath the metropolis.

As the narrative shifts from the basement barber shop to the English homestead of Mr and Mrs Pearson, we are introduced to another intimate space. This time, however, it is a solitary one:

> The lavatory is a place of privacy, Collis thought. You may leave the door open, and others will pass, pretending not to see you, but no one will enter. If the door is locked, no one will knock. In a stranger's house, a fortnight from home, he had discovered the consoling privacy of this place. He hadn't gone there to relieve himself, but to rescue his sanity. (138)

The West Indian Collis is visiting the Pearsons after being given their address in the Caribbean. Like the policeman's trespass of the basement, Collis's presence in this unfamiliar environment signals a breakdown in communication, characterised by progressively tense and faltering conversations (hence his retreat to the lavatory). In contrast to the banter of the basement, the Pearsons' 'behaviour followed a certain order known only to them' (137). The lavatory, like the barber shop for Tornado and the others, provides for Collis a sanctuary from the white world that exists beyond it. Again, the emigrants' ability to manipulate and manage spatial environs to their advantage is demonstrated. The doorways of both thresholds (basement and lavatory) delineate public and private territories that operate symbolically to contain, exclude and protect.

Like the basement barber shop, the Pearsons' walls reflect and circumscribe the identities of the people they house: 'The telephone was on a shelf built into the walls above the radio, and there was a television set into another corner' (139). The radio, telephone and television signify more than a material shift upwards from the basement, they are *interfaces* that connect the Pearsons' home with the white metropolis beyond it. The white couple move easily between the private domain of the house and the public world outside. Similarly the views described through their windows contrast with the barred, viewless window of the basement. The Pearsons' living room marks a sense of belonging to a broader built environment, an environment that is unavailable, or unaccommodating, to the emigrants. Their 'borderless' house contrasts with the hermetic dwellings of the settlers.

At the same time Collis is struck by the 'unnatural silence ... which seemed to reign over the entire house' (142). In contrast to the dwelling places occupied by the West Indian characters (the barber shops, the hostel, Lilian and Tornado's basement) which are all communal, group territories, this dwelling is a space of individuation marked by a strong sense of ownership and possession: 'Mr Pearson did not sit in the chair. He belonged to it. When he left it to serve the sherry, it was not only unoccupied. It became incomplete' (136). The furniture composes a hierarchy of power structures within the living room, with Mr Pearson located at the centre. While his guest is in the lavatory, Mr Pearson 'looked at the chair where he had been sitting, and then at Collis's as though he were trying to measure the distance between them' (139–40). This English homestead cannot 'accommodate' Collis, whose 'rudimentary shelter' (139) at the hostel marks his geographical and cultural distance from the Pearsons.

From the Pearsons' house the narrative returns to the basement location and another West Indian gathering (this time exclusively female), at Miss Dorking's home and hair salon. There are important similarities between the basement rooms of Fred Hill and Miss Dorking. Spatial composition and narrative event replicate one another at these two sites, emphasising the symbolic significance of the subterranean dwelling place:

> This was a womb which the world (meaning those other than you) was not aware of. The world passed by on the outside, intent or callous, but ignorant of the intimacy and the warmth of this house, in this corner, where those

women were seated around a table, a small table with three legs and a rectangular surface, old, polished and efficient. (148)

Again here, there is a strong sense of division between outside (white, cold and callous) and inside (black, warm, intimate) worlds. The view from Miss Dorking's window, like that from Fred Hill's, indicates the segregated cityscape beyond the insular community basement setting: 'the view was abruptly blocked by houses which came up like a wall between two foreign territories' (151).

Congregating around a small table, there is an 'intimacy' to the women's conversations that was absent at the Pearsons', where furniture marked individuation, distance, separateness. The sense of community in both basements that derives, in part, from the hostile white environment around them is underscored through their collective remembrance of the Caribbean. Here the metropolitan basement room becomes the site at which a local West Indian landscape is conjured, offering a familiar territory, a communal reference point for conversation beneath the alienating streets of London. This act of remembrance involves more than a nostalgic 'look back' to the homeland. As the Caribbean landscape – 'down town Port-o'-Spain', 'Marine Square' (145), 'the Savannah' (146) – begins to accrue within Miss Dorking's basement, the foundations of the white metropolis are symbolically disturbed, forced as they are to house an environment that normally exists 'out-of-bounds'.

It is no coincidence then that Miss Dorking uses her rented basement, illegally, as a hairdresser's. Like the dwelling places of the opening section, the basements of *The Emigrants* are notable for their disturbance of the boundaries governing English law. 'You know you ain't suppose to do it without a licence, an' I ain't think she got any licence,' says one of her customers (150). "Tis different from back home where you could set up a little place an' it ain't nobody's business. Here every damn thing is something for papers, permission and signing here an' there, an' the income tax an' all that. You got to be so careful' (150). Unlike the Pearsons' home, which is circumscribed by a strict set of laws, codes and conventions, Miss Dorking's underworld turns its back on English jurisdiction. This 'little place' is run as it would be 'back home': the basement represents a 'pocket' or enclave that rehouses the Caribbean within the white metropolis.

The visit from the police officer at Fred Hill's basement is echoed at Miss Dorking's with the arrival of the mysterious Frederick (a failed African missionary), whom the women take to be the police:

stumbling down the steps and along the dark corridor … He found the knob and turned it, but the door remained shut. It was bolted on the inside. He tried the knob again but no one opened … Frederick rapped at the door again, while Miss Dorking extracted the rolled strip of brown paper from the partition and peeped through the crease of light. Frederick looked about him, trying to take in the geography of the place, and Miss Dorking saw him clearly. (169–70)

Like the policeman earlier, who appears uncertain of the environment in which he finds himself, Frederick struggles to 'take in' this alien territory as he blindly stumbles in the dark. Both Frederick and the policemen find their progression arrested at the threshold between symbolic territories. In both cases it is the West Indian community that regulates the borders of their domain. Miss Dorking is given the power to police her property and carry out a secret surveillance of its threatened threshold.

The last basement dwelling depicted in Lamming's novel belongs to the West Indian couple, Lilian and Tornado. It is now six months since the emigrants arrived in England, the hostel has closed and the Caribbean community is more dispersed than ever. As such this basement represents a precious site of gathering: 'As a meeting place for emigrants and their friends, it was as popular as the barber's shop' (184). Again, this basement is governed by a set of codes, customs and conventions different from that of the Pearsons', structuring itself around the superstitions and mythologies of the Caribbean: Lilian moves a bottle from in front of the mirror to a corner, "Tis better there … I always hear the ol' people say, never let glass stare glass in the face' (183–4). Each of these subterranean dwellings – Fred Hill's, Miss Dorking's, Lilian and Tornado's – is subject to new forms of spatial ritual, appropriation and usage in the novel: they have each become susceptible to a kind of internal colonisation by the West Indian settlers. In Lilian and Tornado's basement, pots of water boil in preparation for potatoes, 'some rice' and 'A piece o' rabbit', and the 'room reeked with the odour of onions and garlic … the smoke came up from the corner and spread across the ceiling' (183).

The main room in the house is cramped, but close-knit. Like the other basements in the novel, it functions as a sanctuary, an escape from the outside world. At the same time there is a growing sense of dissatisfaction with the limits of this black enclave which circumscribes and limits the communal sense of belonging to the private, internal, subterranean boundaries of the house:

They had worked, returned home, and now in the early night which had suddenly grown thick outside they were together in a small room … In another climate, at another time, they would ramble the streets yarning and singing, or sit at the street corners throwing dice as they talked aimlessly about everything and nothing. Life was leisurely. But this room was different. Its immediacy forced them to see that each was caught in it ... Alone, circumscribed by the night and the neutral staring walls, each felt himself pushed himself to the limits of his thinking. All life became an immediate situation from which action was the only escape. And their action was limited to the labour of a casual hand in a London factory. (192)

This passage signposts a shift from the first weeks of contentment that typified the earlier basement scenes. Previously the basement, as a site of imprisonment, was constantly being destabilised by the basement as enclave. Here, as darkness closes in like the walls in which they are 'caught', there is a growing sense of claustrophobia, heightened by memories of a more 'leisurely', outdoor life in the Caribbean. Increasingly since their arrival, the basement, and by extension England, are questioned as sustaining sites of accommodation, nourishment and growth for the West Indian community.

This growing sense of dissatisfaction with the dwelling place is qualified in the final section of the novel, 'Another time'. The only 'dwelling' within this section is the Mozamba club, owned by the Governor and the African, Azi. Although this 'habitable pocket hidden somewhere under the dark heart of the city' (230), appears to house an exclusively black clientele, including the characters from earlier sections, it ultimately signifies in terms of its refusal to accommodate, house, gather. At the novel's close a new group of West Indians arrives in England on the same *Golden Image* taken by Tornado and his countrymen two years before. The arrivants crowd together in a cul-de-sac outside the club in the hope of gaining shelter, but the Governor refuses: ''Tis a club' (279), he says. His justification reveals how much things have changed since 'Rooms and residents'. Earlier, the barber shops of Fred Hill and Miss Dorking functioned as both private businesses and sites of communal accommodation. In contrast, at the Mozamba, the line between business enterprise and communal accommodation has been clearly drawn. Azi and the Governor seem to be surviving in Britain, but only by embracing its capitalist work ethic.

The unaccommodated crowd, we are told, 'remained in the cul-de-sac ragged and bewildered' (271). The cityscape, like the threshold of the basement in the previous section, symbolically confines the emigrants from any positive, productive encounter with England. The cul-de-sac signifies their larger confinement within a metropolis of racialised 'dead-ends' and limits.[47] This sense of the metropolitan landscape as an essentially boundaried, exclusionary location threatens to foreclose the possibilities of any dialogue or growth between the nascent black community and Britain.

In 'Another time' the communal settings of the basement have been exchanged for a more impersonal, exterior London. The emigrant community of the novel now appears more internally divided and remote. As if to signpost this, the closing section opens with a street scene, away from the intimate gatherings of the dwelling place that have preceded it. The sense of estrangement that attends this experience is forged through a return to the first-person narration with which the novel began:

> This was an afternoon like any other, familiar, uneventful, obedient. The street was still there, almost empty ... I had walked this street for more than two years, at first curious, with a sense of adventure which offered me the details of the houses and the fences. Now it was my street. It seemed I had always walked it. It was a convenience which had been created for me. (231)

Despite a new sense of loneliness here, the repetitious pedestrian rhetoric (walking the street for two years) of the 'I' narrator also carves out a previously unavailable site of accommodation within London. The narrator's journey indicates a development within the novel, an emergence from the underworld of the basement. Earlier the street (above, white, exterior) was 'out-of-bounds', the opposite of the subterranean dwelling (below, black, interior). As such it represented a strange, unfamiliar or 'curious' world, signifying only in terms of 'houses' and 'fences' (both symbols of segregation within the novel). In time however, the city streets have become a 'familiar' territory, a setting to which the emigrant narrator does not merely belong, but which also belongs to him.

At the same time, the 'I' narrator's new sense of attachment to a wider urban environment does not appear to signal a simple utopian shift in *The Emigrants* from alienation to belonging. The act of walking described above has also become something metaphorically 'pedestrian', dull, monotonous: it has lost its earlier sense of adventure. Equally, as the sedentary conditions of 'Rooms and residents' are replaced with a more dynamic itinerancy, the mobile black body would seem to demarcate a new space of individuation and privacy within the novel, hinting at a wider fragmentation and dispersal of the emigrant community. In this context Lamming's visions for the future of black London are perhaps more pessimistic than they first appear.

However, it is important to note that, even as *The Emigrants* ultimately seems to signpost a movement away from Britain, the emigrants' potential departure from the landscape is performed through a self-conscious settling of, and settling within, the English landscape. The border tactics employed within the black basements of *The Emigrants* disturb dominant representations of the dwelling place in racial discourse of the early postwar period (where the black settler is consistently figured on the other side of the domestic threshold), turning them *inside out*. If Lamming's novel refuses the possibility of broader negotiations with the city of London, then it manages to symbolically destabilise the ways in which its spaces are racialised by dwelling, albeit temporarily, on figures of accommodation and habitation.

### Lyons and the Circus: naming and dwelling in Selvon's London

On a cold, dead night I walked into a cul-de-sac in Chelsea which they call World's End. It was my beginning. (Sam Selvon)[48]

*The Emigrants* is remarkable for the extent to which it narrates the migrant experience in Britain as a sedentary experience. The novel is stubbornly bound to a series of basement interiors from which the narrative, and its characters, rarely stray. Within Sam Selvon's 'London' fictions (a body of writing that extends beyond the writer's own stay in the city, from short stories such as 'Finding Piccadilly Circus' (1950) to the final novel of the 'Moses trilogy', *Moses Migrating* (1983)), the dwelling place is also a key chronotope. Moses's basement room exerts a magnetic pull upon the boys drawing them together from various parts of the city. It is here that the boys congregate, and exchange stories:

Nearly every Sunday morning, like if they going to church, the boys liming in Moses room, coming together for a oldtalk, to find out the latest gen, what happening, when is the next fete … Always every Sunday morning they coming to Moses, like if is confession, sitting down on the bed, on the floor, on the chairs, everybody asking what happening but nobody like they know what happening, laughing kiff-kiff at a joke … How many Sunday morning get-togethers gone like that? It look to him as if life composed of Sunday morning get-togethers in the room: he must make a joke of it during the week and say: 'You coming to church Sunday?' (138)

This 'small room' in which the boys are 'Lock up … with London and life on the outside' (140) describes a discrete world similar to the basement rooms of Lamming's novel. Housing is an exclusionary environment in *The Lonely Londoners*, imposing an architecture of segregation and individuation: 'It have people living in London who don't know what happening in the room next to them, far more the street … It divide up into little worlds, and you stay in the world you belong to' (74). These 'little worlds' contain and separate families and cultures, keeping at a distance the different ethnic communities of the city. At the same time, Selvon's basement fictions repeatedly disrupt the public/private thresholds installed by the English dwelling place. The basement described here is also 'church', a site of congregation and public exchange. Moreover, the majority of tales and anecdotes that comprise *The Lonely Londoners* unfold *indoors*. The basement in this context becomes an important repository for a group consciousness. It is here that the boys elaborate upon and establish a communal memory. Crucially in terms of the debates of this chapter, these memories are not just of Trinidad and the homeland but of London and their personal histories of being 'here'. Indeed it will be argued that having a history 'here' is crucial in terms of the power relations between the boys and the pecking order that is established among them. The dwelling place, in this context, becomes a key site for dwelling on the recent past.

Selvon's dwellings need distinguishing from the stifling interiority with which they become associated in *The Emigrants*. In *The Lonely Londoners* basement banter more often than not opens up a series of itineraries across the streets of London. There is a much more sustained, optimistic engagement with the built environment beyond the domestic interior in this text. Outdoors, which tends to operate as a site of exclusion in Lamming's novel, is more frequently a point of departure in *The Lonely Londoners*. Where pedestrian space appeared as a cul-de-sac in *The Emigrants*, associated with closure rather than progression, 'the boys' of Selvon's fiction are to be found 'liming' and 'coasting' the streets, inscribing London with an alternative pedestrian rhetoric, opening up new pathways and destinations across the city. Selvon's novel is ultimately less claustrophobic and housebound than Lamming's, moving beyond the bounds of the basement to explore the sites of an increasingly familiar, ever-expanding metropolis. The remainder of this chapter pursues the issue of dwelling within this broader context of the metropolis to consider how Selvon's 'boys' *domesticate* and make themselves at home within a wider urban environment beyond the basement.

Selvon's first 'London' novel, *The Lonely Londoners* (1956), has been seen as pivotal in 'charting' the black metropolis. Despite the publication of a range of black British writings before it (including *The Emigrants* two years earlier), its location has been granted a special, 'originary' status. The *Financial Times* reviewed *The Lonely Londoners* as 'The definitive novel about London's West Indians'.[49] Edward Baugh meanwhile described the novel as a 'landmark'.[50] More recently, in a book-length study of the writer, Mark Looker credits Selvon with, as the title of one chapter puts it, 'Inventing black London': 'In his stories, but more particularly in *The Lonely Londoners*, Selvon accomplishes that rare thing: he creates a world whose byways would be mapped by writers that followed.'[51] Looker's formulation here is interesting for the way in which it figures Selvon's predecessors as 'cartographers' of Selvon's originary 'creation' in a manner which seems to efface *The Lonely Londoners'* existence as discourse or representation.

Such individual evaluations are part of a wider critical perception of Selvon's literary landscapes as unreconstructed, authentic, or definitive. In an uncharacteristic piece of early literary criticism, Stuart Hall compares the work of Lamming and Selvon, noting that: 'Where Lamming begins as poet, Selvon begins as reporter. His [Selvon's] sense of fact, combined with the naturalism of his style, gives the impression of art without artifice, of content without technique.'[52] The perceived 'naturalism' of *The Lonely Londoners* has even led to its appropriation *outside* literary discourse. Within a range of empiricist accounts and studies (historical, political, sociological) of postwar black Britain, Selvon's fictions have been called upon as 'evidence' in the substantiation or validation of a black British past.[53] His black London is granted a quasi-empirical status in this context, as an uncontestable 'source' that is somehow able to transcend its own textuality.

The evaluation of *The Lonely Londoners* in terms of its reflection rather than its construction of the city has been exacerbated by the language debates surrounding Selvon's work. As one of the first novels to use a 'modified Caribbean dialect' (Selvon's phrase) throughout, the linguistic experimentation of *The Lonely Londoners* has received more critical attention than any of its other aspects.[54] Critical debate extends from the novel's episodic, 'ballad'-like structure, adapted from Trinidadian calypso, to its various rhetorical strategies: '"ole talk", "picong", "mamaguy", abuse'.[55] I am less interested in the specific details of these language debates here than I am with the ways in which they have been used to authenticate and essentialise the narrative 'voice' of that text. Selvon's use of dialect was interpreted by writers and critics of the 1950s and 1960s, notably George Lamming and Edward Brathwaite, as 'folk-sources' (Brathwaite), capable of tapping an 'essential' West Indian 'peasant sensibility' (Lamming).[56] Such interpretations are dependent upon problematic notions of dialect's 'instinctual' qualities, its naturalness, transparency, immediacy, or closeness to a genuine, or 'core' Caribbeanness.

language

Writing on language in *The Lonely Londoners* in 1977, Frank Birbalsingh observes that Selvon's 'dialect narrative imparts … a degree of Caribbean authenticity not easily found elsewhere in West Indian literature. When this narrative is combined with the tape-recorded dialogue, what we get is as faithful a copy of Caribbean life as exists in literature.'[57] In the same year, Peter Nazareth states that 'In *The Lonely Londoners*, Selvon tells his story in the artistic representation of Trinidadian dialect to create the authentic West Indian consciousness.'[58]

Selvon's modified dialect is entirely referential for these early critics, it appears capable of rendering a pure, unmediated and authentic West Indianness. On the other hand, Selvon's own comments on the linguistic experimentation of *The Lonely Londoners* highlight the constructedness of its language:

> I did not pick the Jamaican way of talking in London. I only tried to produce what I believed was thought of as a Caribbean dialect. The modified version in which I write my dialect may be a manner of extending the language. It may be called artificial or fabricated. The way I treat the language is not the way it is spoken in Jamaica, or Barbados, or Trinidad either, for that matter. I only resorted to a modified Trinidadian dialect because, much more than Jamaican or Barbadian English, it is close to 'correct' Standard English, and I thought it would be more recognizable to the European reader … I only modified it so people outside the Caribbean would be able to identify it.[59]

In contrast to his early critics, Selvon is keen to stress the artifice of his language: 'I only tried to produce what I believed was *thought of* as a Caribbean dialect.' More significantly, the passage questions the 'origins' and destination of Selvon's linguistic experimentation, which so far have been considered as firmly rooted in an uncontaminated Caribbean landscape. In this quotation dialect is described as offering a dialogue or site of negotiation between Caribbean and metropolitan landscapes. His language does not simply modify a West Indian vernacular but is also loosely structured around 'Standard English' in order to give it a signifying potential to the 'European reader'.

However desirable it may have been for critics such as Lamming and Brathwaite to reclaim the black metropolitan literatures of the 1950s for a specifically Caribbean context, the impact of these literatures for a burgeoning black British community was being reductively denied by them: 'Writers like Selvon … they never really left the land' wrote George Lamming in *The Pleasures of Exile*.[60] What is forgotten here is the relationship between Selvon's modified dialect and the landscape in which it actually appears: London. Dialect's destination, it would seem, is always outwards, away from England and towards the Caribbean: on the other hand the 'hereness' of Selvon's language and its situatedness within the metropolitan landscape of London is neglected.

In an important essay by Gordon Rohlehr published in the early 1970s the reliance of pioneering critiques such as Lamming's and Brathwaite's on an essentialising 'folk' mentality was questioned. Rohlehr argues:

> The 'boys' as Selvon calls his innocents abroad, reconstruct the 'lime' and the language of the 'lime', and through imposing their language on the great city, they remake it in their own image. Sometimes they shrink it by the use of a reductive simile. Hoary Paddington slums reveal walls which are cracking 'like the last days of Pompeii'. The winter sun, symbol of the devitalised misery of megalopolis, is 'like a force-ripe orange'. The 'boys', who have originated from a world of language, recreate in the big city a world of words in which they move, and through which they grope for clarity in the midst of experience as bewildering and vague as the London fog.[61]

The potential of Selvon's dialect for a reinvention of the landscape in which it emerges is identified here. It is this possibility of language (as well as a whole range of other signifying practices) to 'reconstruct', 'impose' and 'remake' the city that I shall pursue in this section.

At the same time there remains a problematic sense, within Rohlehr's account, that Selvon's modified vernacular 'originates' in the Caribbean. The boys, we are told, negotiate the city inside 'their' language, while trying to come to terms with the grim reality of the city outside it. In contrast to the originary 'world of language' that is the West Indies is an equally problematic sense of London as an extra-linguistic space, a space that exists before or outside of language. It is this dislocation between (Caribbean) lexis and (metropolitan) landscape that for Rohlehr means London is ultimately a 'strange world' in which the boys remain fragmented, partial personalities'.[62]

Extending Rohlehr's observations in her recent, illuminating work on Selvon, Susheila Nasta has proposed that the linguistic strategies of *The Lonely Londoners* create a 'city of words'. Selvon's dialect, she argues, facilitates 'the reclamation of an authentic language for identity', while forging 'a distance between the narrative voice and the city whilst establishing an intimacy between the reader and the story teller'.[63] This distance between language and metropolis ultimately creates 'voices in the wilderness', so that 'The black London of Selvon's "boys" has become by the close only a city of words' in which the boys 'remain adrift whatever the situation'.[64] As Nasta suggests, by the end of the novel the characters appear to be becoming increasingly detached from the city, the dynamism characterising much of the text seems increasingly exhausted: there 'is a great aimlessness, a swaying movement that leaving you standing in the same spot' (125). As with Lamming's *The Emigrants*, dwelling in the city has become directionless and disoriented by the end of the novel, no longer a strategy of survival but a sign of stagnancy.

However, within a narrative that privileges what John Thieme has called 'becoming, change and renewal' over linearity and closure (a novel in which the final paragraph appears to gesture metafictionally towards its actual beginning as 'writing'), to place too much emphasis on the ending would be dangerous. If the language of *The Lonely Londoners* signals its characters' 'disorientations', then it is also through language, and the process of naming in particular, that the boys make themselves at home in the city, transforming its alien landscapes into familiar dwelling places. What follows is an attempt to extend the historic body of criticism outlined above, in which language (understood as a transparent projection of the 'West Indian consciousness') tends to get detached from the metropolis (a pre-linguistic 'reality', always already there) through a consideration of these processes of naming.

The following extract from Selvon's early short story 'Finding Piccadilly Circus' (1950) tells the story of a Trinidadian's first encounter with London, and his attempts to locate Piccadilly Circus:

> Ah don't know how to begin to look for this circus. Ah hear so much about it. Everybody who comes back to Trinidad does tell yuh to go to Piccadilly Circus, that that is a hot place. And yuh pardner want to see this circus with lion and t'ing ...
>
> So Ah broach a policeman, and Ah say, 'Batch, is which part de circus is?' Well, he start to rub he chin, like he thinking hard, and then he say, 'Oh,' and he tell me where to go.
>
> But when Ah reach this place, Ah can't see de circus at all. Ah looking all about, but all Ah could see is a statue with ah little fella shooting ah bow and arrow. Ah stand up puzzle. Ah can't see no lion or no circus only Ah see ah people all over the place and car and bus.[65]

Lost in the city, the narrator is repeatedly misunderstood at, and misguided across, its symbolic spaces: 'Is which part yuh think I land up? In front ah place mark: Lyons. Ah had to laugh, boy, to see how people can't even spell "lion". So yuh pardner went in to buy a ticket, and ah woman behind ah counter ask, "Peas, cabbage or mix veg?" Ah stand up puzzle. Ah say, "Is de lions an t'ing Ah looking for"' (126). On the one hand, the narrator's inability to pin the city down, or locate it in any concrete sense,

appears to symbolise a fracture between the language of a local, vernacular subjectivity and the pre-existing, official landscape of monumental
London. At the same time the narrator of this story foregrounds the city
as a discursive landscape that was never simply already there: 'Everybody
who comes back to Trinidad does tell yuh to go to Piccadilly Circus, that
that is a hot place.' The narrator has encountered, invented and learned
London ('ah hear so much about it') well in advance of his arrival. These
earlier discursive encounters with the city make the one he finds on
arrival in England an incompatible, contestable space, which is not
'common-sense' or merely 'there'.

If London exists only as a city of words within the colonial Caribbean,
however, then the London that the emigrants encounter 'face-to-face'
does not somehow represent the 'real', unreconstructed, 'warts-and-all'
metropolis. To arrive in London, in Selvon's writing, is not simply to
demythologise the city, to uncover its 'harsh realities'. London remains,
for the boys of *The Lonely Londoners* a city composed of signs:

> Always, from the first time he went there to see Eros and the lights, that
> circus have a magnet for him, that circus represent life, that circus is the
> beginning and the ending of the world. Every time he go there, he have the
> same feeling like when he see it the first night, drink coca-cola, any time is
> guinness time, bovril and the fireworks, a million flashing lights, gay
> laughter, the huge posters, everready batteries, rich people going into tall
> hotels, people going to the theatre, people sitting and standing and walking
> and talking and laughing and buses and cars and Galahad Esquire, in all
> this, standing there in the big city, in London. Oh Lord.[66]

'Standing there', in the midst of the frenetic to-and-fro of the city's traffic,
Galahad appears mesmerised by his encounter with central London, the
beginning and ending of the world. What is striking is the extent to which
this real London is actually a landscape teeming with, and manufacturing
itself from, a proliferation of signs, images, narratives, performances. The
city encountered here is composed of theatres, statues and monuments,
as well as a proliferation of posters and advertisements. Coca-Cola,
Bovril, Guinness, Everready: these are products that Galahad is likely to
have already 'consumed' (as advertisements, or commodities) in colonial
Trinidad. And yet within the account above it is as if Galahad is seeing
them for the first time, as if he has entered a hyperreal landscape in which
London *is* Coca-Cola, Guinness, Bovril. Galahad's exploration of the city
does not uncover a 'real London' but confirms its reality as collection of
signs:

whenever he talking with the boys, he using the names of the places like they
mean big romance, as if to say 'I was in Oxford Street' have more prestige
than if he just say 'I was up the road.' And once he had a date with a frauline,
and he make a big point of saying he was meeting she by Charing Cross,
because just to say 'Charing Cross' have a lot of romance in it, he remember
it had a song called 'Roseann of Charing Cross.' ...

   Jesus Christ, when he say 'Charing Cross', when he realise that is he, Sir
Galahad, who going there, near that place that everybody in the world know
about (it even have the name in the dictionary) he feel like a new man. (84)

This passage in which Galahad's love affair with the city's women is paralleled with his love affair with the city itself in many ways typifies Selvon's
London. Both the female body and the 'body' of the metropolis become
eroticised 'sites' of a fetishistic surveillance and exploration by 'the boys'.
Moreover, Galahad's understanding of the city and the agency he attaches
to it here is centred on earlier representations of London's symbolic
landscapes: 'You remember that picture *Waterloo Bridge,* with Robert
Taylor?', Galahad asks Moses, 'I went down by the bridge the other night,
and stand up and watch the river' (85). Like the narrator of 'Finding
Piccadilly Circus', Galahad foregrounds London as a primarily *imagined*
geography composed through a range of disparate sign systems: music
and song, film, literature, conversation. 'It even have the name in the
dictionary', says Galahad of Charing Cross: his is an above all discursive
knowledge of the metropolis, a knowledge that has been acquired through
a range of social and institutional apparatuses in colonial Trinidad.

   What is being witnessed here is much more than the discursive power
of an imperial landscape (exported, for instance, as colonial education)
and the helplessness of the boys in the face of it. It is by illuminating the
city as a discursive site that Selvon is able to open London up and make it
susceptible to a rewriting, to alternative signifying processes. The metropolitan centre, as it was encountered by the boys in the colonial West Indies,
is not fixed or absolute but begins to accrue new meanings as 'the boys'
gradually settle in the metropolis. The veteran Londoner, Moses, responds
to Galahad's romantic naming of the city by telling him to 'Take it easy' (85):

   Ah, in you I see myself, how I was when I was new to London. All them
   places is like nothing to me now. Is like when you back home and you hear
   fellars talk about Times Square and Fifth Avenue, and Charing Cross and
   gay Paree. You say to yourself, 'Lord, them places must be sharp.' Then you
   get a chance and you see for yourself, and is like nothing. (85)

For Moses the names lovingly invoked by Galahad have become part of a
meaningless, empty inventory. Like the vocabularies of the narrator in

'Finding Piccadilly Circus', they have gradually become part of a redundant syntax, incompatible with the symbolic landscape of black London. The result is not silence, however, but the emergence of a new set of codes with which to name, enlist and map the city. It is by naming the city, that London is effectively 'settled' by the boys, becoming more than simply a site of dislocation and alienation, but also a landscape of belonging, of accommodation and of dwelling.

From the long opening sentence (also the opening paragraph) of *The Lonely Londoners*, this tension between alienation and familiarity is clearly evident:

> One grim winter evening, when it had a kind of unrealness about London, with a fog sleeping restlessly over the city and the lights showing in the blur as if is not London at all but some strange place on another planet, Moses Aloetta hop on a number 46 bus at the corner of Chepstow Road and Westbourne Grove to go to Waterloo to meet a fellar who was coming from Trinidad on the boat-train. (23)

The frozen, foggy and inhospitable streets of London announce an alien, alienating territory, a landscape described by Kenneth Ramchand as 'a nightmare world', a 'deathly universe'.[67] Yet this wasteland, like 'some strange place on another planet', is also, ironically, a city with which we are 'at home'. The opening draws upon a range of familiar literary archetypes of London: the fog, night, winter, 'unrealness', only to defamiliarise or *alienate* them through the voice of the narrator.[68] The 'standard' register of the metropolis appears otherwise within Selvon's modified Caribbean dialect. From the outset the narrator's location within and relationship to London is ambivalent. This is a speaker who appears both 'knowing' of, and a stranger to, London.

The opening description of the unreal city is further destabilised as the passage shifts to focus on Moses as he casually grabs a bus to the station. If this is a 'strange place' then Moses is no stranger too it. He seems to 'belong' to this environment. Moses has an intimate knowledge of his surroundings: he knows exactly where he is going. His instinctual move, as he 'hops' on to the number 46 (not any old bus), betrays an habitual, local knowledge of the area. There is a shift, during the course of this passage, between a sense of disorientation that is underlined in the drifting fog (we are given no bearings in this city) and a sense of orientation that is reinforced in the purpose and direction of Moses's movements, as he carves out a clear path through the metropolis. This shift between alienation and belonging is most clearly articulated through the naming of the landscape. In the opening words of the paragraph, the reader is confronted with a London void of locality, or place: the fog and the blur of lights produce an obscured, myopic geography in which it is difficult to gain orientation, or render familiar: this is the 'another planet' of which we are told. As the paragraph progresses, however, the city is made familiar through a precise topography which effectively localises London for the reader: Chepstow Road, Westbourne Grove, Waterloo.

Travelling back to Moses's basement on the Underground (subterranean London is as much a symbolic venue for Selvon as it is for Lamming) after picking up the 'fellar' (Henry Oliver) from Waterloo, Moses is quick to re-christen the arrivant 'Sir Galahad' (35). Sir Galahad, on the other hand, nicknames Moses 'mister London' (39). These names do not signify a detachment from the metropolis but an intimacy with both its geography (mister London) and mythology (Galahad). For Henry and Moses it is through nicknames that the two men establish friendship, turning their strangeness into a more casual familiarity. In this context I would want to challenge the notion that naming in *The Lonely Londoners* is, as Rohlehr posits, merely a sign of individuation, or fragmentation.[69] Names also offer a communal semantics for Selvon's West Indians, a collective code that allows new forms of spatial reference to develop. Nicknames are not just given to other West Indians, but also to the landscapes they inhabit. Like Moses and Henry Oliver's nicknames for one another, these names operate to domesticate the cityscape, to render it familiar.

Galahad's interminable questions on the underground as Moses takes them back to his Bayswater basement continually emphasise this dual significance of naming for both characters and cartographies within the city:

> 'Which part you living?' Galahad say.
> 'In the Water. Bayswater to you until you living in the city for at least two years.'
> 'Why they call it Bayswater? Is a bay? It have water?' (35)

Moses takes Galahad to 'the Water'. Selvon's use of names here, both for the city and for its characters, is clearly suggestive of a quasi-religious, Christian iconography and landscape.[70] Initiating Sir Galahad (as well as a larger group of West Indians) into the various rituals and ceremonies of black London, Galahad's journey to 'the Water' with Moses has a baptismal significance that is confirmed in Moses's naming of him. This act of naming signals Sir Galahad's 'rite of passage' into the local black community: Henry Oliver is known only by his new name from this point in the novel, not just by the characters, but also by the narrator. Names and the act of naming function throughout *The Lonely Londoners* to create a body politic, an imagined cultural community that is capable of regulating and reinforcing the boundaries between members and non-members, insiders and outsiders.

Moses's nickname for Bayswater ('the Water') carries a communal significance, it operates as the repository for a group consciousness, as a name that is available only to the established black settler communities of London. This is emphasised through Moses's questioning of Galahad's access to it (his communal membership is still on trial), as well as this newcomer's own inability to make 'Bayswater' signify. Moses uses 'the Water' as a nickname to underline his own sense of belonging, familiarity, his almost casual sense of being 'at ease' within the local landscape. When he tells Galahad he cannot use the name 'for at least two years', Moses is contrasting the arrivant's 'newness' in the metropolis against the length of his own stay and his agency as a veteran Londoner. Naming is used repeatedly in this way in *The Lonely Londoners* to historicise a presence within England and thereby assert and confirm personal status or power within the context of the local black community.

It is for similar reasons that Big City, another West Indian character in the novel, explodes when 'the boys' imply that he does not 'know' London because of his mis-namings of it:

> You think I don't know London? I been here ten years now, and it ain't have a part that I don't know. When them English people tell strangers they don't know where so and so is, I always know. From Pentonvilla right up to Musket Hill, all about by Claphand Common. I bet you can't call a name in London that I don't know where it is. (101)

While the comedy of this scene derives from Big City's mis-naming of the metropolis, its effect is not simply to represent the dislocations of a 'stranger' or 'newcomer'. Big City has spent a decade in England. Mis-naming, like naming in the novel, functions as a form of dissent, a disrespectful corruption of its proper nouns. Such acts display an irreverence towards the official 'language' of the city, symbolically disrupting its dominant geography, while simultaneously supplementing it with a vernacular landscape that operates outside the received, 'standard' London. A reinscription of London's official geography is rendered by these kind of shifting terms of address, opening up slippages that disrupt existing accommodations while at the same time depositing new ones.

Like Moses, Big City also uses names in order to underline his knowledge of, and intimacy with the city. A characteristic trait of Selvon's early London fictions is their characters' claims to, and boasts of, a superior knowledge of England, which they legitimise through reference to both

the length of their stay in the city and their intimacy with its geography.
In 'Waiting for Aunty to cough', a short story in Selvon's collection *Ways
of Sunlight* (1957), Brackley, who is seeing a 'girl' in the suburbs, boasts:

> you-all don't know London! You think London is the Gate and the Arch and
> Trafalgar Square, but them places is nothing. You ever hear about Honor
> Oak Rise …
>           That is a place in London man! I mean, look at it this way. You live in
> London so long, and up to now you don't know where that is.[71]

Names become a way of inserting oneself into, as well as disrupting, both
the national landscape and national memory of 'Brit'n' (again, note
Selvon's corruption and 'domestication' of proper names). In *The Lonely
Londoners* to 'know' England best and gain most respect from 'the boys', is
to have lived there the longest, to have forged an 'internal memory, or past,
a history that is *inside* England: 'You think this winter bad? You should
have been here in '52' (140). Such exchanges between the boys create a
hierarchy, a 'pecking order', with Moses/Mr London (the longest-standing
Londoner) at the top. Naming becomes closely bound up with the act of
dwelling in this context. It is part of a claim to a kind of lingering
historical and geographical 'situatedness' within the metropolis, not as a
form of passive assimilation (the vernaculars used to 'settle' this landscape
ensure this), but as an active assertion of residency, accommodation, 'at-
homeness'. This relationship between naming and dwelling processes is
not a discrete, cartographic issue but is bound up with the ways in which
the boys negotiate and inhabit the locations they have redefined.

### A 'little land' in London: the Gate, the Arch and the Water

> to the city boys, as soon as you start to hit Clapham Common or Chiswick
> or Mile End or Highgate, that mean you living in the country, and they out
> to give you tone like … 'You could get some fresh eggs for me where you
> living?' (Sam Selvon)[72]

On the one hand Selvon's naming of the city reconfigures London as a
global village, re-imaging it through the filter of a Caribbean lexis and
landscape so that, to quote Rohlehr's classic example, the 'winter sun'
becomes 'like a force-ripe orange'. On the other, Selvon's city is less significant as a site of transnational crossing than it is as a working-class
locale. Unlike *The Emigrants*, which narrates the lives of a broad cross-
section of West Indian settlers (from students to workers), Selvon's London
fictions of the 1950s and 1960s focus specifically on working-class West
Indian communities. For all the potential black Atlantic journeys that

*The Lonely Londoners* evokes, the actual itineraries of its characters are notably uncosmopolitan, confined as they are to central London and the monumental landscapes of the 'tourist' city.[73] Within this 'regional' locale, even Clapham and Highgate are exotic, pastoral landscapes beyond the city limits. *The Lonely Londoners* needs differentiating here from texts such as V.S. Naipaul's *The Mimic Men*, where the city is 'two-dimensional', lacking in substance: 'I would play with famous names as I walked empty streets and stood on bridges. But the magic of names soon faded. Here was the river, here the bridge, there that famous building … My incantation of names remained unanswered.'[74] The performative function of naming in *The Lonely Londoners* is crucial to the boys' 'settlement' of London. The dialogue they generate contrasts with the empty, isolated incantations of Naipaul's protagonist, Ralph Singh. Where Singh appears worldly and distanced, capable of transcending the city (living as he does in a 'far-out suburban hotel' (11)), Selvon's boys are firmly rooted within a local landscape, what one early reviewer termed 'little London':

> an exotic London, bounded, on the west by 'the Gate' (Notting Hill) in the East by 'the Arch' (Marble Arch) and in the north by 'the Water' (Bayswater). Londoners of longer standing will hardly recognise this little land, less than two square miles in area … It is not quite a real London; but it is a measure of Mr. Selvon's skill and sympathy that he convinces the reader that it is indeed the London perceived by his characters.[75]

As the boys rename the city, its boundaries are redrawn. The 'familiar' city is disrupted, making it almost unrecognisable to 'longer standing' Londoners. More importantly it is through the habitual repetition of these new names ('the Arch', 'the Water', 'the Gate'), that the boys *inhabit* or domesticate London for themselves. The ritual of naming renders the metropolis familiar and available to the new community. The names by which the boys' London is 'bound' are as significant as the boundaries themselves here.

If this confined space outlines the borders of Selvon's London, its limits are not simply markers of the boys' enclosure. The clustered patterns, the gatherings and congregations that characterise the process of West Indian settlement in and around 'the Water' (Bayswater) sees a restructuring of London in terms of the Caribbean. Tanty's choice of dwelling place is informative in this sense: 'Like how some people live in small village and never go to the city, so Tanty settle down in Harrow Road in the Working Class area' (80). Tanty's settlement in London is founded on a village-based existence exported from the Caribbean and is part of a more sustained communal establishment of location within *The Lonely Londoners*.

Like the dwelling places already explored in Lamming's novel, these emergent sites of accommodation appear as pockets or clusters at which the narrative tends to 'dwell' within a predominantly white urban environment. As the text gravitates towards these dwelling places, alternative maps of the city emerge. Such localised or 'regional' centres of West Indian settlement provide vernacular havens, which, while being inescapably metropolitan, also clearly transplant the values, practices and geographies of a culture left behind.

This transformation of the local metropolitan landscape is epitomised in Tanty's shopping excursions. Constantly engaging 'in big oldtalk with the attendants, paying no mind to people waiting in the queue' (80), her penchant for spreading gossip around the local community means 'it didn't take she long to make friend and enemy with everybody in the district' (78). Tanty's regular sorties to the grocer's effectively transform the local store. Through her bullying banter, her demands for West Indian foodstuffs and a credit system for the local Caribbean community – 'One day she ask the shopkeeper if he know about trust', 'Where I come from you take what you want and you pay every Friday' (80) – Tanty reorganises the shop in terms of the West Indian market. As she 'spread the ballad' (79) of her victory in the grocery among the local community of West Indian women, the shop is colonised by the new settlers:

> It does be like a jam-session there when all the spade housewives go to buy, and Tanty in the lead. They getting on just as if they in the market-place back home: 'Yes child, as I was telling you, she did lose the baby ... half-pound salt-fish please, the dry codfish ... yes, as I was telling you ... and two pounds rice, please, and half-pound red beans, no, not that one, that one in the bag in the corner ...' (78)

This emergence of a 'market-place back home' within the English corner shop echoes the kind of unofficial urban economies already encountered at the barber shops of Fred Hill and Miss Dorking.[76] Such locations are important 'centres' for the black communities of *The Lonely Londoners*. The East End tailor shop near Aldgate station is 'full up with spades' (77), because of its emphasis on a marketplace culture based on customer loyalty, privileges and trust (free cigars and options to return or get refunds on garments). In a manner reminiscent of Fred Hill's basement, the walls of this shop are lined with photographs 'of all the black boxers in the world, and any photo of any presentation or function that have spades in it' (77).

The success of such businesses is dictated not by the broader economic climate of London but by the dissemination of local gossip and rumour among the boys. If the popularity of this tailor shop depends on 'word-of-mouth', then another tailor shop, run by a 'Jew feller in Edgware Road', is given a wide berth by the boys because 'once he make a cheap garbadeen suit for a Jamaican and hit him twenty-five guineas, and since that time the boys give the shop a long walk' (78).

In this shift away from a strictly First World capitalist economy to one based on barter, negotiation, exchange, 'trust', gossip and rumour, the emergence of a marketplace rhetoric within Selvon's London can be traced:

> The grocery it had at the bottom of the street was like a shop in the West Indies. It had Brasso to shine brass, and you could get Blue for when you washing clothes, and the feller selling pitchoil. He have the pitchoil in some big drum in the back of the shop in the yard, and you carry your tin and ask for a gallon, to put in the cheap oil burner. The shop also have wick, in case the wick in your burner go bad, and it have wood cut up in little bundles to start coal fire. Before Jamaicans start to invade Brit'n, it was a hell of a thing to pick up a piece of saltfish anywhere, or to get thing like pepper sauce or dasheen or even garlic ... But now, papa! Shop all about start to take in stocks of foodstuffs what West Indians like, and today is no trouble at all to get saltfish and rice. This test who had the grocery, from the time the spades start to settle in the district, he find out what sort of things they like to eat, and he stock up with a lot of things like blackeye peas and red beans and pepper sauce, and tinned breadfruit and ochro and smoke herring. (76–7)

This lengthy descriptive account is particularly noteworthy within a novel that is mostly structured around the shifting dialogues of the boys: it marks out a significant narrative dwelling place within the text. The meticulous inventory of hardware and foodstuffs indicates something of the narrator's intimate knowledge of this West-Indian-style grocery: it appears as a familiar narrative venue in the text, a site at which the narrator appears 'at home'. The wares it offers sustain and seduce a West Indian community, offering provisions only otherwise available in the homeland. While signalling something of its customers' social status as an economic underclass, the grocery is also significantly modelled on the pragmatics of a market-based, day-to-day economy: pitchoil is available by the tinful, along with exchangeable wicks and bundles of wood.

At the same time the store does not ultimately signify a straight-forward West Indian 'colonization' of the city. If the grocer's is on one level suggestive of the marketplace, then it remains to a large degree structured around the overdeveloped world's capitalist value-systems.

The owner's transformation of the shop is a sign not of his sensitivity towards the cultural values of a new community but of his commercial enterprise: 'as long as the spades spending money he don't care, in fact is big encouragement, "Good morning sir," and "What can I do for you, sir" and "Do come again"' (77). Nevertheless, it is through the grocer's accommodation of Caribbean commodities and provisions that a West Indian community is sustained, and a potentially transitory, provisional street life is encouraged to settle.

In addition to the local streets of working-class London, *The Lonely Londoners* also sees the boys hanging about at the central, monumental landscapes of the city: Piccadilly Circus, Trafalgar Square, Hyde Park, Marble Arch. 'The Arch' is a favourite gathering point during summer months, providing a dwelling place, beyond the confines of the basement: 'It have no other lime in London that Big City like more' (98):

> On any Sunday in the summer ... all the boys dressing up and coasting lime by the Arch, listening to all them reprobates and soapbox politicians, looking around to see if they could pick up something in the crowd. From east and west, north and south, the boys congregate by the Arch. (98)

At the Arch the dispersed representatives of London's West Indian community draw together from all points of the compass. Situated at the imaginary borders of Selvon's 'little land', the Arch is also a crossroads at which the boys meet. Again, the process of 'nicknaming' the city (as Marble Arch becomes 'the Arch'), displays something of the boys' familiarity with this location. Big City is attracted to the Arch because he likes to 'listen to them fellars [at Orators' Corner] talking about how the government this and that, or making big discussion on the colour problem' (98). Similarly Galahad, visiting the Arch for the first time, is 'amaze at how them fellars saying all kind of thing against the government and the country, and the police not doing them anything' (98). If the radio and the newspaper are the official channels for the dissemination of racist mythologies in Selvon's *The Lonely Londoners*, then the Arch offers a counter-discursive venue at which a potentially subversive black politics might articulate and organise itself.[77] However this potential remains unrealised in Selvon's novel. There is a certain trivialization of, and lack of commitment to, the mobilisation of a black 'political' community by the boys of *The Lonely Londoners* that distinguishes them from black literary subjects of the 1970s. When Galahad makes a stand 'on the colour problem' (99) at Orators' Corner, any political impact of his words is diminished by the cajoling and heckling of the boys (99).

Equally, Galahad's inability to vocalise or articulate his plight is symptomatic of a more general inability, among black settlers of the early postwar period to narrate or galvanise themselves into a political community. In contrast to the literatures considered in Chapter 3, where the city plays an instrumental role in the 'expression' of politicised black cultural formations, the black metropolis of the 1950s is as often a sight of self-gratification and pleasure-seeking. As the narrator of *The Lonely Londoners* puts it at one point: 'Piccadilly is my Playground'. For all its harshness, Selvon's city is also a 'circus' to the boys who inhabit it, a space of adventure, of spectacle, a site of entertainment, play and hedonistic excess.

## Conclusion: 'A place to retire to ...'

The question of having a roof overhead becomes very important in a cold country ... From my observation of the immigrants in London, these are the things they strive for most desperately. It also becomes very difficult for them to even get a room to stay in because of social pressure and therefore, it acquires a greater desperation, a greater need and urgency to make sure that you have a room at least that you can return to, that you can at least retire to.

That is the sort of situation that exists, the type of building that a black immigrant gets to buy is one that is about to be demolished. He hasn't got a great deal of choice of houses. He has to take what he gets, but menial as it may be, it is still something to possess his own house in a strange country. (Sam Selvon)[78]

Here Selvon reflects on the difficulty of finding accommodation as a black settler in early postwar Britain, a consequence of the tensions surrounding housing and immigration discussed in the opening section. Even the property that *is* available here is derelict or 'about to be demolished'. At the same time, his account signals the importance of 'having a roof over head', of finding a home and settling in. Paradoxically, the bleak housing conditions facing black settlers in this period only *increases* emotional investment in the dwelling place according to Selvon. Within the wider, less tenable landscape of the London he portrays here, the home represents a vital locus of 'return' and 'retirement'. In spite of everything, the house 'is still something to *possess*'. Of course, these dwellings are in many ways fragile: they don't appear to offer permanent foundations for the boys. It is significant then that the vast majority of property in early postwar writing is rented, or temporary (though Selvon's *Moses Ascending* and *The Housing Lark* have blacks buying, or struggling to buy, houses).

However the extent to which fictions of the early postwar period dwell on property and the search for it distinguishes it from contemporary black British writing where the home has been all but abandoned. Where the home tends to function as a refuge, a site of gathering in fictions of the 1950s and 1960s, contemporary black British writing has privileged it as site of flight, a point of dispersal or departure. The centripetal force that housing ritually exacts in early postwar literature has since the 1980s become an increasingly centrifugal one. The kind of claustrophobic anxiety that is symptomatic of Karim Amir's desire to be 'always somewhere else' in *The Buddha of Suburbia* (see Chapter 4) typifies a more general distaste for the dwelling place in recent writing. This shift over the postwar period is perhaps indicative of the growing influence of a poetics of itinerancy in contemporary diasporic writing, as well as the changing history of the black British homestead over the past fifty years. The distaste for dwelling that emerges in much contemporary literature is frequently explained in terms of the new lifestyles home accommodates. For example, the often idealised, all-male gatherings that form a substantial part of the close-knit basement culture in writings of the 1950s have since given way to family lives, frequently divided along gender and generational lines. Here the dysfunctional domestic worlds experienced by Hyacinth in Joan Riley's *The Unbelonging* (1985), or Dele in Diran Adebeyo's *Some Kind of Black* (1996), hint at a much more widespread sense of alienation from the dwelling place. The possibility that Karim's relatively privileged middle-class background makes available to drift between a range of different houses in *The Buddha of Suburbia* needs differentiating from Selvon's black underclass. For Selvon the house *cannot* be abandoned, offering as it does a site of survival within a broader context of 'social pressure', 'desperation' and 'urgency'. These factors make having a 'roof overhead' only *more* important.

The basements and bedsits of Lamming and Selvon signal the lowly status of their black characters. Nevertheless, they also make available spaces at which to undermine the city's foundations symbolically. In both *The Emigrants* and *The Lonely Londoners* rooms offer temporary sanctuary: they are public, rather than private spaces associated with gathering and the establishment of a communal politics. Moreover, Selvon's fiction proposes a domestication of London that stretches well beyond the domestic interior (nicknamed 'the yard' in *The Lonely Londoners*). Renaming 'Proper London' through the language of the boys, Selvon does not just 'defamiliarise' the city, he also transforms it into a 'homely' location.

## Notes

1   Lord Kitchener, 'My landlady's too rude…', in Sheila Patterson, *Dark Strangers: A Sociological Study of the Absorption of a Recent West Indian Group in Brixton, South London*, London: Tavistock Publications, 1963, p. 209. Patterson tells us that this calypso was 'composed and sung by Lord Kitchener in *A Man from the Sun*, a play given on BBC television in 1956'. Also in James Procter (ed.) *Writing Black Britain 1948–1998*, Manchester: Manchester University Press, 2000, p. 20.

2   Donald Hinds, *Journey to an Illusion – The West Indian in Britain*, London: Heinemann, 1966. Hinds was a bus driver and part-time writer in London in the early postwar period. *Journey to an Illusion* is a valuable compilation of accounts by a range of West Indians made during the 1950s and early 1960s.

3   Ruth Glass, *Newcomers: The West Indians in Britain*, London: Centre for Urban Studies and Allen & Unwin, 1960, p. 50.

4   Notably Charles Booth's *Life and Labour of the People of London* (1891–1902). Although there is not space within this book to offer a genealogy of racial vocabularies in Britain, it is important to note that the language of black racial discourse in the 1950s and early 1960s was not simply 'invented' for the new postwar black settler. Rather, it borrows from and modifies a much earlier imagery from the nineteenth and early twentieth centuries, an imagery previously applied to Eastern European and Irish immigrants as well as the working class.

5   Ruth Glass observes in *Newcomers* that 'In the four issues of the *Kensington Post* from 27th November to 18th December, 1959, there were 645 advertisements for furnished accommodation inserted by private landlords. Only two of these private advertisements were "pro-coloured": but 102, one in six, were "anti-coloured", as compared with one in eight in the earlier account [taken a year earlier]', p. 60.

6   Glass, *Newcomers*, p. 46.

7   These vocabularies were used across a wide range of texts in the 1950s and 1960s. See, for example, Claudia Jones, 'The Caribbean community in London', in *I Think of My Mother: Notes on the Life and Times of Claudia Jones*, London: Karia Press, 1985 (originally published 1964), p. 148; Glass, *Newcomers*, p. 57; Patterson, *Dark Strangers*, p. 186; Edward Pilkington, *Beyond the Mother Country*, London: I.B. Tauris, 1988, pp. 53–68.

8   The term *laissez-faire* was first used in this context by A. Sivanandan according to Stuart Hall, 'Racism and reaction', in *Five Views of Multi-cultural Britain*, London: Commission for Racial Equality, 1978, p. 27.

9   Anthony Richmond, *Colour Prejudice in Britain: A Study of West Indian Workers in Liverpool, 1941–1951*, London: Routledge, 1954, p. 73.

10  *Picture Post*, 30 October 1954, p. 23.

11  Hall 'Racism and reaction', p. 27. For a discussion of housing shortages in the 1950s see Pilkington, *Beyond the Mother Country*, p. 53.

12 Patterson, *Dark Strangers*, p. 183.

13 Patterson, *Dark Strangers*, pp. 182–3.

14 Ironically, it was the black settlers who were often the first to renovate and modernise these dilapidated properties, see D. Hiro, *Black British, White British*, London: Eyre & Spottiswoode, 1971, p. 72.

15 E.J.B. Rose, *Colour and Citizenship: A Report on British Race Relations*, London: Oxford University Press, 1969, p. 123. Also see Paul Gilroy, *There Ain't no Black in the Union Jack*, London: Routledge, 1987, pp. 79–80. Section two pursues these debates over the density of black housing further in terms of the 'shebeen'.

16 Patterson, *Dark Strangers*, p. 183.

17 In this period pathogenic paranoia surrounding relationships between black men and white women meant that miscegenation was not only construed as 'deviant' but was 'seen to violate the sanctity of white British womanhood, the bearer of national culture'. (W. James and C. Harris (eds) *Inside Babylon*, London: Verso, 1993, p. 64). The Royal Commission Report, published in 1949, provided the following cautionary narrative: 'Immigration on a large scale ... would only be welcoming ... if the immigrants were of good stock and were not prevented by their religion or race from intermarrying with the host population and becoming merged with it' (R. Miles and A. Phizacklea, *White Man's Country*, London: Pluto, 1984, p. 24).

18 'The dark million – 6', *The Times*, 23 January 1965.

19 Rex Collings (ed.) *Reflections: Selected Writings and Speeches of Enoch Powell*, London: Bellew Publishing, 1992, p. 166.

20 Peter Griffiths, *A Question of Colour?*, London: Leslie Frewin, 1966, p. 119.

21 Patterson, *Dark Strangers*, p. 198.

22 Griffiths, *A Question of Colour?*, p. 91.

23 See chapter 3 of *There Ain't no Black in the Union Jack*.

24 'The dark million – 4', *The Times*, 21 January 1965.

25 Elspeth Huxley, *Back Street New Worlds*, London: Chatto, 1964, p. 65.

26 'The dark million – 4'.

27 Helen Tiffin, 'New concepts of person and place', in P. Nightingale (ed.) *A Sense of Place in the New Literatures in English*, St Lucia: University of Queensland Press, 1986, p. 23.

28 V.S. Naipaul, *The Mimic Men*, London: André Deutsch, 1967.

29 O.R. Dathorne, *Dumplings in the Soup*, London: Cassell, 1963.

30 Timothy Brennan, *Salman Rushdie and the Third World: Myths of a Nation*, London: Macmillan, 1989, pp. 69–70.

31 The basement is not just a recurrent venue in the fiction of Lamming and Selvon; it is also a key symbolic space in African-American writing. See Richard Wright's 'The man who lived underground' (1944) and Ralph Ellison's *Invisible Man* (1952).

32 See Kobena Mercer, *Welcome to the Jungle*, London: Routledge, 1994, p. 100.

33 In his essay 'Black hair/style politics' Kobena Mercer notes the preponderance

of barber shops in black neighbourhoods and the possibilities they open for 'expressing the aspirations of black people historically excluded from access to official social institutions of representation and legitimation in urban, industrialised societies of the capitalist First World'. The barber shops in this section operate in a similar way, to open up territories for black expression.

34  George Lamming, *The Emigrants*, London: Michael Joseph, 1964, p. 129.

35  Homi Bhabha, *The Location of Culture*, London: Routledge, 1994, p. 4.

36  This is not to suggest that Bhabha has 'got it wrong'. It was never his intention to offer a 'situated' account of diaspora experience. Indeed, his spatial metaphors have stimulated some productive research. On their own however, and as they have been taken up within the academy, they have prompted a proliferation of abstract, dislocated geographies which it seems to me refuse to commit themselves to a *politics* of diaspora experience.

37  Mike Phillips and Trevor Phillips (eds) *Windrush: The Irresistible Rise of Multiracial Britain*, London: HarperCollins, 1998, p. 135. In an alternative account within the same book the stairwell or kitchen is remembered in similar terms: 'you come home in the afternoon and you put your ten pence, five pence in the meter, and somebody will even move your pot over when you've gone back in your room, and you come back, there's no money in the cooker but your pot isn't cooked' (pp. 130–1).

38  Robert Moore, 'Housing', in Richard Hooper (ed.) *Colour in Britain*, London: BBC, 1965, p. 67. Similarly Ruth Glass in *Newcomers* points out: 'It is difficult to avoid quarrels when several families share a cooker on a landing and an antiquated W.C.' (p. 56).

39  Patterson, *Dark Strangers*, p. 183.

40  Patterson, *Dark Strangers*, p. 204.

41  Patterson, *Dark Strangers*, p. 204.

42  Trevor Philpott, 'Would you let your daughter marry a Negro?', *Picture Post*, 30 October 1954, p. 21.

43  Enoch Powell, 'To the Annual Conference of the Rotary Club in London', in Collings (ed.) *Reflections*, p. 175.

44  This simile seems appropriate given the criminalised underworld the men are about to enter: later in the text the basement is visit by a policeman following the arrest of Higgins as a suspected drugs peddler. As the Jamaican remarks in response to the policeman's enquiries, 'they think there is some black underground connecting every one of us' (p. 159).

45  As one critic puts it, *The Emigrants*' 'corresponding images of obscured vision and constricted life' are best understood as they intensify 'at the very bottom of the stairwell firmly establish[ing] the theme of an underground that is both prison and hell'. Sandra Paquet, *The Novels of George Lamming*, London: Heinemann, 1982, p. 37.

46  This is also true of Lamming's *Water with Berries* (1971).

47  The cul-de-sac is also a metaphor used by Kamau Brathwaite in an early essay on the state and status of Caribbean writing in 1950s Britain to describe what

he felt was 'the disintegration of the old West Indian folk personality': 'The novels so far written in London by West Indians are novels of disorganisation, of misunderstanding'. Brathwaite, 'Sir Galahad and the islands', *Bim*, 7:25 (1957), pp. 8–16.

48  Sam Selvon, 'A leaf in the wind', *Bim*, 4:16 (1952), p. 287.

49  Front and back cover of the Longman edition of *The Lonely Londoners*.

50  Edward Baugh, 'Friday in Crusoe's city: the question of language in two West Indian novels of exile', in S. Nasta (ed.) *Critical Perspectives on Sam Selvon*, Washington DC: Three Continents Press, 1988, p. 240. I am grateful to Susheila Nasta's important bibliographical and editorial work on Sam Selvon for drawing my attention to a range of literary criticism in this area.

51  Mark Looker, *Atlantic Passages: History, Community, and Language in the Fiction of Sam Selvon*, New York: Peter Lang Publishing, 1996, p. 60. Similarly, Susheila Nasta describes the novel as a 'pioneering work ... emblematic in its creation of a black colony' (p. 79) while noting that Maya Angelou has spoken of Selvon as the 'father of Black Literature in Britain' (p. 72).

52  Stuart Hall, 'Lamming, Selvon and some trends in the West Indian novel', *Bim*, 6:23 (1965), p. 176.

53  See, for example, Glass, *Newcomers*; Patterson, *Dark Strangers* and Pilkington, *Beyond the Mother Country*.

54  See Michel Fabre, 'Samuel Selvon: interviews and conversations', in Nasta (ed.) *Critical Perspectives on Sam Selvon*, Washington DC: Three Continents Press, 1988.

55  Gordon Rohlehr, 'The folk in Caribbean literature', *Tapia*, December 1972, in Nasta (ed.) *Critical Perspectives on Sam Selvon*, Washington DC: Three Continents Press, 1988, p. 39.

56  Brathwaite, 'Sir Galahad and the islands', p. 22. George Lamming, *The Pleasures of Exile*, London: Michael Joseph, 1960, p. 225.

57  Frank Birbalsingh, 'Samuel Selvon and the West Indian literary renaissance', *Ariel*, 8:3, in Nasta (ed.) *Critical Perspectives on Sam Selvon*, Washington DC: Three Continents Press, 1988, p. 154.

58  Peter Nazareth, 'The clown in the slave ship', *Caribbean Quarterly*, 23:2/3, in S. Nasta (ed.) *Critical Perspectives on Sam Selvon*, Washington DC: Three Continents Press, 1988, p. 234.

59  Michel Fabre, 'Samuel Selvon', p. 67.

60  Lamming, *The Pleasures of Exile*, p. 45

61  Rohlehr, 'The folk in Caribbean literature', p. 41.

62  Rohlehr, 'The folk in Caribbean literature', p. 41.

63  Susheila Nasta, 'Setting up home in a city of words', p. 83. Nasta elaborates on some of these points in her recent book *Home Truths: Fictions of the South Asian Diaspora in Britain*, Basingstoke: Palgrave, 2002.

64  Nasta, 'Setting up home in a city of words', pp. 87 and 79.

65  Sam Selvon, 'Finding Piccadilly Circus', *Guardian Weekly*, in K. Ramchand and S. Nasta (eds) *Foreday Morning: Selected Prose 1946–1986*, Harlow: Longman,

1989, p. 125. All further references are to this edition and are included in the text.

66  Sam Selvon, *The Lonely Londoners*, Harlow: Longman, 1956, p. 90. All further references are to this edition and are in the text.

67  K. Ramchand, 'Songs of innocence, songs of experience: Samuel Selvon's *The Lonely Londoners* as a literary work', *WLWE*, 21:3 (1982), p. 226.

68  Selvon's play with a modernist London, notably the 'unreal city' of T.S. Eliot's 'The Waste Land', is clear here. Susheila Nasta has also noted its echoes of canonical texts such as Eliot's 'Prufrock' and Dickens's *Bleak House* in Nasta (ed.) *Critical Perspectives on Sam Selvon*, pp. 223–33.

69  'the boys remain fragmented, partial personalities … they have nicknames, not real names. Perhaps, nicknames are an acknowledgment of individual richness … but they are also suggestive of an incompleteness of self' (Rohlehr, 'The folk in Caribbean literature', p. 41).

70  Speaking on the subject of diaspora and the manufacture of national identities in a very different context, Paul Gilroy has cited a useful passage from Rousseau on the history of the Children of Israel that is particularly illuminating in terms of Selvon's novel: '[Moses] conceived and executed the astonishing project of creating a nation out of a swarm of wretched fugitives, without arts, arms, talents, virtues or courage, who were wandering as a horde of strangers over the face of the earth without a single inch of ground to call their own. Out of this wandering and servile horde Moses had the audacity to create a body politic, a free people … To prevent his people from melting away among foreign peoples, he gave them customs and usages incompatible with those of other nations; he over-burdened them with peculiar rites and ceremonies; he inconvenienced them in a thousand ways in order to keep them constantly on the alert and to make them forever strangers among other men' ('Diaspora and the detours of identity', in K. Woodward (ed.) *Identity and Difference*, London: Sage, 1997).

71  Sam Selvon, *Ways of Sunlight*, Harlow: Longman, 1957, p. 129. All further references are to this edition and are included in the text.

72  'Waiting for Aunty to cough', in *Ways of Sunlight*, p. 127.

73  Despite the settlement of blacks in other British cities and other *parts* of the city, there are surprisingly few fictional accounts of these places in early postwar black British writing.). There are of course some notable exceptions, for example G.R. Fazakerely's novel *A Stranger Here* (1959), which is set in Liverpool. The boys' 'discovery' of the city is frequently paralleled with the carnivalesque excesses of a working-class tourism. See the visit to 'Hamdon Court' in *The Housing Lark* for an instance of this.

74  Naipaul, *The Mimic Men*, p. 19.

75  Bruce Hamilton, *Bim*, 7:25 (1956), pp. 61–2.

76  This sort of marketplace landscape becomes an increasingly substantive symbolic venue in black British writing of the 1970s and early 1980s (see Chapter 3), where it tends to constitute an emphatic marker of (black) cultural

difference within the city. By the late 1980s and early 1990s, however, these locations were being abandoned for alternative modes of narrating the relations between commodification and the black subject: I will be considering these alternatives in Chapter 4 in terms of Meera Syal's *Anita and Me* and Hanif Kureishi's *The Buddha of Suburbia.*

77  As the narrator puts it in a section describing white myths of black settlement, 'Newspaper and radio rule this country' (p. 24).

78  Peter Nazareth, 'Interview with Sam Selvon', in S. Nasta (ed.) *Critical Perspectives on Sam Selvon*, p. 89.

# 3

# The street

## Introduction

> ... the race issue had entered the streets. (Stuart Hall *et al.*)[1]

On 30 August 1970 an article by two commentators appeared in the *Sunday Times* entitled 'Blacks and police – how the rot set in'. Although it was published on the day of the Notting Hill Carnival, the streets of Notting Hill, the article states, are empty. The carnival has been cancelled after confrontations, three weeks earlier, between police and Notting Hill's West Indian community over raids on a Caribbean restaurant and meeting place: the Mangrove.[2] However, it is not with the Mangrove itself that the *Times* article concludes, but with the image of a black pedestrian strolling along the streets outside: 'A tall, lithe Negro walking elegantly down Ladbroke Grove wearing a vivid Dashiki (African shirt), woolly hat, blue trousers and patterned moccasin is the personification of everything an Englishman isn't.'[3]

The pedestrian body of this article is called upon to inform deteriorating relations between blacks and the police. Racial alterity is not only embodied in this street figure in such a way that it comes to constitute a categorical difference: walking, it insinuates, *makes* the difference. In the *Times* article perambulation and street occupation appear as racially determined acts. The height of the 'Negro', his 'litheness', the 'elegance' of his walk are used to diagnose an essentialised and innate 'negritude' that has its origins in nature, not culture, that is expressive of an unquestionable racial taxonomy. His walk is the 'personification' of some absolute difference between blacks and the English, African-Caribbeans and the police.

Where the *Times* article presents walking and street occupation as racially determined acts, this chapter explores them as culturally encoded practices. The 1970s saw a move away from the formal, 'stiff' dress codes and postures epitomised in the suits and Sunday bests of the boat train

"Nobody can accuse me of
discrimination, Sambo -
Now move on ! "

2  *Race Today* cartoon, February 1973

crowds (see Chapter 6). With the arrival of reggae and rastafarianism, black British youth began to fashion what Dick Hebdige calls a 'natural image' of itself.[4] Of course this shift in style was by no means 'natural'. It was part of a wider cultural and political shift away from the kind of ideologies of whiteness and civility that Wole Soyinka associated with early postwar dress in 'Two in London' (1961): 'My dignity is sewn / Into the lining of a three-piece suit. / Stiff, and with the whiteness which / Out-Europes Europe'.[5] However, such shifts in style did involve appro-

3   Horace Ove, *Pressure*, 1974

priating the *language* of 'naturalness'. Here the pristine, 'starched' styles
of the 1950s and 1960s were exchanged for an 'uncultivated', 'wild',
untended, dishevelled look. This 'looseness' or slackness can be read in
the development of an alternative pedestrian posture in the 1970s: the
change in gait, the relaxed, or 'lazy' perambulation, which recreates
something of what Hebdige calls the 'slowness', the 'ponderous and
moody rhythms' (31) of reggae. In this period the black body is ritually
figured propping up walls and lamp-posts, lingering on street corners,
hands in pockets, the body exaggeratedly slouching (see figures 2 and 3).

Such transformations in pedestrian style and stance took place at
precisely that moment when black was being remobilised in Britain as a
political category, detached from its earlier, negative connotations and
rearticulated as a positive signifier: 'black is beautiful'. The 'dishevelled'
look of rasta style played an important role in this process of rearticula-
tion, transforming markers of shame into markers of pride. In this
context the black pedestrian body becomes part of a positive and politicised assertion of 'racial' difference and of opposition. The oppositional
qualities of black street occupation were perhaps most visible in the
military accent of black clothing in the seventies: 'On every British high

street stood an army surplus store which supplied the righteous with battle dress and combat jackets: a whole wardrobe of sinister guerrilla chic'.[6] Military regalia was a 'theme' of the 1978 Notting Hill Carnival (see figure 4) and uniforms were central to black power organisations such as the British Black Panthers in the 1970s, offering an important means of identification.

What is striking about many of these street styles is the extent to which they are dependent upon a range of diasporic attachments elsewhere: Africa, Jamaica, the United States. Dick Hebdige has stressed the 'cut-and-mix' qualities of black British style, and the uptake of a 'refracted form of Rastafarian aesthetic, borrowed from the sleeves of imported reggae albums and inflected to suit the needs of second-generation immigrants' (43). Kobena Mercer, on the other hand, has spoken of the 'diasporean' nature of black hair and style politics and the desire they express to 'return to the roots'.[7] If such transatlantic correspondences signal a kind of cultural itinerancy then they need also to be understood at a local level as part of territorialised pedestrian culture. The appearance of black military outfits and uniforms on the street might have been informed by shifts in urban style in the United States, but they also worked to signify black solidarity 'here', a communal stance against 'white oppression' on Britain's inner-city byways. The vivid dashiki, moccasins and woolly hat of the black pedestrian in the *Sunday Times*'s article points to a series of affiliations with locality and the communal black politics emerging within Notting Hill at the time. By the early 1970s 'The very way black youth moved implied a new assurance – there was more deliberate "sass", more spring, less shuffle'.[8] Importing the rhetoric of black power and black pride from the United States, the assured dress sense and 'elegance' of the *Sunday Times*'s pedestrian signify a figure both *of* the street ('streetwise') and *of* the immediate black environment where such styles were being played out more generally. The circulation and reproduction of such styles on the streets was a means of establishing an 'imagined community' within the neighbourhood.

What the military dress of the 1970s also foregrounded was the extent to which the street had become a specifically *masculine* site of self-fashioning in this period. Although women played a key role in politics and street protests in this period, it was the heroic, macho stand of the black male that held centre stage in images and accounts of such events.[9] Writing on 'black masculinity and the contest of territory' in the early 1990s, artist Keith Piper gestures to the significance of masculinity within the protests of the 1970s. Recollecting an image from the *Observer Review*

**Play Mas With Race Today Renegades**

As we have outlined in the Man Free Column, Race Today Renegades will portray 'Forces of Victory' at the 1978 Notting Hill Carnival. Below are our designs for each section of the band. If you are interested in playing, contact 01-737 2268 or 01-737 2813 for further details.

Drum Majorette: Purple, blue, green, yellow, orange and red: Satin.

Frogman: purple cotton jersey.

Sailor: blue/purple.

Airforce Officer: light blue. Army Officer: green. Naval Officer: dark blue.

Airman: light blue.

Guerrilla: green/camouflage.

Airman/Paratrooper: yellow.

Victorious People: orange/red.

**4** *Race Today* carnival drawings, July/August 1978

of 1975, he describes a running battle between black youth and the police during the 1975 Notting Hill Carnival 'which generates resonances of "Custer's last stand", or that film "Zulu" with Michael Caine':

> Facing them [the police] across the page is a single Black male. His friends are behind him, attempting to draw him back, but essentially he is the focus of the image. It is essentially his 'stand', his aggressive defiance, and, we are to read, the disarray which the ferocity of his defiance has wrought upon the power of the state police, which becomes the subject of the headline. It reads: 'Young, Bitter and Black'. I was confronted by this image as a coloured boy of 15 years, wrestling, as one does at that age to orientate one's self, and to map one's social, political, cultural and sexual presence. The image acted for me, as it must have done for a whole range of my peers and contemporaries, to aid the crystallisation of a whole body of unfocused but romantic assumptions around what it was to be young, Black and male in Britain of the 1970's.[10]

As we shall see, the kind of heroic black 'stand' described by Piper was by no means a unique or isolated street event. In spite of its anecdotal relationship to the overall article, the way in which the *Sunday Times* article chooses to foreground local pedestrian space (Ladbroke Grove) to articulate larger national anxieties over 'race' is far from coincidental. Such accounts are part of a much larger turn in the symbolic location of black culture in the 1970s and early 1980s (the period covered by this chapter), away from the basement and towards the pavement. Within this context it is important to recognise that what follows is not an account of black street literature in general but an exploration of masculine pedestrian representation in particular. It is overwhelmingly the black *male* that comes to embody anxieties and fears surrounding racialised street venues in this period, whether in the form of the hedonistic Rastaman, the militarised machismo of the black power movement or the sexualised threat of the mugger.

## From basement to pavement

Chapter 2 argued that in the early postwar period a distinct range of narratives converged at the dwelling place. Private, domestic territory was mythologised in this period: it was a primary site in the imagination of black settlement. By the 1970s the locus of major racial confrontations in Britain had shifted to the city's public venues: its pavements, clubs, cafés and shop floors. As Cecil Gutzmore has observed:

our culture was expressed in extremely private ways, primarily between '58 and '75 in this society ... In particular the black masses – the men and women who work for their living – in churches, in clubs, in shebeens, in 'roots'/basement restaurants, in private gambling dens and so on ....

It was only in 1975 that we went onto the streets in large and challenging numbers ... throughout the '60s and '70s blacks were systematically brutalized in shebeens and house parties and so on ... And that, as I say, is largely because the culture of the black masses was expressed indoors.[11]

It is important to emphasise that the shift Gutzmore outlines here was never entirely consistent or wholesale. Within the 'house-bound' racial discourse of the 1950s and early 1960s, outdoor space was already playing an important, if subordinate role. The Notting Hill and Nottingham riots of 1958, the presence of a 'colour bar' across a range of urban institutions – pubs, clubs, churches, dance-halls, and (beyond Lamming's obsessively internalised London) the emergence of public space in the early fictions of postwar black British experience, and Selvon's writing in particular, are suggestive of areas of racial conflict other than housing in this period.

Similarly, from the 1970s onwards, housing remained a key arena of contestation, with the fiercely fought campaigns of the Bengali Housing Action Group, the persistent criminalisation of shebeen culture and house parties, and the 'New Cross massacre' of January 1981, in which thirteen children were burned to death.[12] Clearly then, the dwelling place was not just an important site of racial contestation within the early postwar period. Such moments are testament to the persistence of domestic space as a mobilising category well into the 1980s.

Nevertheless, between 1970 and 1985 pedestrian space did become a focal point for black communal expression and mobilisation in a particularly concentrated way: in marches and demonstrations, carnival events, sit-down protests, in riots and running battles with the police, in 'muggings' and other forms of street crime.[13] Streets like Brick Lane, Ladbroke Grove and Railton Road became notorious venues over this period, acquiring a mythical status within and beyond the national imaginary.[14]

In 1958, and in the aftermath of the Notting Hill riots, Lord Justice Salmon sentenced nine teddy-boys, claiming that 'everyone, irrespective of the colour of their skin [has the right] ... to walk through our streets with their heads erect and free from fear'.[15] In 1979 after insurrection in Southall and the death of Blair Peach at the hands of an SPG (Special Patrol Group) officer, the Metropolitan Police Commissioner commented: 'If you keep off the streets in London and behave yourselves, you won't have the SPG to worry about.'[16] In the two decades that separate these comments, the black settler had become acutely aware of the changes that pedestrian space had undergone. This section pursues the progressive 'hardening' of the street surface over the 1970s and 1980s.[17]

To focus on the street would at first seem to imply a move away from the discourses of dwelling explored in the opening chapter. Within European cultural theory the street has been privileged as a site of transit. 'Benjamin, Baudelaire, de Certeau, the situationists, and a host of other writers and wanderers have been followed on their *dérives*, their *flâneries*, their saunters.'[18] Similarly, cultural anthropologists and geographers have privileged the street as a site at which to observe the homeless of the Western metropolis.[19] As a site of peripatetic excess, the street offers a particularly compelling chronotope when translated into the travelling poetics of diaspora discourse. Itself a metaphor for 'wandering, mobility, arrival and departure' the street would appear the *locus classicus* for an exploration of the migrant condition.[20]

This chapter pursues another route. Focusing on the politics of pedestrian acts such as loitering, rioting, revelling, mugging and demonstrating, it considers the extent to which the street, as a site of travel or flow, is disrupted in the 1970s and early 1980s. Images and accounts of rioters blockading streets; of carnival crowds congesting the city; of protesters making a 'stand'; of lingering inner-city youths turning streets into 'no go' areas were a major source of anxiety in this period. Black pedestrians were routinely asked to 'move on!' (see figure 2). The 'errant' forms of street occupation pursued in this chapter reveal an alternative pedestrian rhetoric in which the pavement is privileged as a territory, rather than a site of transit. By subjecting the street to certain sedentary modes of occupation, it is reconfigured against the dominant flow of traffic advocated by the law.

We need to be wary at this point of romanticising and idealising black struggles in and over the street. The emergence of a black street culture was in part the result of heavy policing in and around black off-street recreational facilities in the early 1970s. Repeated raids upon clubs, cafés and other social centres in this period literally pushed black youth out on to the pavements. Again though, the names given to those black groups arrested at leisure venues in the early 1970s – the Mangrove Nine (arrested August 1971), the Metro Four (arrested May 1971); the Oval Four (arrested March 1972); the Brockwell Park Three (arrested June 1973), the Swan Disco Seven (arrested September 1974); the Cricklewood Twelve (arrested October 1974), the Stockwell Ten (arrested October 1974) – tell another story. These appellations do not remember the individuals 'responsible' for the crimes, or the crimes they allegedly committed, but the *location* at which black youth came into confrontation with the police. As such, these names hint at the broader territorialisation and localisation of black inner city geographies in the 1970s and early 1980s.

In order to appreciate how black pedestrians have 'deviated' from the formal functions of the street we first need to recognise its antithetical potential as on the one hand a site of dispersal and mobility and on the other a site of gathering and dwelling. Within traditional Western architecture, the street has two main functions: 'it is, at one and the same time, both path and place'.[21] As place, the street is privileged less as a site of travel and more as a site of interaction and gathering; a location 'serving to bind together the social order of the polis ... the local urban community'.[22] The street facilitates the formation of territories and communities even as it appears to breach their 'boundaries' by encouraging movement across them. However architects have argued that this place-making function of pedestrian space has declined in recent years. The street tends to function as path rather than place in the modern period as it increasingly becomes 'just a place to pass through' rather than a 'place to stay'.[23]

In Western Europe and the United States, the decline of the street as dwelling place cannot be detached from the emergent politics of 'race' and the new social movements of the 1960s and 1970s. Vietnam, student activism in Europe and black power demonstrations in the United States prompted a period of prolonged insurrection as protesters in France, Germany, America and Japan took to the streets in 1968. In light of the events of this period, pedestrian space gained a growing reputation as a site of violence, disorder and civil unrest. Such events help to explain Britain's increasingly authoritarian approach to pedestrian space in the 1970s and early 1980s. In Birmingham in April 1968 Enoch Powell justified his calls for repatriation by envisioning the streets of the future as rivers of blood: 'That tragic and intractable phenomenon [black insurrection in the United States] which we watch with horror on the other side of the Atlantic ... is coming upon us here by our own volition and our own neglect.'[24] Two years later, Powell spoke of how 'civil government itself has been made to tremble by the mob – in its modern form, the demonstration ... by the fact or the fear of crowd behaviour'.[25]

In their ground-breaking analysis of mugging in the 1970s Hall *et al.* pursue the kinds of anxiety present in Powell's speeches to argue that muggers do not 'suddenly appear on Britain's streets'. Rather, mugging is a *signifier* imported from America that *articulates* 'race' and 'crisis'. Hall *et al.*

conclude that the image of the mugger is so powerful in 1970s Britain because it condenses wider national anxieties surrounding black settlement in the aftermath of events like those across the Atlantic in Watts and Detroit. Within the specific context of this chapter we might also argue that one of the reasons mugging (as opposed to other forms of crime) became such a powerful signifier of national anxiety in this period was that it is an act that *unfolds in the street.* Already a signifier of lost innocence, 'alienation … violence and crime' within postwar Western culture, the street was clearly mobilised as a *symbolic* venue in the 1970s and 1980s in order to police a lingering black presence within pedestrian landscapes.[26] It is perhaps no coincidence that the dominant forms of black crime in this period were overwhelmingly forms of *street* crime: mugging, obstruction, affray, assault, possession, looting. Within this context 'Loitering on street corners', or 'hanging about outside', was pathologised as a specific form of black 'anti-social behaviour'.[27]

To hang about in pedestrian space was to court surveillance and arrest in the 1970s and early 1980s. Stop and search policing and 'sus' laws (which date back to the Vagrancy Act of 1824) were to prove key issues in causing the Brixton riots. Targeting the street, they allowed police to stop, search and detain anyone suspected of intending to commit street crime. Sus laws made 'loitering', in effect, a criminal act.[28] Within this context Railton Road, the symbolic centre of Brixton's black community and the riots of 1981, became a paradigmatic example of the territorialisation of street space. A key site of confrontation between blacks and the police in the 1970s, Railton Road was referred to locally as the 'front line'. This imagined geography is suggestive of a broader symbolic and strategic appropriation of street space in the period. The term translates a passage into a border. Travelling space becomes an embattled frontier in need of defence from 'outsiders': the police. Within this context loitering and rioting are not simply symptoms of dispossession: they are also territorial acts of repossession and reclamation. To demarcate the street as a front-line location transforms a space of negotiation into a site of tenacious dwelling.

The symbolic stress on territorial defence suggested in Railton's front-line geography emerged largely in response to the wider threat of deterritorialisation suffered by the local black community in the run-up to the Brixton riots. The Nationality Act, the New Cross fire and saturation policing all played a key role here. The Nationality Act abandoned the *ius soli* ('law of the soil') which had been used to define British citizenship for the past nine hundred years. The *ius soli* determined that to be born

*[margin annotation: LINK – not just cultural relation but space reclamation.]*

on British soil (or the soil of its empire) was a guarantee of Britishness. By abandoning the law of the soil, Margaret Thatcher's government brought an end to primary immigration from Britain's former colonies. The Bill caused outrage among Britain's Asian and African Caribbean communities because it threatened their citizenship rights.

Another major contributing factor to the riots was the New Cross fire in Deptford, which killed thirteen black youths in January 1981. Although the police handling of the tragedy was a major source of dissatisfaction among the black community, it was the event's muted coverage within the national media that prompted the greatest outrage. The public condolences normally communicated after such tragedies by the Prime Minister and the Queen never came. The New Cross protest, which fed directly into the riots, was fuelled by the black community's sense of invisibility and unbelonging within the wider national community. Perhaps most tangible in terms of the deterritorialisation of locale in the run-up to the riots, was the increased use of saturation policing and SPG officers in the Brixton area. Such surveillance strategies were encapsulated in SWAMP '81. A highly intrusive police operation which started just days before the riots, SWAMP '81 was designed, in the words of the police, to 'flood' the streets of Brixton and carry out as many stop and searches as possible. Such invasive tactics were read by the local community as an attempt to reclaim the inner city. Collectively the Nationality Act, New Cross and saturation policing help to explain why streets like Railton Road became highly territorialised sites of contestation in the late 1970s and early 1980s. In such contexts *locale*, and street locales in particular, became key sites for the mobilisation and expression of a community denied access to *national* discourses of representation.

In his official report into the Brixton 'disorders' of April 1981, Lord Scarman identifies the street as a key site, not just in the riots themselves but in the build-up to the riots. For Scarman the street makes available the conditions for insurrection. In his exploration of the background to the riots he notes that black youths' alienation from the institutions of the family, education, and employment produced 'a people of the street'.[29] 'Without close parental support, with no job to go to and with few recreational facilities available, the young black person makes his life on the streets and in the seedy commercially run clubs of Brixton' (29). The result of this situation is that 'street corners become the social centres of people, young and old, good and bad, with time on their hands and a continuing opportunity, which, doubtless, they use, to engage in endless discussion of their grievances' (22). Scarman identifies the origins of the riots in the black community's dislocation from the local environment (from parents, the job market, recreational facilities) and their subsequent *relocation* in the street. For Scarman the black pedestrian shares a parasitic relationship to street space, feeding off the arterial routes of the inner city in a manner that suggests an anti-social relationship to the 'host' community. Foregrounding the street as a place of (anti-) social exchange rather than perambulation, Scarman's street corner is a 'centre' at which blacks disseminate their 'grievances':

> the limited opportunities of airing their grievances at national level in British society encourage them to protest on the streets. And it is regrettably also true that some are tempted by their deprivations into crime, particularly street crime – robbery, car theft and the pick-pocketing offences: in other words some of them go 'mugging'. They live their lives on the street, having often nothing better to do; they make their protest there; and some of them live off street crime. (35–6)

Without access to 'national' modes of representation, Scarman suggests, it is the locale of the street that provides the dominant channel for the communication of a politicised black consciousness. The street is an unhealthy, dangerous place for Scarman because of the vital role it plays in mobilising the black community. Within the above passage the apparently unconnected acts of street protest and street crime are continually bound together. If Scarman's easy slippage between rioting and 'mugging' is highly questionable then it is also 'common sense' within the context of the racialised street venues outlined so far in this chapter. It is within the context of such a 'logic' that Lord Scarman proposes the intervention of the police in local planning projects in order to regulate and manage pedestrian landscapes of the inner city:

> It is vital that the law and order implications of environmental and social planning should be taken into account at the earliest stage. A good illustration of the need for this is provided by the Stockwell Park Estate, whose garages, pedestrian walkways and numerous small recesses, though a planner's dream, have provided opportunities and escape routes for thieves and vandals, and create major policing problems. (160)

Ominously, the increasingly authoritarian surveillance of the street during the 1970s was clearly not enough for Scarman, writing in the aftermath of the Brixton riots. The 'labyrinthine' city, he suggests, is a utopian project, a planner's dream. Instead he calls for a city without recesses or escape routes, a carceral city in which black pedestrian life is required to remain permanently on display and has no place to hide. Here Scarman advocates a territory unavailable to the kind of territorialising strategies employed in the Brixton riots.

The territorialisation of black street culture in the 1970s did not occur in isolation, but emerged alongside an increasingly localised policing. In fact the state responded to black locale in very different ways in the 1970s and early 1980s. Paul Gilroy has noted that some Labour councils changed street names ('Britannia Walk' became 'Shaheed E Azam Bhagot Singh Avenue') in a way that seemed to acknowledge the emergence of new localities in Britain.[30] However it was the changing approach to policing local space that this period is remembered for.

In *Policing the Crisis* (1978) Hall *et al.* note that black crime became '*located and situated* ... geographically and ethnically, as peculiar to black youth in the inner-city "ghettos"'.[31] They argue that media coverage of 'muggings' did not have to refer to the 'race' of the alleged attacker: the 'specification of certain *venues*' was enough to reactivate 'earlier and subsequent associations: Brixton, Clapham' (329). The displacement of crime from the black body on to the black metropolis registers something of the symbolic potential urban geography had come to accumulate in the 1970s. If 'Brixton' became a codified way of registering black criminality, then it did so as part of a relatively coherent racial discourse in which urban crime and black territory was a common-sense equation. At stake here is the emergence of metropolitan space, and the street in particular, as a racialised, criminalised venue. Increasingly from the 1970s, the street surface functions as the crossroads at which 'race' and 'crisis' intersect, and the stage upon which the spectacle of black settlement is located and policed.

It is to the inner city that the eye of authority repeatedly shifts in accounts of black communities during the period covered in this section. Such a shift in urban surveillance is outlined by Poulantzas, who, in describing the consequences of technological advance on policing strategy, usefully clarifies the move from criminal body to the *location* of that body:

> duplication of the official police by private surveillance networks ... involves a lifting of the traditional boundaries between normal and abnormal ... thus control is shifted from the criminal act to the crime-inducing situation, from the pathological case to the pathogenic surroundings, in such a way that each citizen becomes, as it were, an a priory [*sic*] suspect or a potential criminal.[32]

Poulantzas's observations indicate a break with the 1950s and early 1960s where anxiety and authoritarian surveillance tends to centre upon the black body, clustering, most notably around the syntax of sexuality (black male virility and white permissiveness, miscegenation, venereal disease). In the 1970s the black body certainly remains a focal point of official anxiety, subject as it was to routine police surveillance, not to mention more overt police brutalities. However, it was the city's geography that became the centre of an authoritarian investigation, an anxious scrutiny, on an unprecedented scale during this period. Stop and search policing, sus laws, Special Patrol Groups, saturation policing (mostly notably SWAMP '81) and community policing all privileged geographical locality in targeting those areas of the inner city most densely populated by blacks.[33]

## Off-street locations: the Mangrove restaurant

This chapter opened with the image of a black man walking the streets of Notting Hill. The image appeared within the context of a newspaper article about the cancellation of the Notting Hill Carnival following a street protest in defence of the Mangrove restaurant. Standing on All Saints Road, the Mangrove was the first of a number of off-street institutions to play a key role in mobilising street protest during the 1970s and 1980s.[34] A consideration of this venue provides an insight into the way in which local black communities responded to the increasingly territorialised policing strategies outlined above.

Like several other black off-street venues at the time, the Mangrove was identified as a space outside the law. The restaurant first became notorious when its Trinidadian owner Frank Critchlow was fined for serving food outside licensing hours after being declined a permit to open after midnight. The restaurant was targeted as an anachronistic location that stubbornly refused to submit to the standard hours of the city.[35] Critchlow's defence was that he gave food to his friends rather than throw it away at closing time.[36] What is important here is not whether Critchlow was guilty or not guilty, but the way in which the Mangrove became a staging post for a dramatisation of black criminality through the disjunction between official time (food licensing laws) and unofficial time. Subsequently, the restaurant became a key venue in the narration of racial conflict more generally over the 1970s and early 1980s and played a vital role in articulating the new police intolerance and black activism of the early 1970s.

The street protest in defence of the Mangrove restaurant (organised in response to repeated police raids) was one of the earliest instances of a politicised black community 'taking to the streets' in defence of local territory. On 9 August 1970 between one hundred and one hundred and fifty protesters gathered to demonstrate against police harassment in the restaurant and in the neighbourhood more generally. The Mangrove

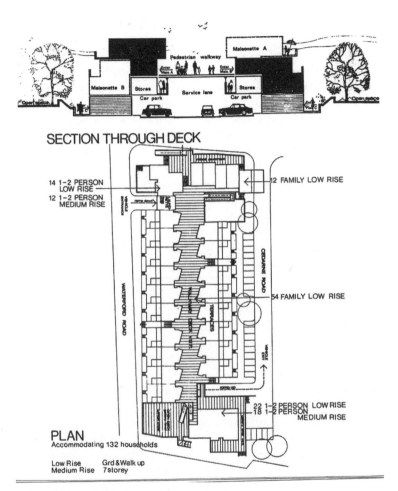

SECTION THROUGH DECK

PLAN
Accommodating 132 households

5  'The village in the sky', *Race Today*, July 1971

formed the start and finish point of this march, structuring the demonstration, and orienting its signification. Although the protesters were arrested on Portnell Road, they were named by the black community as the 'Mangrove Nine', a title that, like the appellations enlisted earlier, privileges locale in the symbolic appropriation of urban geography.

Although the Mangrove's role in local black politics was confined to the early 1970s, its significance cannot be detached from the wider cultural geography of Notting Hill in the postwar period. Since at least 1958 the area had been synonymous with racial conflict. The riots in August of that year resulted in the publication of numerous sociological studies, fictional accounts and histories of the locality over the postwar period. Notting Hill came to be seen as a 'problem area' and was the target of numerous regeneration schemes and self-help projects. For example, in July 1971 *Race Today* published an article on a housing redevelopment project in Golbourne, a predominantly black area of Notting Hill famous for hosting the carnival (see figure 5). The project hoped to improve the local environment in which ill-health, 'Dampness and overcrowding' were reckoned to be rife.[37] The proposed solution was a four-storeyed building known as the 'village in the sky'. Bordered by trees and exchanging the congested street surface for open space, the 'village in the sky' was to work to purify, or cleanse the contaminated black inner city through an appeal to non-urban environments. Praised by the then white-run journal *Race Today*, the project's liberal desire to 'improve' the locality also conceals a dangerous racial politics, calling into play the worrying tactics of erasure, distillation and purification in the rejuvenation of black inner city space.

The pastoral, 'village' rhetoric of this redevelopment plan hides an architecture of containment in which the local black community is in effect elevated and removed from the streets. With its own internal economy of shops and services and its walkway, vertically segregated from the pavements below, there is an advocation of enclosure, confinement and ghettoisation in this 'village in the sky'. The project threatens to 'refine' the local landscape in the same way that the syntax of the countryside does in racial discourse more generally.

Such attempts to 'distil' the black inner-city landscape of Golbourne came to the fore in subsequent conflicts over the Notting Hill Carnival during the 1970s. The carnival takes place annually over the August Bank Holiday and its beginnings have been traced back to the early 1960s. However, it was not until the 1970s that tensions between the carnival's participants and those policing it fully emerged. In 1974 members of the crowd wore prison uniforms in order to signal the increasingly intrusive policing of Notting Hill.[38] The 1976, 1977 and 1978 carnivals 'hosted', in the words of Paul Gilroy, 'the most bitter confrontations to date between blacks and the police'.[39] The restrictive 'containment' strategies adopted by police worked to control and hinder movement through the streets across which the carnival normally progressed. The responses of two black political commentators who took part in the 1976 carnival are indicative here:

They closed off the streets and alleys and people, including myself, got arrested, allegedly for trying to take down barriers and re-open alleyways so that there could be the normal flow of people, both in the context of the carnival and also within the community, because those alleyways are places that we traverse normally.[40]

At the junction of Acklam Road and Portobello Road, new and established bands played from a big stage to a cheering crowd. This was a focal point for the revellers. No bands passed through. Someone said the police had decided. Coming up Portobello Road, I saw many of them ... they multiplied in hundreds as the dusk set in. They paraded the streets, they moved with the floats and bands, they directed traffic on bordering streets ...

Apparently they had organised routes and divided the whole carnival area into six sectors. No movement between sectors. Up Westway there were more ominous signs: telescopic lenses, cameras and other sophisticated surveillance hardware pointed down at the revellers.[41]

These two accounts are notable for the extent to which they highlight pedestrian space as the focal point of conflict between the crowd and the police. Policing the carnival expresses as its ultimate goal, the containment or confinement of the black pedestrian body. To attempt to negotiate or traverse the limits of these fortified street venues is to risk discipline and arrest. These issues of pedestrian containment and surveillance were not restricted to the carnival *per se*, but represented, in a concentrated form, the territorialised policing of pedestrian traffic as it appeared across Notting Hill more generally in the 1970s.

The extent to which the street had become a carceral location within the black community is indisputable in these accounts. Between 1975 and 1977 the police and local authorities campaigned for the Notting Hill Carnival to be relocated at White City Stadium, Hyde Park or Chelsea Football Ground.[42] Black street occupation, it seemed, had to be banished at all costs. By 1978 the prison uniforms had been replaced by military floats and costumes (figure 4). The change of clothing is telling, suggesting as it does a move from passive to active street occupation and a more militant pedestrianism. These outfits signalled a symbolic attempt to defend street space and to police it from within. It is within this context that Stuart Hall has referred to the Notting Hill Carnival as a 'kind of re-colonisation': 'People had never seen the costumes before, had never seen dancing in the street like that'.[43]

The Mangrove played an important part in the carnivals of the mid-1970s, both hosting and organising events for it. However, it was for the police raids and the Mangrove protest of 1970 that the restaurant is remembered in accounts and histories of the period. Across such texts the

Mangrove emerges, not just as a pre-eminent location at which the black community took a stand, but as a *discursive* dwelling place; a site to which accounts of the period repeatedly return to, circulate around and elaborate upon. The Mangrove was not only exemplary in terms of the levels of 'policing' and 'panic' it provoked, or the forms of black counter-protest it prompted, but for the extent to which it became narrativised and *claimed* as a symbolic venue by the black community.

Of course, while the restaurant became a key venue in the narration of racial conflict in the 1970s and early 1980s, it was never available for the inscriptions of a single community and was always essentially, a contested terrain. The police, who repeatedly raided the restaurant in 1970, regarded it as a menacing underworld. PC Frank Pulley referred to the establishment as 'a den of iniquity' in the trial of the Mangrove Nine: 'The place is a haven for criminals, prostitutes, ponces and the like. Anyone going there is likely to be corrupted if not corrupted already.'[44] Here we have an expression of what Poulantzas earlier identified as a new emphasis on location in police surveillance, where citizens become *a priori* suspects or potential criminals. The Mangrove is imagined as a site of dangerous social exchange for Notting Hill's back street communities. Like Scarman's street corner, it is the point at which black criminality circulates and disseminates. The easy slippage between the emergence of black consciousness and criminality made by Scarman is also clearly evident in accounts of the Mangrove.

The restaurant was one of the first venues to be diagnosed in terms of those strains of crime and insurrection being watched with 'horror' on the other side of the Atlantic and was seen to have provoked 'a situation which may well explode into a Watts or a Detroit'.[45] The protest march against the disruptive policing of the Mangrove in August 1970 was aligned in these terms by the British press as a worrying expression of black power.[46] Police action against the Mangrove was ritually justified by pointing out that it was 'frequented by coloured people sympathetic to the Black Power Movement'.[47] Detective Inspector Stockwell, in defence of the over-policing of the protest, recalled that 'outside the Mangrove Restaurant just before the procession started, Godfrey Millett, another of the accused, was seen either distributing or selling copies of a Black Panther newspaper'.[48] Underlying these expressions of paranoia and panic by the police and public, is a common understanding of the Mangrove as an illicit communications network, a site of politicised exchange and subscription. Within such accounts the Mangrove emerges as an early signifier of 'crisis', a symbolic venue at which the moral panics and anxieties surrounding black life in the early 1970s came to be structured and articulated. The arrest of the Mangrove Nine was instrumental in the Home Secretary's decision to commission a report into the growth of black power and an independent, unofficial enquiry into police/black relations.[49] These issues would come to play a dominant role in the narration of 'race' and nation throughout the 1970s.

In contrast the local Caribbean community regarded the Mangrove restaurant as a 'social centre', or 'unofficial advice bureau' and after the police raids in 1970 it became 'a symbol of black enterprise and resistance'.[50] The drug raids (none of which led to charges), along with police patrols outside the restaurant, led to a decline in the Mangrove's patronage and was felt to be an attempt by the police to 'break the backbone of the black community'.[51] The anatomical metaphor used here is not coincidental, suggesting something of the importance of the Mangrove as a 'nerve centre', or communications network for the local West Indian population. At the same time the dispute over the Mangrove was not confined to the locale of Notting Hill. The Action Committee for the Defence of the Mangrove distributed a statement on the eve of the protest to (among others) the Home Office, Prime Minister and High Commissioners of Jamaica, Guyana, Trinidad and Barbados, demanding 'an end to the persecution of the Mangrove Restaurant'.[52]

These events were documented within a diverse range of black publications, from *Savacou*, the artistic journal of the Caribbean Artists Movement (CAM), to the political magazine *Race Today*. Through such publications the Mangrove was mythologised and 'written-up' as an emblematic site of black political expression in a way that would have been unthinkable in the 1950s and 1960s. *Race Today* perhaps played the most crucial role in aiding the event's passage into communal memory. At key moments in the 1970s and 1980s, and supplementing its circulation in popular, everyday folklore, the Mangrove was routinely reproduced in its columns as an empowering symbolic venue. In July 1976, within the immediate context of Gurdip Chaggar's murder and growing police brutality more generally, the magazine published a list of 'Cases to Remember', headed by the Mangrove Nine.[53] Similarly, in a series of articles that ran between 1980 and 1981 on the theme of black resistance, the story of the 'Mangrove Struggle' played a pivotal role:

> It was this event ... that altered completely all the methods through which our struggles against the police and the courts had been conducted. It would lay down the guidelines which would haunt all future political activity ... it was an historic event.[54]

In these kinds of account the Mangrove rarely exists as a discrete or isolated location, but operates as the site from which a larger history of black struggle and resistance in Britain is projected and recollected: from the Notting Hill riots of 1958 and the raids on leisure venues, shebeens and youth clubs such as The Metro (at which Frank Critchlow was a leader) in the 1970s, to the more recent commemorations of the *Windrush* anniversary in the late 1990s.[55] The Mangrove restaurant helped, and continues to help, structure what had previously been a dispersed, sporadic articulation of black protest and rebellion into a collective narrative. It played a part in the organisation of subsequent black conflicts through an appeal to local territory. In this context the Mangrove restaurant emerges as a pioneering dwelling place within the black community. Not only this, as a discursive site it structured and 'stored' a folk archive and a history of black resistance at a crucial point, *before* the more substantial 'official' histories of black resistance came to be written and recorded.

### Rioting and writing: the street and representation

> The street is not only a means of access but also an arena of social expression. (Cliff Moughtin)[56]

In 1974 the CAM's literary and artistic journal *Savacou* published a series of photographs depicting the Mangrove street protest alongside poems, short stories, essays and drawings by artists active in the movement at the time. Entitled 'Writing away from home', this issue signals the extent to which artistic production had become overtly politicised by the 1970s. The Mangrove photographs, first used as empirical evidence in the trial of the 'Mangrove Nine', now appeared alongside pen and ink drawings by Christopher Laird and within a self-consciously 'artistic' journal. The traditional boundaries between 'art' and 'politics' are effectively eroded in this special issue focusing on black British cultural production. More specifically, 'Writing away from home' invites us to read empirical evidence as art and artistic production as politics in a manner that encourages a slippage between poetics and the political.

Located immediately before the Mangrove photographs, Christopher Laird's drawings (see figure 6) are evocative of the lingering pedestrianism outlined elsewhere in this chapter.[57] Both the materials *from* which these boots are composed (tyre treads) and those *in* which they are composed (pen and ink) suggest a subaltern street rhetoric. Not only does the image imply a lack of access to materials or materiality, but also a lack of access to the dominant systems of representation. Yet the drawing is less a

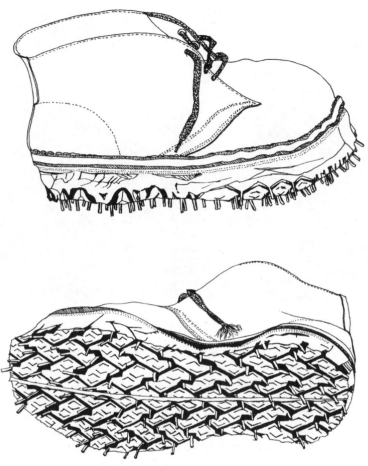

**6**  C. Laird, 'Song treads one and two'

critique of lack or absence then it is a celebration of reappropriation: of tyres as boots, of pen as paint and, it will be suggested, of walking as dwelling. Although they are not worn, these boots certainly advocate a particular style of perambulation, a style that privileges grip and purchase and which facilitates a stubborn, lingering street presence. As I have suggested already, images of the black pedestrian pondering, or 'hanging about' on the street were perceived in racial discourse of the 1970s and early 1980s as deeply menacing acts, a threat to law and order. The 'loitering' black body was criminalised in this context. The kind of

**7** 'The Mangrove protest'

street 'tenacity' implied in the soles of Laird's boots appears symbolic of a black pedestrian rhetoric more generally in this period. From the masculine 'stand' of the black youth recollected by Keith Piper to images of street-corner youth hanging around in Lord Scarman's report, to the kind of steadfastness and perseverance exhibited by the Mangrove demon-strators (figure 7), the street as path is reappropriated as dwelling place.

The treads of Laird's boots are significant for the traction they appear to offer, they suggest a certain 'hold' upon the street surfaces of inner-city Britain. The soles facilitate anchorage, they imply a stubborn refusal to move on. It is this poetics of situatedness, stasis, positionality that I would suggest partly informs the politics of loitering as an act of resilience within the landscape. The points that extend from the soles of these boots have been exaggerated and enlarged, they become ambiguous structures, suggesting spikes or roots. Laird's footwear insinuates a potential street violence then, they are invested with a capacity to puncture, to scar the face of the city. At the same time they would appear to extend the black pedestrian's adherence along the city streets, they offer rootedness. It is precisely this kind of street tenacity that is exhibited in the photograph of Mangrove protesters by Horace Ove in figure 7. The man squared up to the policeman embodies the ability of this crowd to menace the authorities by 'staying put', by refusing to move on. Anchored to the streets of Notting Hill, the body of this black youth is, like the placards reading 'hands off', an explicit sign of territorial defence. 'Staring out' the policeman, his stance also signifies a stand, an aggressive, 'heroic', confrontational act of defiance. Physically, his body works to reclaim a locale that has been 'invaded' by the police.

By placing Ove's photographic 'evidence' (already circulated in the court room) within the context of an artist journal, 'Writing at Home' reveals the extent to which the street had become both a site and a *product* of representation. Earlier in this chapter it was noted that the street facilitates two contradictory movements. On the one hand, it encourages travel and dispersal across locations. On the other, it encourages gathering, interaction and what Moughtin refers to above as 'social expression'. For black Britons of the 1970s and early 1980s the street was a vital territory at which both to gain access to representation and to contest dominant modes of representation.

Exemplary in this context was the 'national march' held on 2 March 1981 after the New Cross fire in which thirteen black children died. This protest was not simply motivated by the fire itself, but by the lack of national media attention given to the tragedy. Not only did the march follow a route past London's dominant institutions of representation (Fleet Street, the Courts of Justice, Speakers' Corner), but it was a protest *about* representation: '13 Dead and nothing said' was the resounding chant throughout the march.

The New Cross demonstration was by no means unique in illuminating the vexed relationship between (local) protest and (national) representation during the early 1980s. As we have seen, Scarman's report on the disorders of 1981 reveals an anxiety about black street-corner society using pedestrian space as a site at which to 'air grievances' that cannot be communicated at a 'national level'. Meanwhile Paul Gilroy has observed that the Brixton and Handsworth riots saw blacks confronting not just police but the journalists seeking to represent them.[58]

Developing the work of Touraine and Melucci on new social movements, Gilroy argues that street protests are informed less by black people's rejection of conditions of labour than by a tendency 'to refuse mediation of their demands by the political system against which they have defined themselves' (226). He goes on to argue that rioting privileges 'direct participation and direct action', an 'authentic, immediate politics' over a 'politics of representative delegation' (232). Gilroy's point here is not that rioting is anti-representational, what Scarman might call 'disorder'. It is also an attempt to re-order, re-present, to create a new order. If, as Gilroy suggests, rioting is a rejection of representative *delegation* then street insurrection does not foreclose the possibility of representation as *intervention*, an act of representation that privileges directness, immediacy and authenticity.

There are striking similarities between the politics of representation that Gilroy argues inform insurrection here and the dominant poetics of representation informing black artistic production over the same period.[59] The qualities of immediacy, directness and authenticity that Gilroy associates with rioting are echoed in Kobena Mercer's assessment of the aesthetics of documentary realism in black film over the same period:

> The reality effect produced by realist methods depends on the operation of four characteristic values – transparency, immediacy, authority and authenticity – which are in fact aesthetic values central to the dominant film and media culture itself. By adopting a neutral or instrumental relation to the means of representation, this mode of black film practice seeks to redefine referential realities of race through the same codes and forms as the prevailing film language whose discourse of racism it aims to contest ... By presenting themselves as transparent 'windows on the world' of racism and resistance, black films in the documentary realist mode emphasise the urgency, immediacy and 'nowness' of their message ... this is a contextual necessity, as such films perform a critical function by providing an alternative version of events so as to inform, agitate and mobilize political action.[60]

Discussing films such as *Pressure* (1974), *Forward Youth* (1977) and *Riots and Rumours of Riots* (1981), Kobena Mercer argues that documentary realism's privileging of immediacy and authenticity provided an effective discourse through which to contest dominant media representations of 'race'. In a period when black representations were few and far between, the documentary mode allowed film-makers to 'put the facts straight' and 'tell it how it really is'.

Writing within a very different context to Paul Gilroy, Kobena Mercer sees black film production in the 1970s and early 1980s as symptomatic of precisely the same historical conditions of representation that Gilroy associates with rioting. Both film and rioting, they individually suggest, are informed by a lack of access to the dominant modes of representation, whether at the level of politics or in terms of arts funding. Rioting and film might be characterised in this context in terms of their suspicion of representation. Filmic representation effaces its own existence as representation, embracing a 'reality effect' that values 'transparency, urgency,

authority and authenticity'. Rioting emerges out of a refusal to be mediated, delegated, or spoken for by dominant (racist) systems of representation. It is an attempt on the behalf of the rioters to 'define themselves';
through directness, authenticity and immediacy.

I want to extend Gilroy and Mercer's observations on rioting and film
now to the context of writing. Black literary discourse was informed by
similar vexed relations to the dominant institutions of representation
during the 1970s and early 1980s. Indeed *Savacou*, the literary and artistic
journal with which this section opened, was created in response to a sense
of being excluded from those institutions. As Kamau Brathwaite, the
CAM's founding member (along with Andrew Salkey and John La Rose),
recalls:

> I didn't see West Indian writers, painters and only a very few actors (and
> these in stereotyped parts) on British Television ... I was not hearing their
> voices or the sound of their work on radio. They didn't seem to be partici-
> pating in the literary and arts pages of the newspapers and magazines that
> were concerned with these things in this country. This was a remarkable
> change from the 50s when West Indian writing was the 'new thing'.[61]

Brathwaite highlights the Caribbean artist's lack of access to key sites of
representation within the metropolis, a factor which clearly disabled the
possibilities of exchange across and mobilisation within the black
community at a crucial moment in its development. This in contrast to
the 1950s and 1960s when aspiring West Indian writers flocked to London
because of its reputation as what Henry Swanzy termed a 'literary head-
quarters'. In the early postwar years the BBC *Caribbean Voices* programme
and Caribbean little magazines such as *Bim* provided important sites at
which a dispersed community of black British writings were gathered
together and disseminated. By the 1970s such forums had either disappeared or were fading fast. Meanwhile black British artists were, according to Brathwaite, failing to gain access to the mainstream British media:
radio, television, magazines and newspapers. Although it was active only
between 1966 and 1973, CAM provided an invaluable forum for the
black artistic community of Britain through the regular meetings it
organised and through *Savacou*. Spanning a key phase in black cultural
history, CAM played a crucial role in politicising black literary production over that period, and Linton Kwesi Johnson has since spoken of its
impact on his own development as a poet.[62]

If in the early CAM sessions there seems to have been serious doubt as
to whether its artistic concerns should be bound up with the 'grassroots'
political struggles of black Britain, then by 1968, this uncertainty had

passed. On 4 April that year Martin Luther King was assassinated; on 20 April Enoch Powell made his famous 'Rivers of blood' speech in Birmingham, and on 3 May the CAM session held a minute's silence 'to mark the passing of liberal conscience'.[63] Brathwaite went on to say: 'It is no longer a matter of being committed or not being committed. We have not any CHOICE' (147). Brathwaite called for the writers and artists of CAM to cease making a distinction between political action and intellectual or creative action: 'The two men must be part of the same man ... part of the same plan' (147).

Brathwaite's call for a new politics of representation anticipated a commitment to politics in black British writing that would prevail across the 1970s and early 1980s. Like film over the same period, literary discourse turned to realist modes of representation in order to redefine what Mercer refers to above as the 'referential realities of race'. Where black film turned to the genre of documentary realism, literature was dominated by autobiography as a discourse of documentation, a genre that privileges the realist conventions of immediacy, transparency, authenticity and authority. Buchi Emecheta's early autobiographical novels, *In the Ditch* (1972) and *Second Class Citizen* (1976), describe the trials and tribulations of being a single mother in London. Similarly, Beryl Gilroy's classic autobiography, *Black Teacher* (1976), documents the writer's experiences as a working mum in various inner-city schools. Meanwhile, in South Asian writing, Tariq Mehmood's semi-autobiographical account of the Bradford Twelve (of which he was a member), *A Hand on the Sun* (1983), articulates the politicisation of Pakistani school-leavers and factory workers in the north of England. In very different ways these narratives intervened in dominant representations of black people at the time by (as Paul Gilroy put it within the context of insurrection) 'defining themselves'. They exploit the authority and transparency of autobiographical discourse in order to 'tell it how it really is'.

Realism (in the sense that Mercer uses it) is also the dominant value in black fiction and poetry of this period as novelists and poets worked to articulate and contest the 'referential realities' of the time. Farrukh Dhondy produced a range of short stories and novels during the 1970s and early 1980s recording the politicisation of South Asian and African-Caribbean youth through fictional accounts of actual events. *Seige of Babylon* (1978), for instance, was based on the Spaghetti House siege. Even poetry, that most 'ahistorical' of genres, was reclaimed as a discourse of documentation in dub and protest poetry of the period. Many of the poems left over from this period are framed by epigraphs and footnotes, 'peritexts' that have the effect of situating the work in terms of concrete historical contexts. Poets such as Benjamin Zephaniah, Marsha Prescod, Valerie Bloom and Linton Kwesi Johnson all display a desire to record, to produce a document of black events and struggles in their writing. Prescod writes about the fight to keep the Notting Hill Carnival; Zephaniah about battles between racists and anti-Nazi campaigners; Johnson about everything from the arrest of black Britons such as Darcus Howe and George Lindo to the New Cross massacre of 1981. Many of these writers did not simply work to displace one version of reality with another; they sought also to challenge dominant media representations head on. In Prescod's 'May the force be with you' the speaker imagines a future Notting Hill Carnival in which everyone masquerades as the police: 'De Press gon go mad, / (Because you know dey like to take de same fucking / picture every year of Police at carnival).'[64]

Such overt contestation of the dominant modes of representation signals a difference between literature and film, which Mercer argues adopts 'a *neutral* or instrumental relation to the means of representation' in this period. Moreover where Mercer argues that his four characteristic values (transparency, immediacy, authority and authenticity) are central to the traditional aesthetic values of film and media culture *itself*, literary discourse might be characterised in terms of its self-consciousness, its tendency to highlight its own constructedness, its lack of authenticity. Directness, immediacy, authenticity and presence are compromised here by literature's foregrounding of distance, deferral, artifice and absence. The literary texts considered below appear ultimately more self-conscious about the problems of black representation than the films enlisted by Mercer. Unlike those visual narratives, which are saturated with images of street protest and riot, there is a notable absence of insurrection within black British literatures of the same period. From the outset it is as if riot constitutes a certain *problem* of representation within this writing. Those texts that do narrate insurrection tend to foreground it as a *problem* of narration, rather than as the transparent object of its narrative.

What follows is an extended account of these issues of representation in relation to postwar black British writing. Focusing on the chronotope of the street, it extends our consideration of pedestrian space as a site *of* representation (protests, marches, riots) to explore its conditions *in* representation (novels, short stories, poems). While at the centre of this discussion is literary discourse of the 1970s and early 1980s, and the work of Linton Kwesi Johnson and Farrukh Dhondy in particular, I have found it necessary to locate these texts in terms of the literary production either side of it. This involves a survey of pedestrian rhetorics in postwar black writing, from the *flâneur* in fictions of the 1950s to the postmodern nomad of the late 1980s. It is only by placing cultural production of the 1970s and early 1980s in relation to this wider literary context that the specific conditions of representation in those years can be identified.

## Touring the city: the black British *flâneur*

The street becomes a dwelling for the *flâneur*, he is as much at home among the facades of houses as a citizen is in his walls. (Walter Benjamin)[65]

He used to find time to think about those parts of the pavement which have never felt the pressure of a foot. When he walked on them, he looked for those places. Up near the base of the wall, where dust and dirt and moss gathered, where people never walked. He used to walk there deliberately, his trousers wiping the dirty walls, ankles knocking each other as he trod virgin ground. Just for the hell of it. (Samuel Selvon)[66]

In 1966 Hunter Davies published *The New London Spy*, a popular guide to 'unofficial' London. Subtitled *An Intimate Guide to the City's Pleasures* and inspired by Ned Ward's heavily censored *The London Spy* (1703), the book markets itself as an 'underground' guide, sign posting an illicit, taboo and often 'scandalous' London.[67] One section, 'Foreign London', divides the city up into six discrete territories, including 'Indian London' and 'West Indian London', locations that are imagined as firmly outside the national landscape. These 'unexplored' pockets of the metropolis are made available for discovery, investigation and adventure by Davies's guide. Like Huxley's shebeen in Chapter 2, they work to map the city's *terra incognita*, writing into existence those enclaves of the metropolis 'which haven't been charted before' (7). The guide advertises the black city for a local as well as a tourist 'audience'. These are quarters of the city made visible to the visitor through *spying*: 'It is invaluable for the foreigner to know where these areas are ... It can also be a pleasure, perhaps a revelation, for the natives to discover them as well' (267).

Underscoring the bourgeois, imperialist vocabulary of *The New London Spy* is the rhetoric of the *flâneur*. Primarily associated with nineteenth-century literature and the writings of Charles Baudelaire and Edgar Allen Poe, *flânerie* refers both to the activities of the artistic idler, strolling the street in search of stories and a literary trope *within* writing. The *flâneur* is no casual stroller, but a detective of the street, capable of discerning its various pleasures and attractions; its smells, sounds, characters, and, most importantly of all, its *sights*.[68] The *flâneur* is driven by a scopophilia that is marked by gender, race and class. The object of this restless, voyeuristic gaze tends to be (as the chapters of *The New London Spy* imply), the urban exotic within the metropolis: women and prostitutes, the working-class, immigrants. Rob Shields argues that the *flâneur* engages in a 'tactile encounter with representative Others from the far-flung colonies and outposts of empire', he 'mimics the action of the explorer who not only maps but also describes, designates and claims territory'.[69]

In the last chapter it was suggested that walking around and naming the city were also tactics used in Selvon's writing to 'domesticate' the city and make it home. As de Certeau has argued, walking in the city is also a 'tactic', a way of making the city 'habitable' (105). To repeat the names given to the various parts of the metropolis, its streets, squares and districts, is also to open it up 'to the diverse meanings given them by passers-by'. The 'emptying-out and wearing-away' of the city's proper names 'insinuate other routes into the functionalist and historical order of movement' (105). It is by liming the streets of London and by renaming its various spaces that the boys come to mimic the tactics of the *flâneur*, exploring its streets in order to 'describe', reinscribe and claim them. As the epigraph from Selvon above implies, dawdling on the streets is also a (heavily gendered) means of dominating the city, of taking possession of it.

The image of the solitary male, wandering and/or observing the streets is a recurring one in black British writing of the early postwar years, where the black pedestrian is ritually figured as a *flâneur* touring and discovering the monumental venues of the city. Soyinka describes a street encounter with a prostitute in Hammersmith, as does Lamming as he walks from Gloucester Place to Kensington Gardens in *The Pleasure of Exile*. Ralph Singh of Naipaul's *The Mimic Men* drifts through the streets of the city alone, trying to unravel its mysteries. Meanwhile, Kamau Brathwaite observes the various street characters passing by in 'Letter from Cambridge' (1953): 'I am here, high up above the street, sitting on the ledge outside my window … Below is the street, busy with poking tourists and summer cyclists with their pink and brown legs, and the walking sticks and neatly rolled umbrellas of the dandies taking the air.'[70] Louise Bennett offers a rare glimpse of the *flâneuse* in her poem 'De Victory parade' as she views the London crowd from the vantage point of the Victoria Memorial! Literature of this period is frequently populated by characters for whom the public venues of the city are, as much as the domestic interior, spaces of 'dwelling'.

Johnnie Sobert, the narrator of Andrew Salkey's *Escape to An Autumn Pavement* (1960), appears most at home in the streets between his bedsitter in Hampstead and the 'Dantesque night club' (p. 145) in which he works: 'I felt compelled to get out and go for a long walk. Anywhere. I walked up Whitcomb street. Into Leicester Square. Up Charing Cross Road. Up to Cambridge Circus. Into Piccadilly. And down towards Green Park. I was heading nowhere in particular' (208).[71] Johnnie's account is typical of literary constructions of pedestrian space in the 1950s and 1960s where the street frequently signals a space of liberation. The network of pavements outside Johnnie's workplace signify freedom or 'escape' from a stagnated indoor life. The momentum conveyed through this passage's short sentences and its rapid accumulation of place names contrast with the stagnancy of his life indoors, and is suggestive of an emancipatory negotiation of the city, a dynamic pedestrian rhetoric. If his aimless itinerary on the one hand suggests a sense of dislocation in the city, his repetition of street names is also a means of claiming it. As with Selvon's boys, Johnnie's walk is also suggestive of the 'I' narrator's knowledge of the city. His naming, his *articulation* (conjoining or voicing) of the streets is a sign of his intimacy with its public spaces: there is no hesitancy here, he knows the streets, his passage across the city appears almost 'instinctual'. This unimpeded pedestrian body, free to wander 'anywhere', contrasts with the carceral street venues within literary discourse of 1970s. In the 1950s negotiating the city is often a leisurely, pleasurable activity associated with 'play' rather than 'politics'.

The hedonistic delights made available by the city's public spaces have, as we saw at the close of Chapter 2, been most radically imagined in Selvon's work:

> I'll tell you what I did one night. One night I skated down Regent Street, sliding with effortless ease, leaping from bus top to bus top, balancing on one hand on top of Eros' head in Piccadilly Circus. Then I made one tremendous leap and stood poised on top of Nelson's Column in Trafalgar Square and made a graceful swan dive into one of the fountains.[72]

This passage comes from an autobiographical essay, 'Little drops of water' (1967) in which Selvon interweaves accounts of journeys across the city with apparently random thoughts on the difficulties of writing. In this extract the city appears as a kind of fairground, or circus, in which Selvon, the unlikely trapeze artist, skates, leaps, jumps and swings across the monumental spaces of Regent Street, Piccadilly Circus and Trafalgar Square. His body occupies a disturbing, disrespectful position within this deeply symbolic post-imperial landscape. The city's grand, imposing architecture here becomes little more than the apparatus of play, pleasure and freedom. Elsewhere, Selvon's writerly sketches of the artist taking an 'amble' (57) or a 'sally' (58) through the city evoke the classic image of the *flâneur* as 'the man abandoned in the crowd' (55):

> Standing there [outside Trafalgar Square Underground station], shoved and pushed by thousands of unseeing people who are rushing home, I've imprinted the scene time and time again on my mind – the constant traffic, the faces of the people, the pale yellow lights in office buildings and the starlings chattering like background music as if they were trying to drown out the noise below them. (57)

Selvon's evocation of the writer wandering through the metropolis suggests an artistic self-consciousness absent in the realist fictions of the 1970s and 1980s where walking tends to have a purpose or goal.

The kind of affection that Selvon's ramblings reveal for the street is typically shared by an affection for its women. His street narratives are underscored by a male subjectivity, and are written from within the masculinist tradition of the *flâneur* in which women ritually appear as the focal point of urban investigation. The destination of the pedestrian gaze in early postwar black writing is typically the female body:

> This is Syl coming up from the underground: from the time he left the train, his eyes making a quick scan for something to appreciate ... the selection move off, and Syl bringing up the rear. It don't matter where the selection going, east, west, north or south, up the road or down the road. Whatever Syl's original destination forgotten long ago, whither thou goest I will go.[73]

The pleasures of the street are difficult to ignore in Selvon's fiction where the pedestrian movements of West Indian men are governed primarily by quests for the (white) female body. Women's bodies constitute a significant spectacle in early postwar writing by men, an object on display and of consumption. The eroticisation of the cityscape is perhaps most explicitly presented in Andrew Salkey's *The Adventures of Catullus Kelly* (1969), a novel in which the West Indian protagonist fucks his white girlfriend against the plinth of Nelson's Column. *The Adventures of Catullus Kelly* tells the story of a Jamaican's forays in and around London in a way that, as the title suggests, mimics and subverts the conventions of the colonial travel narrative. On the advice of longer-standing members of the black community he makes regular sorties into London, visiting the White Defence League offices in Notting Hill; Soho; Temperate Broadcasting Unit; Chico's barber shop; Kenwood House and so on. These quests are intimately bound up with his sexual conquests in the city, both of which he links closely in his imagination:

The sensations, in both instances, of cracking cells, yielding warrens, exploding taboos, were alike. He recounted: surfaces are, often, securely draped and set apart from the spectator, but they were, obviously, intended to be touched, encouraged into some kind of intimacy, especially with the drifter, and uncovered and enjoyed.[74]

For Catullus the female body and the 'body' of the metropolis have become inseparable symbolic destinies: the objects of a lustful male fantasy. Both represent tantalising, seductive, eroticised 'sites' of exploration available for the unhindered and tactile perusal of the *flâneur*: their draped surfaces are there to be pulled back, uncovered and enjoyed. The metropolis of early post-war black British writing tends to be a feminised, supine landscape in this sense. Available for the surveillance, exploration and penetration of the questing black male, the streets of the city offer a passive geography which is made to yield, expose itself and open up beneath the advancing urban explorer.

These pedestrian rhetorics of the early postwar period tend to be optimistic, even utopian in terms of their potential to provide sexual gratification, relief and freedom. In the literatures considered so far, the street tends to provide an escape route from the more constraining, racialised venues of the city, such as the dwelling place or workplace. At the same time walking is more than a therapeutic act within these different texts. Perambulation across the city is closely associated (as Selvon's 'Sir Galahad' suggests) with a 'quest' for and conquest of the city. Traversing the street is part of a symbolic recolonisation of London, a means of establishing new viewpoints and perspectives that intersect, compete with and appropriate the dominant imaginative mappings of the metropolis. The black pedestrian body is reinvented in these literatures, as investigator rather than the site of investigation, consumer, as opposed to producer, spectator, more than spectacle. However, the juvenile nature of these street acts, as these street figures fantasise and boast about their various performances in the city, ultimately conceals something of their political immaturity or naivety. Their lustful fantasies of sex in the city are part of a more general inability to empower or mobilise themselves as blacks within London. Behind their male bravado lies a certain impotency.

## 'Doun de Road ...': Bluefootedness

As the casual, imperialist gaze of white urban investigators such as Hunter Davies in the early postwar period were replaced by more formal, authoritarian modes of street surveillance, the kind of youthful, exuberant narratives outlined above dried up. The policing of the pavement during the 1970s and early 1980s meant that the streets were unavailable for the kind of leisurely idling associated with *flânerie*. From the late 1970s onwards, the street is figured more regularly as a site of protest and insurrection than it is as a site of play or perambulation. The literary itineraries of early postwar literature took readers on excursions across monumental landscapes like Trafalgar Square, Piccadilly Circus, the Victoria Memorial and Hyde Park. By the 1970s this tourist scene had been exchanged for the 'mean' inner-city street. These venues were not just the setting for riots and social unrest; they also became the stage for a new body of literary and artistic production. Farrukh Dhondy's Spital-fields, Isaac Julien's and Linton Kwesi Johnson's Notting Hill, David Simon's and Faustin Charles's Brixton, Tariq Mehmood's Manningham, Derek Bishton's and John Reardon's Handsworth are indicative of some of the new, increasingly dispersed artistic venues to be mapped in the 1970s and early 1980s.[75]

It was not just the location but the mood of pedestrian space that changed over this period. What had been predominantly a site of pleasure in the early postwar period, had become, by the 1970s, a symbolic locus of pain. *Bluefoot Traveller,* an early anthology of black British poetry first published in 1976 was suggestive of the new agonies associated with walking the street in this period. 'Bluefoot', Berry tells us in the intro-duction to his collection, is a Jamaican term used to describe:

> an outsider, a man from another county or parish who has come to settle among new villagers. The term arises because such a man is supposed to have bruised his feet by walking barefoot along hot roads and railway tracks with his belongings, looking for a new home. And even when this new-comer finds his new home and marries and settles he is still referred to as the Bluefoot Man.[76]

Bluefootedness is more than simply a metaphor for a mode of trans-atlantic nomadism. It also connotes a particular form of pedestrian pain that had become painfully familiar within the racially fraught context of 1970s Britain. Beyond the 'parish', and along the 'hardening' street surfaces of England's inner cities, the metaphor is implicated within a more literal, referential context of violence and bruising that recurs in black British literature of the period.

> Stirred steps
> you better know your guard ...
> You didn't make these nets

of footways
These streets are minefields
every brick and stone
ammunition[77]

In these lines from Berry's 'Worst days among another tribe' (1979) the pavement is not a site of liberation as it was for Selvon and Salkey, but a landscape of entrapment or entanglement. The street is a battleground, a scene clearly informed by the increasingly militarised policing of pedestrian space in the 1970s. Yet this (a)venue is no unambiguously carceral location, either. If on the one hand it threatens to inflict violence on the black pedestrian body ('these streets are minefields'), then it also provides the raw materials for counter-insurgency ('every brick and stone / ammunition').

These tensions between the street as a site of Babylonian violence and the street as a site at which the black community comes to 'stand its ground' are particularly acute within dub and protest poetry of this period. The kind of disengaged, passive, solitary idling of the bourgeois *flâneur* is replaced here with the communal voice of the black working class. Linton Kwesi Johnson's work is exemplary in this context, reversing the *flâneur*'s privileging of rituals of consumption over activities of exchange. Poems such as 'Forces of victory' describe the black crowd marching through the streets, not from the perspective of the isolated or detached stroller but from *within* the collective body of the crowd:

wi mek a lickle date
fi nineteen-seventy-eight
an' wi fite an' wi fite
an' defeat di State
den all a wi jus' forwud
up to Not'n' Hill Gate

we're di forces af vict'ry
an' wi comin rite through
we're de forces af vict'ry
now wat y'u gonna do[78]

Published in 1979, 'Forces of victory' is indicative of the changing figuration of street space in the 1970s. The poem celebrates the 'victory' of the Notting Hill Carnival of 1978, which had survived despite attempts to police it off the streets. As we move from the crowded street scenes of central London in the 1950s to the street crowd of Johnson's Notting Hill in the 1970s, we also travel from anonymous public space to local black territory. A new pedestrian rhetoric becomes apparent here as the confrontational crowd ('now wat y'u gonna do') asserts its right to occupy the neighbourhood. The loneliness and detachment of the black British *flâneur* are exchanged for a communal street scene. 'Forces of victory' privileges a collective, griot voice that is underlined in the repetitious 'we', 'wi', 'we're'. Gone here is the writerly individual within the anonymous, randomly strolling crowd. Play is replaced by politics; detachment by commitment; passive consumption with active production, as the carnival crowd is described in military terms 'advancing' down the street. Pedestrian space is less a site of voyeuristic pleasure than a *territory*, a 'front line' battleground at which to make a stand. The surface of the pavement is no longer a space to simply be strolled over or meandered across; it becomes a dwelling place, a point of confrontation at which *tenacity*, a prolonged defence and occupation of the street is privileged.

At stake in the distinctions being made here between pedestrian rhetorics of the 1950s and the 1970s is the issue of representation. In contrast to the self-reflexive artistry exemplified in the figure of the *flâneur*, literary discourse of the 1970s and 1980s might be characterised in terms of its turn to realist modes of representation. The militarised street metaphors in both Berry and Johnson's poem are not simply part of an imagined geography. 'Forces of victory' records the actual title and military dress codes adopted by the 'Race Today Renegades' at the 1978 carnival.

Commenting on his own work, Linton Kwesi Johnson has said that 'from the very beginning I saw myself as giving voice to, and documenting, the experiences of my generation'. Johnson privileges a politics of representation strikingly similar to that outlined by Mercer; a politics of representation premised on delegation ('giving voice to') and realism ('documenting') over self-conscious artistry. Many of Johnson's poems narrate actual events (the New Cross massacre; the Notting Hill Carnival), individuals (Darcus Howe; George Lindo) and issues (sus laws; unemployment) at specific historical moments. They carry a commitment to context (both geographical and historical) untypical within the genre of poetry.

Johnson's agency as a spokesperson for the black community is dependent upon his commitment to a realist aesthetic that privileges immediacy, urgency, 'nowness'. I am thinking here not only of the rhetoric of 'spontaneity' surrounding his 'live' dub performances, but also of the topicality of his poetry, which was often written for and delivered at certain political events *as they unfolded*. The street is more than a recurrent figure within Johnson poetry, it is also the physical site at which many of his poems were originally performed. For example, 'It Dread Inna Inglan' and 'Man Free', eventually published in *Inglan Is a Bitch* (1980), were first recited at, and had as their subject, black demonstrations calling for the release of George Lindo and Darcus Howe. These poems had an important impact 'there-and-then', at street level. Such qualities of 'immediacy' have played a crucial role in promoting and mobilising black political activity on the ground.

However, it has to be said that these same qualities have also led to a critical paralysis in the reception of Johnson's poetry. Its referential aspects have informed a sense of the writing's 'transparency', as if somehow its meaning is self-evident, non-negotiable, 'black-and-white', and therefore in need of no further elaboration. This neglects the performative and self-reflexive qualities of Johnson's writings, many of which are not simply protest poems but poems *about* protest, representations *about the act of* representation:

> an' wen wi march pan Pentonville
> di BPM were dere
> an' wen wi step-it-up to Pentonville
> di BSM were dere
> an' wen wi dally-up to Pentonville
> di CDC were dere
> an' wen wi pickit di Pentonville di RTC were dere[79]

In this extract from 'Man free', a poem which celebrates the release of Darcus Howe from prison, it is not Howe's freedom but the issue of representation that preoccupies the speaker. Like much of Johnson's poetry, it is less concerned with the outcomes of black political struggle than it is with the acts of social expression and representation surrounding them. Interestingly, this act of expression is not communicated via the 'voice' of the protesters but by the accumulative pedestrian rhetoric (marching, stepping, dallying, picketing) which, through its very excess, is used to articulate the sense of liberation and euphoria surrounding Darcus Howe's release. The sheer exuberance of the walking styles described here signal victory in the streets. At the same time the poem's rhythm and its repetitious, *regimented* structure underline that this is a (pedestrian) rhetoric of protest, foregrounding the politics of representation embodied in the 'march' to Pentonville.

That the self-reflexive qualities of Johnson's poetry have not been taken seriously is evidenced in the conspicuous absence of critical analysis on Johnson's work to date. Despite his reputation both within and outside the academy as one of the key poets of the period, it is as if the meaning of Johnson's poetry is self-evident. A key factor in this issue of critical neglect is the cultivation by reggae and rastafarianism (both influential on Johnson's poetry) of what Dick Hebdige calls a 'natural image'. The rhythm of Johnson's poetry, along with its Old Testament rhetoric of violence, blood and fire, clearly borrows from reggae music. Some of Johnson's major influences are deejays such as U-Roy, I-Roy and Big Youth. Yet the commentary that *does* exist on Johnson's work has uncritically privileged this musical context in ways that foreground its spontaneity and naturalness.[80] At the same time there has been a neglect of the textual and literary concerns of Johnson's writing and the way in which it represents a critical and selective *appropriation* of reggae and rasta discourse.

Johnson has argued that the term 'dub poetry', which he originally coined to refer to the spontaneous and improvisatory form of reggae deejays, has since been applied incorrectly to group poets such as himself, Oku Onuora, Mutabaruka and Michael Smith. Such 'dub poets', he says, are different from the reggae deejay, whose 'art is closer to the African oral poets in so far as it's spontaneous'.[81] He goes on: 'there's not that element of spontaneity in dub poetry – you sit down and you work it out and you write it and you compose it and you change this word and that word' (25).

It would be a mistake here to simply reverse the traditional privileging of speech over writing in Johnson's work to assert that the 'scribal' is somehow more important than the 'oral' in his poetry. Nevertheless, it is significant that in interviews Johnson has sought to distance his own work from reggae and the rhetoric of immediacy, authenticity and presence that have come to surround it. In interview Johnson has tended to emphasise the influence of a black *literary* tradition – Du Bois, Césaire, Senghor, Langston Hughes, Kamau Brathwaite – while displaying a certain ambivalence towards rastafarianism. Distancing himself from its religious and philosophical turn to Selassie and the back-to-Africa movement, his writings privilege a local, black British politics: 'From an early age ... I realised that black people were in this country to stay and we had to accept that we weren't going anywhere.'[82] The following lines are from 'Five nights of bleeding':

> Night number two doun at SHEPHERD'S
> Right up RAILTON ROAD;
> It was a night named Friday
> When everyone was high on brew
> Or drew a pound or two worth a kally.[83]

On the one hand 'Five nights of bleeding', as Dick Hebdige has observed, 'draws heavily on the vocal style of Big Youth'.[84] In fact in many ways this is a poem *about* reggae, about music venues and sound systems. At the same time the poem contains intertextual allusions to *Robinson Crusoe* ('It was a night named Friday') and borrows stylistically from the discourses of print culture. By placing certain words and phrases in capitals, Johnson adapts the format of the newspaper headline in a way that signals his commitment to documentary realism. Of particular interest here is the way in which the poem's capitals highlight particular *territories*.[85] Shepherd's, Railton Road, the Rainbow, the Telegraph were all key symbolic venues for Brixton's black communities in the late 1970s and early 1980s. In spite of the poem's disoriented, hallucinatory feel (everyone is high on brew or kally), there is a strong sense of a physical geography here.

At the same time there is no cartographic desire to map the inner city faithfully in Johnson's poetry. Nor can the poetry's referential dimensions be seen as an escape from *figurative* language. Railton Road is not simply a geographical co-ordinate in 'Five nights of bleeding': it signifies more than a front-line venue in and around the years of the Brixton riots. Viewed within the broader context of Johnson's writing, 'the road' also emerges as a recurrent chronotope and organising trope to which his poems repeatedly return.

Although it tends to be discussed and reproduced on its own, 'Five nights of bleeding' is not an isolated poem. It was first published in a sequence of nine poems under the subheading 'Doun de road' which in turn comprises the opening section of *Dread, Beat and Blood*. How does this subtitle structure or organise this section? Immediately it appears to foreground local territory: to be 'doun de road' is to be nearby, close at hand, in the neighbourhood. The poems in 'Doun de road' either denote or evoke Brixton and the front-line territory of Railton Road. They evoke journeys through the black inner city that document the sufferings of black youth; an encounter at Brixton market; the key clubs and music scenes in the area. Alongside these locations, 'Doun de road' presents the reader with a series of more abstract, psychological or imagined street venues.

The first two poems, 'Yout scene' and 'Double skank', have pedestrian narrators travelling down the street, recording the local scene: 'I decide fe tek a walk / doun a BRIXTON, / an see wha gwane.'[86] This quotation comes from the opening of 'Yout scene', a poem divided in terms of both its structure and subject. The first two stanzas describe a Saturday as the speaker witnesses a group of black youths standing and dancing outside a

Brixton club. The last two stanzas are set at night as the black youths are rounded up and beaten by the police. This formula, in which pedestrian speaker encounters the injustices and suffering associated with black urban experience, is a recurrent one in Johnson's poetry. Not only does it signpost the street as an epicentre of racial tension, it works to turn the street into a specular locale and a key symbolic channel for the dissemin-ation and representation of the black community's plight. Elsewhere in 'Doun de road' the names of black individuals and groups who either were involved in confrontations at or were killed on Britain's streets are recorded: David Oluwale, Joshua Francis, the Black Panthers and Leroy Harris. In spite of this attention to referential black experience, there is a constant slippage between the literal and the metaphorical in 'Doun the road'. Indeed the street of this sequence can be read as a border location at which the public and the private, physical and psychological, interior and exterior, literal and figurative both intersect and collapse.

In 'Five nights of bleeding' the 'cruel infighting' among blacks is described figuratively as 'rebellion rushing down the wrong road'.[87] 'Rage' describes a black man's escape from psychological imprisonment or 'colonisation' in Babylon via a physical assault (mugging?) on a white pedestrian: 'Soon some white will stroll by, / and strike he will to smash / the prison / and let his stifled rage run free.'[88] Meanwhile, in a manner that is both direct and elusive, 'Street 66' describes a house party that is interrupted by the arrival of the police. The scenario is a familiar one (the black house party was a persistent target of police raids at the time the poem was published) and yet it is 'estranged' by the rhetorical figures used to describe it. The opening line both establishes and disturbs the scene: 'de room woz dark-dusk howlin softly'.[89] The metaphor of the room as howling dusk is a disorienting one. Not only is a concrete location figured here in abstract terms, but an interior space (the room) is imagined as elemental exteriority (dark-dusk howlin). The opening line turns location and signification inside out. As 'Street 66' progresses, the disturbance of the boundary between interior and exterior is pursued:

> 'Open up! It's the police! Open up!'
> 'What address do you want?'
> 'Number sixty-six! Come on, open up!'
> Western feelin high reply:
> 'Yes, dis is Street 66;
> Step rite in an tek some licks.' (19)

The police investigating the party ask to be allowed into a house (number 66), while Western, the black man in charge of the party, gives them access to a street. As with the open line, inside is figured as outdoors. Of course, these lines cannot be simply understood in terms of their internal dynamic or play. The slippage between house and street within this poem is central to the black communal politics outside it at a time when 'private' space (the house) was perceived as being under threat from a black community that transforms it into a 'public' venue (the shebeen).

'Doun de road' is a sequence of poems that takes the reader on a detour beyond Railton and on a metaphorical and metaphysical journey towards black consciousness. There is a sense of movement or development in the sequence as we move from the early poems of 'fatricide', of fighting amongst the rebels, to the later poems where blacks begin to unite against 'white oppression'. The road becomes a site a transformation in this context, the point at which the black community emerges as a politicised force. The last three poems of the sequence, 'Doun de road', 'Time come' and 'All wi doin is defendin', all claim an intention to take a stand against Babylon. The poem 'Doun de road' articulates a journey, a 'rough route' in which 'fatricide is only the first phase'.[90] It ends prophetically: 'the first phase must come to an end / and time for the second phase to show' (23). 'Time come' imagines this second phase via a confrontational pedestrian scene in which the speaker is 'de shadow walking behind yu / is I stannup rite before yu / look out'.[91] The black youths that are figured in the early poems fleeing from, or being beaten by the police, have, by the time of 'All we doin is defendin' taken to a territorial defence of the streets against 'de truncheon', 'de Special Patrol', 'de riot squad'. Within the closing poems of 'Doun de road' the street is no longer figured as a site of escape or travel, but as the point at which to 'stand ground', to stay put: 'no ... no ... / nuh run, yu did soun yu siren an is war now...', 'wi will fite yu in de street wid wi han ... get ready fe tek some blows'.[92]

## Brick Lane: Dhondy's 'Iqbal café' and Rushdie's *The Satanic Verses*

This chapter closes with a location that is streets away from the West Indian enclave of Railton Road. Brick Lane, in London's East End, is predominantly associated with South Asian and Bengali settlement in the postwar period. As such it offers an alternative, though not unconnected perspective on street discourse in the 1970s and early 1980s. Unlike Railton Road, a high-profile front-line location now well trodden in post-insurrection sociological studies of 'race', Brick Lane's symbolic status within the black community has received comparatively little attention.[93] Stretching from Whitechapel to Bethnal Green, Brick Lane and the surrounding streets of Spitalfields became the focus of a persistent National Front campaign in the 1970s. In 1978 events came to a head when Altab Ali was murdered in Adler Street. The killing prompted a protest in which the local community marched from Brick Lane to Downing Street. The event was described in the Trades Council Report as 'one of the biggest demonstrations by Asians ever seen in Britain'.[94] As with Railton Road and other street venues looked at so far, Brick Lane became a front-line territory during this period as an anti-racist campaign was organised to 'defend Brick Lane' (12). In 1978 protesters created a human barricade across the entrance to the street in order to block a National Front march. Similarly, groups of black and Asian youths patrolled the streets in cars at night in order to protect the local community. As a result of this reclamation and territorialisation of street space, Hackney and Tower Hamlets Defence Committee observed that 'far fewer racist attacks have taken place in Brick Lane over the last few months'. '[T]he local people attribute [the drop in attacks] not to the increased police pressure but to the active defence which is being carried out by black people and anti-racists' (12).

The interpellation of the local Bengali community as 'black' here is suggestive of the collaborative relationship between Asians and African-Caribbeans in the struggle over Brick Lane and the extent to which 'black' had come to articulate African, Caribbean and Asian ethnicities more generally by the 1970s. The struggle over Brick Lane was well documented in the black political monthly Race Today. In the 1970s the magazine ran headlines like 'Come what may we're here to stay' and 'No retreat from the East End'.[95] Such accounts not only demarcated the street as a contested terrain and a site of tenacious dwelling; within the context of an African-Caribbean periodical they participated in the construction of an imagined black British community comprising settlers of African and Asian descent.

Farrukh Dhondy, himself a member of the Race Today Collective, was the first writer to fictionalise Brick Lane and the Asian communities of London's East End in short-story collections such as Come to Mecca and East End at Your Feet, as well as in the pages of Race Today. Dhondy was a member of the Black Panthers, and his writing of the late 1970s and early 1980s needs to be understood in terms of its broader identification with the black imagined community alluded to above. Like Johnson's, Farrukh Dhondy's writing adopts a realist mode of representation in this period.[96] He was a schoolteacher at the time, and much of his early fiction was written for young adults. As such it carried a particularly heavy 'burden of representation', working to challenge and 'correct' dominant, negative constructions of blackness prevalent in the media.

Dhondy's short story 'Iqbal café' recalls many of the events that took place in Brick Lane in the 1970s. It describes National Front activity in the marketplace at the corner of Brick Lane and Bethnal Green Road. It alludes to the Bengali Welfare Association, the Naz cinema and the Asian cafés in which the local community gathered before the 1978 protest. It describes the growing violence and the Bengali community's self-defence of Brick Lane and the surrounding streets as they become involved in the black power movement.[97] Yet despite the overt politics of the short story, 'Iqbal café' is also an allegorical narrative, a self-reflexive story *about* the issue of representation, or more specifically the Asian community's lack of access to it.

The story describes a white liberal reporter, who, as the *East London Herald*'s Asian specialist, works to document racial tensions in Brick Lane. The reporter is a frequent visitor to the Iqbal café, where he goes in search of material: 'Some of the boys he knew would fill him in on the goings-on around Brick Lane. He'd pick up things other reporters couldn't get.'[98] The reporter shares an uneven, parasitic relationship to the community he 'represents' in the pages of the *Herald*, as his name, Clive (an allusion to Clive of India), makes explicit. Unlike the articulate, middle-class reporter, the working-class and unemployed Asians who frequent the Iqbal café have no access to the dominant modes of representation; they appear incapable of representing themselves.

The very name of this off-street institution points to a certain failure of representation. Referring to the Persian poet Iqbal, the appellation fails to speak for the Asian community it gathers. As one of the Bengali youths notes, 'you should change the name after the Bangladesh war. Iqbal is a Pakistani poet' (49). The youths politicise the signifier 'Iqbal', which can no longer be said to represent the community after Bengal's fight to gain autonomy from Pakistan. In contrast, for the owner Langda, Iqbal is a universal signifier capable of trancending political conflicts: 'I like Urdu poet. Most sweetest language in the world just next to Bengali and English. Iqbal, Tagore, Nazrul, Shakespeare, all artists, all brothers' (49). Art and representation are beyond politics for Langda, who names his café after a Persian poet but decorates its walls with French art and who, when a window is smashed in the riots, papers it over with a giant jubilee poster of the Queen. As the proprietor explains, 'when I first came to Brick Lane I saw all those stupid peoples and I'm thinking, this restaurant must be giving some knowledge, some beautiful' (49). With its connotations of eloquence and of linguistic mastery, 'Iqbal' carries a certain irony within the context of Langda's broken English and the illiterate, inarticulate inhabitants of the café. Ultimately the name foregrounds the Bengali community's inability to communicate or represent itself, its powerlessness in the face of dominant modes of articulation and signification. The 'beauty' Langda sees the restaurant bringing to Brick Lane is debatable, raising questions about the relationship between aesthetics and politics, representation and reality. The name 'Iqbal café' in this text ultimately asks us to be suspicious of representation and to consider its political motivations.

It is precisely this suspicion of representation that mobilises the Bengali youth at the end of the story. After sleeping in one Sunday morning, Clive arrives in Brick Lane late, only to find that he has missed a scoop. Asian and white youths have been rioting in the area, but the police will not give the reporter any further information. Clive turns to the café for the full story: 'He walked briskly down the street. The Bengali shops even those that stayed open on Sundays had closed down. There was a kind of hush in Brick Lane' (55). On entering the café he observes a change in atmosphere: 'the crowded café look up at him as though he were an intruder and not wanted' (56). The youths, who had previously provided Clive with information, are now openly hostile and speak to him in Bengali. Rafiq, the group leader, who, significantly, cannot read or write, differentiates Clive's role as reporter from theirs as rioters: 'You are writing story in the newspaper. We are knowing for living' (59). Rafiq privileges 'living' over representation and as such he depicts the Bengali community as active subjects, rather than the passive objects of representation for the first time in the text. The youths gathered in the café have chosen rioting rather than writing as their preferred mode of representation. They privilege immediate action over what Gilroy terms a politics of representative delegation. In the closing line Rafiq says 'If you want politics come to Brick Lane ... if you want business go elsewhere' (61). Addressed to Langda, these words refer equally to Clive who makes his living out of the stories supplied to him by the young men and who is now forced to recognise his role as 'scavenger, moving in for news whenever he picked up the scent of a kill' (60). As the café crowd emerge as a militant, politicised force at the close of the text they refuse Clive's attempts to (mis)represent them. 'Newspaper never go against police' (59), states one of the young Bengalis, in a manner that makes explicit the relationship between power and representation in the narrative.

The riots in Brick Lane appear ineffable, not just within the context of Clive's newspaper but in terms of the short story itself, which is structured around the presence of an absence, an act of street insurrection that unfolds 'outside' the text. Yet 'Iqbal café' is less about the failure of representation than it is about the rejection of one system of representation for another. 'Iqbal café' ultimately appears to embrace the kind of politics of representation outlined earlier by Paul Gilroy. For Gilroy street protest involves a refusal to be mediated by the very 'political system' it seeks to challenge. Within this context, rioting offers a means of refusing representative delegation through a privileging of immediacy, authenticity and action, what Rafiq calls 'living'.

Ten years after the publication of 'Iqbal café' Salman Rushdie turned to the streets of East London for the location of his postmodern epic *The Satanic Verses* (1988). Shortly after falling 29,002 feet from a jumbo jet on to a beach in Hastings, the novel's protagonists, Gibreel and Saladin, abandon the nation's limits in pursuit of its centre. In a novel where difference is constantly being destabilised, the alternative journeys taken by these Indian movie stars or migrants is instructive. Saladin Chamcha, who has begun metamorphosing into the devil, moves heavenward into the attic of a café in the East London borough of Brickhall. Gibreel Farishta, who is transforming into an angel, moves underground as he struggles to negotiate the London Tube. Gibreel, who derides Proper London, is driven to tramp its streets. Saladin, who craves it, is banished to the outskirts.

It is these outskirts, beyond the tourist landscape of Gibreel's *A to Z*, that constitute the decentred 'centre' of *The Satanic Verses*. 'Brickhall' is a fictional borough within a real location ('London NE1'), a magic realist setting at which material and imagined geographies bleed into one another. The name is a conflation of two real locations central to South Asian struggles of the late 1970s: Brick Lane and Southall. On the one hand 'Brickhall' extends the symbolic implications of Brick Lane by turning a street into a borough. On the other hand it deterritorialises the street by translating a specific location into a dispersed, deranged heterotopia.[99] Within the anachronistic streets of 1980s Brickhall, the haunting figure of the Granny Ripper is simultaneously haunted by the ghost of Jack the Ripper who stalked the streets of Whitehall and Brick Lane in the nineteenth century. This East London 'street' or borough is a rhizomic location which carries more than a passing resemblance to Jahilia, the Eastern desert city of Gibreel's dreams. Both Brickhall and Jahilia are 'nomadic' centres recently inhabited by migrants (many of whom share the same name); both describe landscapes in a state of constant metamorphosis; both house increasingly 'dangerous streets' in which old women get raped. Brickhall ultimately conjures routes between East and West that extend well beyond the bounds of Brick Lane. For Rushdie, I will suggest, the street is less a referential location at which to participate in the struggle over the politics of black representation than it is a singular (that is non-specific) figure connoting a poetics of travel, itinerancy, nomadism.[100]

At the heart of Brickhall stands the Shaandaar café, a four-storey terrace on the High Street. Run by Hind and Muhammad Sufyan and their two daughters, the Shaandaar is a space of multiple usage, an eatery and B&B; its six rooms are crammed with approximately thirty guests: 'temporary human beings with little hope of being made permanent' (264). It is in this temporary dwelling place of 'misfits and migrants' that the metamorphosing Saladin Chamcha finally finds shelter. A social centre for the local Bengali community and the epicentre of the ensuing riots, the Shaandaar (literally 'full of glory') is, like those earlier off-street venues (the Iqbal café and the Mangrove), a key site in the contestation over representation. At the same time there is a certain irony in the grand names given to these fictional down-market establishments: the Shaandaar and Iqbal. Both seem 'out-of-place' within the local context of Brick Lane, and the extent to which they support, or are parasitic upon, their local communities is open to debate.

Where the Iqbal café paid homage to a 'great poet', the Shaandaar is home to an unsuccessful poet, Jumpy Joshi, whose unpublished book of protest poetry, *The River of Blood*, lies unread on his bedsit desk. Appropriating the central figure of Enoch Powell's 'Rivers of blood' speech, in which the street is reimagined as a bloody River Tiber, the volume is an attempt to 'reclaim the metaphor … Turn it; make it a thing we can use'.[101] Jumpy's poetry reveals his political allegiances to the black power movement and *its* reclamation of the negative signifier 'black' in the 1970s as a symbol of empowerment. As such, *The River of Blood* works within the prevailing modes of black representation of that decade, presenting an oppositional, binaristic discourse that works to contest 'negative' white stereotypes of the black community by translating them in positive terms.

*The Satanic Verses* is certainly parasitic upon *The River of Blood*'s rhetoric of representation. Shortly after moving into the Shaandaar, Saladin Chamcha begins to appear in the dreams of Brickhall's Bengalis: 'rising up in the Street like Apocalypse and burning the town to toast' (285). From these serial dreams, the physically repulsive, devil-like

Saladin emerges within the community's unconscious as an unlikely symbol of black consciousness, a signifier of hope and empowerment. 'At first these dreams were private matters, but pretty soon they started leaking into the waking hours, as Asian retailers and manufacturers of button-badges sweatshirts posters understood the power of the dream, and then all of a sudden he was everywhere, on the chests of young girls and in the windows protected against bricks by metal grilles, he was a defiance and a warning' (286). Here the novel self-consciously alludes to the rise of black power in the 1970s. As the 'symbol of the Goatman, his fist raised in might' (286) gains currency, a negative signifier is reclaimed and rearticulated in positive terms. Rushdie has also argued that the title of the novel itself is an attempt at 'the sort of act of affirmation that, in the United States, transformed the word black from the standard term of racist abuse into a "beautiful" expression of cultural pride'.[102]

However, the novel also places itself at a critical distance from Joshi's verses, which are, like the voiceovers of black deejay Pinkawalla, satirised within the novel. Rushdie does not recover earlier modes of black representation in order to 'authenticate' his narrative, rather he 'quotes' from and parodies them in order to draw into question the very notion of authenticity privileged in black representations of the 1970s and early 1980s. The novel's citation of earlier modes of black representation is not an act of 'recovery' but part of a 'knowing', self-conscious postmodernism that reveals an 'incredulity toward metanarratives'.[103]

In *The Satanic Verses* a realist aesthetic of immediacy and transparency is exchanged for a postmodern aesthetic of hyperreality and depthless-ness in a landscape dominated by VCRs and the flattened surface of the television screen. While 'Iqbal café' appears ultimately to privilege a politics of immediacy and authenticity *beyond* the textuality of the media, *The Satanic Verses* implies there is no such outside text. *The Satanic Verses* proclaims the exhaustion of 'the real' and the impossibility of insurrection as immediacy, presence, transparency. The narrative does not reveal a desire to 'tell it how it was'. Rather it contents itself with a radical deconstruction of those representations, of which rioting is an *effect*.

Unlike the writings of Johnson and Dhondy, which on one level work to anatomise specific, referential instances of insurrection, *The Satanic Verses* plunders the late 1970s and early 1980s seemingly at random in order to produce a hybridised riot in which echoes of Southall, Brixton, Handsworth and Brick Lane are all to be found. Where the riots of 'Iqbal café' take place outside writing in a manner that suggests the need for direct representation rather than representative delegation, *The Satanic Verses* puts the riots into writing in order to expose the limitations of representation *itself*. The rioters of Dhondy's text, become "'rioters'" (454) in Rushdie's: the use of scare quotes here signals *The Satanic Verses*' suspicion of the aesthetic values of immediacy and authenticity privileged at the time in which the novel is set. The 'riots', as they appear in Rushdie's novel, are offered not as pure uncontaminated presence, but via the distorting lens of the camera. The result is postmodern television: coverage in which medium is privileged over message, style over substance, form over content:

> The camera sees broken windows. It sees something burning in the middle distance: a car, a shop. It cannot understand or demonstrate, what any of this achieves. These people are burning their own streets.
>    – Cut. – Here is a brightly lit video store. Several sets have been left in windows; the camera, most delirious of narcissists watches TV, creating for an instant, an infinite recession of television sets, diminishing to a point – Cut. (455)

The conditions for riot emerge following what the authorities claim is a 'growing devil-cult among young blacks and Asians', resulting in the intensification of policing in Brickhall. When Uhuru Simba, a local black activist, is wrongfully arrested for the Granny Ripper murders and later killed in police custody, the local community is galvanised into action. Yet this action is presented to the reader through the distanced, detached images of the camera which observes 'the shadow-lands from afar' (455). The footage it records offers no passive, objective document of insurrection. Filmed using a combination of aerial photography and 'on-the-ground' reporting from the perspective of the police, the camera 'chooses sides' (455). This 'machine of state' (454) actively constructs the event, *it* 'sees' the burning cars and broken windows.

On one level Rusdhie's rendering of riot is a critique of representation through a turn to the postmodern sublime.[104] The camera fails to make the scene signify, it 'cannot understand or demonstrate', it can only watch. The riots appear as a surface event devoid of substance, depth or meaning, a series of signifiers without signifieds. The camera does not offer an unobstructed view of a 'real' riot, it is a mirror not a window: 'the camera most delirious of narcissists watches TV'. *The Satanic Verses* does not claim access to the riots themselves; rather we find ourselves trapped in an anti-representational world of discourse and sign systems, 'an infinite regression of TV sets' that provide no access to the material geographies of East London. In the image of the television watching television we are presented with footage that feeds off itself and which refers to nothing beyond or outside itself.

The 'knowing' reader is encouraged to derive a certain pleasure from these heavily aestheticised, avant-garde 'riots'. At stake here is a 'mass' insurrection that is dependent upon an elite, intellectual audience, sophisticated enough to revel in the text's metafictional digressions and intertextual references. The novel's use of film and television aesthetics is at best ambivalent. The camera is not simply a machine of the state, a tool of power used to manipulate and 'oppress' Britain's migrant communities. The camera is something that the novel *itself* wields (*The Satanic Verses'* language and form throughout borrow heavily from the aesthetics of film). Teeming with actors, VCR addicts and producers, this text uses cinema to produce an extended and celebratory metaphor of the migrant condition. The vertiginous, elevated, weightless perspective of Rushdie's migrants appear strangely close in this context, to that of the aerial photographers in the Brickhall riots.

At the same time *The Satanic Verses* makes it clear that the techniques and technologies of the news team do violence to the riots as they seek to capture them. From the brutal '– Cut –' of the camera to the images of the helicopter '*shooting down*' (454) on the crowd, Rushdie's text makes explicit the power relations at stake in the mediation of riot. Viewed in this context, as a critique, rather than as a celebration of the riot's mediation, *The Satanic Verses* looks remarkably similar to the 'modernist' films that Kobena Mercer says displace realist documentaries of the 1970s. Exploring films such as *Handsworth Songs* and *Territories*, Mercer notes that film-making in the late 1980s is characterised by an awareness of the limitations of 'a mimetic conception of representation which assumes reality has an objective existence "out there"'.[105] These new films, he goes on, draw attention to:

> The decisions and choices made in the selection and combination of signifying elements in sound and image, the new films are conscious of the fact that the reality effect of documentary realism is itself constructed by the formal tendency to regulate, fix, contain and impose closure on the chain of signification. By intervening at the level of cinematic codes of narration and communication, the new films interrupt the ideological purpose of naturalistic illusion and perform a critical function by liberating the imaginative and expressive dimension of the filmic signifier as a material reality in its own right. (58)

Placed within the context of Mercer's analysis of film, the postmodern riots of *The Satanic Verses* are no less 'political' than the realist riots of

Johnson and Dhondy. Here though Rushdie is concerned with the politics of representation itself. If Dhondy and Johnson ultimately seek to contest dominant representations of the black community, *The Satanic Verses* reproduces them in order to de-doxify them. In the next chapter we will consider the new modes of representation Rushdie's text puts into play in more detail.

## Conclusion: yellowbrick lane

If on one level Brickhall is a self-conscious allusion to Brick Lane, then the nearest we actually get to that physical location in *The Satanic Verses* is through the narrator's punning reference to 'yellowbrick lane' (282). What is at stake in this translation of a street name? What does it *do* to 'Brick Lane'? On one level it extends the streets' horizons well beyond the metropolitan boundaries of NE1. Yellowbrick lane posits at least two itineraries. It directs us to the physical geography of a street in East London and to a magical (yellow brick) road that leads West in *The Wizard of Oz*.[106]

In an essay on Frank Baum's film *The Wizard of Oz* written for the BFI film classics series in 1992, Rushdie reads his first fictional influence as a 'parable of the migrant condition'.[107] Rejecting the conservative conclusion of the film which proclaims 'there's no place like home', Rushdie argues that Judy Garland/Dorothy:

> embodies … the human dream of *leaving*, a dream at least as powerful as the countervailing dream of roots. At the heart of *The Wizard of Oz* is a great tension between these two dreams; but as the music swells and that big, clean voice flies into the anguished longing of the song, can anyone doubt which message is the stronger? In its most potent emotional moment, this is unarguably a film about the joys of going away, of leaving the greyness and entering the colour, of making a new life in the 'place where there isn't any trouble'. 'Over the rainbow' is, or ought to be, the anthem of all the world's migrants, all those who go in search of the place where 'the dreams that you dare to dream really do come true'. It is a celebration of Escape, a grand paean to the Uprooted Self, a hymn – *the* hymn – to Elsewhere. (23)

By translating Brick Lane into yellowbrick lane, *The Satanic Verses* invites us to consider an aestheticised and above all utopian version of migrancy. This migrant aesthetic privileges a very different kind of street occupation to that witnessed within the politicised pedestrian contexts of the 1970s and early 1980s. Centred on a rhetoric of uprootedness, departure, elsewhereness and escape, it is very much at odds with the confrontational, territorialised street acts to be found in the poetry of, say, Linton Kwesi Johnson.

Rushdie's ambitious version of migrancy is also ultimately ahistorical and areferential. Even as *The Satanic Verses* recuperates a narrative of postwar insurrection, it appears keen to disengage itself from the politics of locality and territory that this chapter has argued were central to it.[108] In his account of *The Wizard of Oz* Rushdie celebrates the migrant as a transcendental, signifier: Dorothy's journey, he argues is an 'anthem for *all* the world's migrants'. This universal narrative of the migrant everyman effaces economic, geographical and historical differences within and between diaspora communities. It risks unifying travelling communities into a monolithic 'oneness' that *The Satanic Verses* works so hard to contest

Where in *The Wizard of Oz* Dorothy's ruby slippers ensure a safe passage home, for Rushdie they signal 'there is no longer any such place *as* home' (57). As an emblem of perpetual, migrant itinerancy, Dorothy's dainty footwear makes available a very different kind of pedestrian rhetoric to that implied by the sturdy soles of Laird's boot drawings of the 1970s discussed earlier in this chapter. The former facilitate flight and movement, the later offer traction on the street, a means of 'standing ground'. As distinct as the shoes of Van Gogh and Warhol in Frederic Jameson's celebrated essay, this footwear characterises some of the key shifts in pedestrian rhetorics outlined across this chapter.[109] Laird's boots not only privilege a politics of locatedness and location (with their emphasis on tread), they make themselves available for historical grounding in relation to the Mangrove protests and the broader refusal of blacks to 'move on' in that context. On the other hand Rushdie's ruby slippers operate as postmodern signifiers, devoid of referentiality and emptied of history. Not only do the ruby slippers allow Rushdie to celebrate dislocation, they are themselves detached from the historical and geographical contexts of diaspora experience.[110]

## Notes

1  London-based novels such as *In the Ditch* (1972) and *Second-class Citizen* (1976), centre on the politics of familial and domestic space as Adah, a single parent, struggles to bring up her five children.

2  Relations between blacks and police had been deteriorating long before this event. See Joseph Hunte's *Nigger Hunting in England?*, London: West London Standing Conference, 1965, for an early account of this issue. The Mangrove reappears as a key symbolic venue in racial discourse at crucial moments during the 1970s and early 1980s, and we shall return to it below.

3  Derek Humphrey and Gus John, 'Blacks and police – how the rot set in', *Sunday Times*, 30 August 1970.

4  Dick Hebdige, *Subculture: The Meaning of Style*, London: Routledge, 1979, p. 43.

5  In J. Procter (ed.) *Writing Black Britain 1948–1998*, Manchester: Manchester University Press, 2000, p. 25.

6  Hebdige, *Subculture: The Meaning of Style*, p. 43.

7  Kobena Mercer, *Welcome to the Jungle*, London: Routledge, 1994, p. 112.

8  Hebdige, *Subculture: The Meaning of Style*, p. 41.

9  Although there are exceptions (see, for example Amrit Wilson, *Finding a Voice*, London: Virago, 1978), black British feminists of the 1970s and early 1980s tend to focus on the need to recognise the significance of domestic space and the importance of 'the black family' as 'a site of political and cultural resistance' (H. Carby, 'White woman listen! Black feminism and the boundaries of sisterhood', in Centre for Contemproary Cultural Studies (ed.) *The Empire Strikes Back*, London: Routledge, 1982). Similarly, I have been unable to trace a black women's literature of the street in this period. Writers such as Buchi Emecheta, in London-based novels such as *In the Ditch* (1972) and *Second-class Citizen* (1976), centre on the politics of familial and domestic space as Adah, a single parent, struggles to bring up her five children.

10  Keith Piper, *Step into the Arena: Notes on Black Masculinity and the Contest of Territory*, Rochdale: Rochdale Art Gallery, 1991.

11  Cecil Gutzmore, 'Carnival, the state and the black masses in the United Kingdom' (1978), in Winston James and Clive Harris (eds) *Inside Babylon: The Caribbean Diaspora in Britain*, London: Verso, 1993, p. 214.

12  For an account of BHAG see *Race Today*, 10:5 (July/August 1978), pp. 106–10.

13  South Asian and Kenyan Asian women organised controversial strikes outside Imperial Typewriters (1974) and the Grunwick Film Processing Plant (1976). West Indian youth was to come repeatedly into conflict with the police in and around a range of recreational venues. Riots erupted in places such as Chapeltown, Handsworth, Brixton, Toxteth, Moss Side, Southall and St Pauls.

14  For example, when the President of Bangladesh visited Spitalfields in 1980 he received a street sign for Brick Lane which he said he would use to rename a street in Dhaka on his return. See Jane Jacobs, *Edge of Empire*, London: Routledge, 1996, p. 96.

15  A. Sivanandan, 'From resistance to rebellion', in *A Different Hunger*, London: Pluto, 1982, p. 10.

16  Sivanandan, 'From resistance to rebellion', p. 45.

17  I borrow this metaphor ('hardening') from Mike Davies's excellent book *City of Quartz: Excavating the Future of Los Angeles*, London: Verso, 1990.

18  David Bell and Jon Binnie, 'Theatres of cruelty, rivers of desire: the erotics of the street', in Nicholas Fyfe (ed.) *Images of the Street: Planning, Identity and Control in Public Space*, London: Routledge 1998, p. 130.

19  See for example Neil Smith, 'Homeless/global: scaling places', in J. Bird *et al.* (eds) *Mapping the Futures*, London: Routledge, 1993.

20  Bell and Binnie, 'Theatres of cruelty', p. 131.
21  Cliff Moughtin, *Urban Design: Street and Square*, Oxford: Architectural Press, 1992, p. 133.
22  Robert Gutman, 'The street generation', quoted in Moughtin, *Urban Design*, p. 131.
23  C. Alexander *A Pattern of Language* (1977), quoted in Moughtin, *Urban Design*. Also see Jane Jacobs, *The Death and Life of Great American Cities*, London: Routledge, 1961, and Davies, *City of Quartz*, for seminal accounts of the 'decline' of the street in the United States.
24  Powell, 'To the Annual Conference of the Rotary Club of London', in R. Collings (ed.) *Reflections*, London: Bellew Publishing, 1992, pp. 168–9.
25  Powell, 'The enemy within', in *Reflections*, p. 111.
26  S. Aitken and C. Lukinbeal, 'Of heroes, fools and fisher kings: cinematic representations of street myths and hysterical males', in Fyfe (ed.) *Images of the Street*, London: Routledge, 1998, p. 143.
27  *Race Today* (October 1971), p. 346.
28  Lord Scarman, *The Scarman Report: The Brixton Disorders, 10–12 April 1981*, Harmondsworth: Pelican, p. 177.
29  Lord Scarman, *The Scarman Report*, p. 28.
30  P. Gilroy, *There Ain't no Black in the Union Jack*, London: Routledge, 1987, p. 229.
31  Hall *et al.*, *Policing the Crisis*, p. 329.
32  Quoted in John Solomos *et al.*, 'The organic crisis of British capitalism and race: the experience of the seventies', in Centre for Contemporary Cultural Studies (ed.), *The Empire Strikes Back*, London, Routledge, 1982, p. 20.
33  Gilroy has noted that one of the key strategies of community policing was to introduce 'local knowledge in to the control room'. After the riots in Handsworth in 1985 the local police force developed a new computer system that indexed, by beat, 27,000 streets. See *The Empire Strikes Back*, p. 170.
34  For example the Metro club in Brixton and the Black and White café in Bristol.
35  *Race Today*, 3:10 (1971), p. 346.
36  *Race Today*, 3:11 (1971), p. 386.
37  *Race Today*, 3:10 (1971), p. 205.
38  Kwesi Owusu, *The Struggle for the Black Arts in Britain*, London: Comedia, 1986, p. 8.
39  Gilroy, *There Ain't no Black in the Union Jack*, p. 92.
40  Gutzmore 'Carnival', p. 227.
41  Owusu, *The Struggle*, p. 3.
42  Owusu, *The Struggle*, p. 12.
43  Stuart Hall in M. Phillips and T. Phillips (eds) *Windrush: The Irresistible Rise of Multi-racial Britain*, London: HarperCollins, 1998, p. 273.
44  *The Times*, 19 August 1971.
45  *Race Today*, 3:11 (1971), p. 385.
46  *The Times*, 9 August 1970.

47  *The Times*, 19 October 1971.
48  *The Times*, 14 August 1971.
49  *Race Today*, 2:12 (1970), pp. 455–7.
50  *Race Today*, 2:12 (1970), p. 455, and *Race Today*, 3:11 (1971), p. 386.
51  *Race Today*, 2:12 (1970), p. 457.
52  *Race Today*, 11 (1980), p. 37.
53  *Race Today*, 8:7/8 (1976), p. 151. Note the *articulation* of Caribbean and South Asian struggles within the context of a 'black' history here.
54  *Race Today*, 11 (1980), p. 36.
55  See *Race Today*, 4:2 (1972) and M. Phillips and T. Phillips (eds) *Windrush*, for instances of this kind of 'recollection'.
56  Moughtin, *Urban Design*, p. 130.
57  Laird has suggested that the boots, partly composed of tyres, 'symbolically … refer to the way the Third World uses the garbage of Capitalism in a Creative way' (*Savacou*, 9/10 (1974), p. 103). Again here, the images would appear to promote a migrant aesthetic, the product, as they are, of a cross-cultural dialogue between First and Third World. However in terms of the discursive context in which they appear, these boots also have a more immediate political significance.
58  Gilroy, *There Ain't no Black in the Union Jack*, pp. 239, 240
59  Of course such 'correspondences' need to be viewed with caution: rioting cannot be reduced to poetics or textuality. Similarly it is important to acknowledge the difference between isolated, bourgeois acts of representation (such as writing) and those of a popular, communal underclass in rioting. At the same time the boundaries between art and politics became increasingly unstable in this period: when a figure such as Linton Kwesi Johnson performed his work at marches and demonstrations, was he a 'poet' or a 'protester'?
60  Mercer, *Welcome to the Jungle*, p. 58.
61  Kamau Brathwaite, *Caribbean Quarterly*, 14:1/2 (1968), p. 57.
62  Anne Walmsley, *The Caribbean Artists Movement, 1966–72: A Literary and Cultural History*, (London: New Beacon Books, 1992, pp. 297–8.
63  Walmsley, *The Caribbean Artists Movement*, p. 147.
64  Marsha Prescod, 'May the force be with you', in *Land of Rope and Tory*, London: Akira Press, 1985, p. 49.
65  Walter Benjamin, *Charles Baudelaire: A Lyric Poet in the Era of High Capitalism* translated by Harry Zohn, London: Verso, [1969] 1999, p. 37.
66  Samuel Selvon, *An Island Is a World*, London: Allan Wingate, 1955.
67  Hunter Davies (ed.) *The New London Spy: An Intimate Guide to the City's Pleasures*, London: Corgi Books, 1966, p. 8. All further references are to this edition and are included in the text.
68  Walter Benjamin notes 'the preponderance of the activity of the eye over the activity of the ear' (*Baudelaire*, p. 38) in this context.
69  Rob Shields, 'Fancy footwork: Walter Benjamin's notes on *flânerie*', in Keith Tester (ed.) *The Flâneur*, London: Routledge, 1994, p. 74.

70 E.L. Brathwaite 'Letter from Cambridge', *Bim* (December 1953), pp. 256–7. Brathwaite adopted the name Kamau in the 1970s.

71 Andrew Salkey, *Escape to an Autumn Pavement*, London: Hutchinson, 1960. All references are to this edition and are included in the text.

72 Selvon, 'Little drops of water', *Bim*, 11:44 (1967), pp. 246–7. All further references are to this edition and are included in the text.

73 Selvon, *The Housing Lark*, London: MacGibon and Kee, 1965, p. 90.

74 Andrew Salkey, *The Adventures of Catullus Kelly*, London: Hutchinson, 1969, p. 133.

75 See Dhondy's collections of short stories *East End at Your Feet* (1976) and *Come to Mecca* (1978); Julien's film *Territories* (1985); Johnson's *Dread Beat and Blood* (1975); Faustin Charles's novel *The Black Magic Man of Brixton* (1985) and Bishton and Reardon's photographic essay *Homefront* (1984).

76 James Berry (ed.) *The Bluefoot Traveller: An Anthology of West Indian Poets in Britain*, London: Limestone Publications, 1976, p. 6.

77 James Berry, *Fractured Circles*, London: New Beacon Books, 1979, p. 55.

78 Linton Kwesi Johnson 'Forces of victory', in *Inglan Is a Bitch*, London: Race Today Publications, 1980, p. 27.

79 Linton Kwesi Johnson, 'Man free', in *Inglan Is a Bitch*, p. 21.

80 In particular critics have tended to privilege speech over writing in discussions of Johnson's work.

81 Mervyn Morris, 'Interview with Linton Kwesi Johnson', *Jamaica Journal*, 20:1 (1987), pp. 17–26 (p. 25).

82 'Interview: Linton Kwesi Johnson talks to Burt Caesar', *Critical Quarterly*, 38: 4 (winter 1996), p. 69. In this respect Johnson is similar to many British reggae bands of the 1970s, who tended to situate themselves in terms of local, black British struggles. For example, 'Can't walk the streets' by Aswad dealt with the 'sus' laws, while Steel Pulse dedicated their first album, *Handsworth Revolution*, to the people of Handsworth.

83 Johnson, 'Five nights of bleeding', in *Dread Beat and Blood*, London: Bogle L'Ouverture, 1975, p. 16.

84 Dick Hebdige *Cut 'n' Mix: Culture, Identity and Caribbean Music*, London: Routledge, [1987] 1994, p. 101.

85 Early issues of *Race Today* placed key references and territories in capital letters, and Johnson was maybe adopting or adapting these conventions within his poetry.

86 Johnson, *Dread Beat and Blood*, p. 13.

87 Johnson, *Dread Beat and Blood*, p. 17.

88 Johnson, *Dread Beat and Blood*, p. 18.

89 Johnson, *Dread Beat and Blood*, p. 19.

90 Johnson, *Dread Beat and Blood*, p. 22.

91 Johnson, *Dread Beat and Blood*, p. 24.

92 Johnson, *Dread Beat and Blood*, pp. 26–7.

93 The fullest account of this area is probably Kenneth Leech's pamphlet *Brick*

*Lane 1978*, Birmingham: AFFOR, 1980.

94  Leech, *Brick Lane 1978*, p. 11. All further references are to this edition and are included in the text.

95  See, for example, the June 1976 issue of *Race Today*.

96  This contrasts with his more self-conscious experimentation in more recent work such as *Bombay Duck* (1990).

97  There is a tension in 'Iqbal café' between the older, more conservative generation (signalled by Langda) and the younger, politically engaged Bengalis. As Langda puts it 'A big Jamaican leader, he come and say everybodies must do fighting. What these boys knows about fighting?' (p. 125).

98  Farrukh Dhondy, 'Iqbal café', in *Come to Mecca*, London: Macmillan, 1978, p. 47.

99  Foucault coined the term 'heterotopia', which he defined in a notoriously vague manner as 'something like counter-sites, a kind of effectively enacted utopia in which real sites, all the other real sites that can be found within the culture, are simultaneously represented, contested and inverted'. See Foucault's essay 'Of other spaces', *Dialectics* (1996), pp. 22–7.

100  See Peter Hallward, *Absolutely Postcolonial: Writing Between the Singular and the Specific*, Manchester: Manchester University Press, 2001, for a ground-breaking discussion of these issues.

101  Salman Rushdie, *The Satanic Verses*, London and New York: Viking, [1988] 1989, p. 186. All further references are to this edition and are included in the text.

102  Rushdie, 'In good faith', in *Imaginary Homelands* (London: Granta, 1991, p. 403.

103  Lyotard, *The Postmodern Condition: A Report on Knowledge*, translated by G. Bennington and B. Massumi, Manchester: Manchester Unversity Press, 1984, p. xxiv.

104  Lyotard describes the aesthetics of the postmodern sublime as 'an imagination striving to figure that which cannot be figured' in 'The sublime and the avant-garde', in *The Lyotard Reader*, Oxford: Blackwell, 1989, p. 204.

105  Mercer, *Welcome to the Jungle*, p. 58.

106  *The Wizard of Oz* is one of Rushdie's most potent intertexts, both in this novel and elsewhere.

107  Rushdie, *The Wizard of Oz*, London: BFI, 1992, p. 54.

108  In his excellent essay 'The riot of Englishness: migrancy, nomadism, and the redemption of the nation', in *Out of Place: Englishness, Empire and the Locations of Identity*, Princeton: Princeton University Press, 1999, pp. 190–218, Ian Baucom offers a very different, and more sympathetic, reading of similar sections of Rushdie's novel in relation to a 'migrant politics of emplacement' (p. 213).

109  See Fredric Jameson, *Postmodernism, or, The Cultural Logic of Late Capitalism*, Durham: Duke University Press, 1991.

110  For a very different 'diasporic' narrative of Brick Lane see Syed Islam's collection, *The Map-makers of Spitalfields*, Leeds: Peepal Tree Press, 1997,

which, as Roger Bromley argues, is an 'attempt to localise and contextualise the "nomadic", to ground it in a particularising and specific experience of difference' (Bromley, *Narratives for a New Beginning*, Edinburgh: Edinburgh University Press, 2000, p. 128).

# 4

# Suburbia

## Introduction: boredom at the suburban border

> The city tires me and the country bores me. The suburbs are ideal. (Hanif Kureishi)[1]

> Perhaps it is the odd mixture of continents and blood, of here and there, of belonging and not, that makes me restless and easily bored. Or perhaps it was being brought up in the suburbs that did it. (Hanif Kureishi)[2]

> Isn't there a problem in being seen as transgressive all the time? What about the right of blacks and gays not to be exciting? (Paul Gilroy)[3]

Suburbia, it has been argued 'spells the death of the "walking city"'; signalling a retreat into the insular world of the motor car and the semi-detached, it forecloses the possibilities of communal street occupation considered in Chapter 3.[4] Self-consciously distant from the 'multicultural' inner city and detached from the public/political realm associated with it, the curvilinear closes and cul-de-sacs of the suburbs appear a long way from the 'hard' inner-city streets of Brixton and Southall and front line territories such as Railton Road and Brick Lane. Unlike the dwelling place or the street, which have a special 'place' within the context of black struggles over territory, the fictional suburban settings considered below appear lacking in any such referential co-ordinates. Indeed, compared with the other chapters in this book which open with spaces of racialised, territorial conflict (housing in the 1950s and 1960s; the street of the 1970s and early 1980s; the city of Bradford in the 1990s), suburbia seems a somewhat unlikely, uneventful, black British venue. Yet suburbia has also proved one of the most significant settings of black and Asian cultural production in recent years.[5] Putting aside the irony of Kureishi's statement above for a moment then, *what is it* that makes the suburbs 'ideal'? Focusing on two suburban novels of the 1990s – Hanif Kureishi's *The Buddha of Suburbia* (1990) and Meera Syal's *Anita and Me* (1996) –

this chapter dwells on the possibilities of this border landscape for the 'location' of contemporary black British writing.[6]

Suburbia is not as distant from the post-colonial geographies of the city as it would first appear. Recent accounts of the suburbs have exposed its diasporic potential as a landscape *in-between* in a manner that reveals something of its significance here. Excavating the history of the bungalow and its importation from India to England, Anthony King has described suburbia as a 'multicultural' space.[7] Other critics have linked the rise of suburbia in the eighteenth century with the 'early stages of high imperialism'.[8] In the introduction to a recent collection of essays on suburban culture (containing, appropriately, a postscript by Homi Bhabha), Roger Silverstone notes 'the hybridity of suburbia'.[9] Within the context of such accounts it is precisely the inauthenticity of suburbia as what one critic terms a 'mutant zone, lacking organic consistency' that explains its centrality to texts such as Syal's and Kureishi's.[10] These *bildungsroman* novels encourage certain symbolic parallels between the 'inbetweeness' of suburbia and that of their growing protagonists. Kureishi's Karim famously describes himself as an 'odd mixture of continents and blood' (3), whereas Syal's Meena notes feeling at home 'in the grey area between all categories' (150). Announcing liminal settings within a South Asian diasporic context, these suburbs share the rhetorical properties of a migrant landscape, initiating journeys not just between the city and the country but between England and the Indian subcontinent. The 'sandalwood Buddhas, brass ashtrays and striped plaster elephants' (30) that decorate Eva's semi-detached, like the crumbling grounds of the Big House which conceal an ancient statue of Ganesh at the centre of Syal's Tollington, encourage the reader to excavate the post-colonial implications of these apparently all-white settings.

Yet if, as Robert Fishman has suggested, suburbia represents a kind of urban unconscious, 'a testimony to bourgeois anxieties, to deeply buried fears that translate into contempt and hatred for the "others" that inhabit the city' then Tollington and Bromley are also more than sites for a 'return of the repressed'.[11] The versions of diasporic hybridity that emerge in *Anita and Me* and *The Buddha of Suburbia* do not simply haunt suburbia, or reimagine it as cosmopolitan space. On the contrary, this chapter will argue that these two novels are in many ways about becoming local, about a turn away from cosmopolitan versions of migrancy. Suburbia, in the context of this chapter, is as significant as a provincial English dwelling place as it is a syncretic 'third space'. Kureishi has said that today 'England is primarily a suburban country and English values are suburban values'.[12] Such a statement demands that we take seriously the *Englishness* of work by writers such as Syal and Kureishi, an Englishness that Stuart Hall has argued marks the 'originality' of contemporary black British cultural production more generally.[13]

David Sibley has spoken of the suburbs as 'closed communities where the discrepent is clearly identified and expelled'.[14] Similarly Hanif Kureishi has commented on suburbia's 'narrowness of outlook and fear of the different. There is a cruelty by privacy and indifference' (100). Appealing more to the purity of the 'white' English countryside than to the cultural diversity of the city, a situated reading of suburbia's 'geographies of exclusion' complicates the poetics of migrant hybridity announced within these novels. In the semi-rural setting of Kureishi's Chislehurst the roads are not tarmaced but 'deliberately left corrugated with stones and pits to discourage ordinary people from driving up and down' (29). Meanwhile, within *Anita and Me* a much more substantial 'purification' of the suburbs takes place as the local village turns against 'outsiders' when plans for urban development are proposed.

To read the suburban settings of these two novels as deterritorialised, diasporic borderlands is to elide their specific and 'local' conditions; their difference, not just from one another but from the multicultural cosmopolitanism of the metropolitan centres beyond which they lay. Karim lives in Bromley, but the borders of his suburban world stretch from Chislehurst to the east and Penge to the west. Chislehurst, the outer 'edge' of Kureishi's London, actually structures itself in terms of the rural landscape beyond it. Indeed, for Karim Chislehurst *is* 'the country' (29), composed as it is of 'greenhouses, grand oaks and sprinklers' (29), Chislehurst is very different from Penge, at the opposite end of *The Buddha of Suburbia's* south London landscape. Penge is the home of Anwar's corner shop, Paradise Stores: 'closer to London than our suburbs, and far poorer. It was full of neo-fascist groups, thugs who had their own pubs and clubs and shops ... At night they roamed the streets, beating Asians and shoving shit and burning rags through their letter-boxes' (56).

Beyond Penge, central London is host to a post-imperial, international community that includes, or has included, 'foreign students, itinerants and poor people'; 'Ghandi'; 'landlord Rachman'; 'Mesrine' and 'IRA bombers' (126). Karim's accounts of his journeys through London tend to catalogue the diversity of its streets. This is a city that reminds Changez of Calcutta (224) and Karim of Bombay (128). However, Karim's home is in the provinicial suburbs, or 'the sticks' (138) where people go to bed at ten-thirty (62). Cycling down Bromley High Street, the narrator observes, 'there were so few Asians in our part of London' (64), 'the streets were solid with white faces' (65). This, in contrast to the city where 'there were thousands of black people everywhere' (121).

The suburban landscapes of Syal and Kureishi are not just 'in-between' city and country, they are also *peripheral* to those uncompromisingly *urban* 'centres' of black cultural production considered in Chapters 2 and 3. Set respectively in the former mining village of Tollington and the outskirts of south London, *Anita and Me* and *The Buddha of Suburbia* are as close to the green belts of the Black Country and rural Kent as they are to the metropolitan centres of Birmingham, Wolverhampton and London. It is the narrators' self-conscious awareness of being 'beyond' the multi-cultural city that drives their autobiographical narratives and signals something of their difference from the hegemonic settings of black British writing.

Both novels unfold within overwhelmingly white landscapes popu-lated by local English characters. This focus on white communities and cultures allows Kureishi and Syal to provincialise Englishness, revealing and satirising the 'smallness', the *ethnicity* of working-class Brummie or middle-class south London life. Yet while these fictional 'ethnographies' of provincial England allow Syal and Kureishi to poke fun at and distance themselves from 'native' white culture, their accounts also betray the extent to which the protagonists participate in and *belong to* this culture. The outsider status of the anthropologist is lost here as bonds with the locale (underlined through the protagonists' intimate relationships with white locals, Anita Rutter and Charlie Kay) are established and exposed. Taking the part of Mowgli in a production of *The Jungle Book*, Karim disrupts the exoticism of his role: 'suddenly relapsing into cockney at odd times. "Leave it out, Bagheera," I'd say' (158). Such outbursts don't simply foreground identity as performance, they also expose the narrator as local.

This chapter argues that suburbia remains one of the most significant settings of black British writing in recent years, not because of its abandonment of a referential landscape but precisely because of its prolonged engagement with a new politics of locality and locale outside the metropolitan centre and the cosmopolitanism associated with it. If *The Buddha of Suburbia* initiates a series of border crossings, then, it will be argued, they have more in common with the microcosmic back-and-forth itineraries of commuter traffic (between suburbia and the city) than they do with diasporic, transnational journeying. Karim's father's books on 'Buddhism, Sufism, Confucianism and Zen' (5) are not im-ported from India or the East, but come from 'the Oriental bookshop in

Cecil Court, off Charing Cross' (5). These 'manuals' draw attention to a
recently acquired 'Indianness', self-taught from within the bedroom of a
semi-detached in south London. Similarly, the 'scarlet Indian waistcoat
with gold stitching around the edges' (6) that Karim wears to Eva's
'spiritual' evenings, borrows as much from the mainstream London
fashion and music scene (referenced elsewhere in the text via the Beatles,
Pink Floyd, the Rolling Stones and so on) and *its* fetishisation of the
orient in the 1960s and 1970s, as it does from any genuine cross-cultural
dialogue with India. At the end of the novel we are told 'Eva persuaded
Dad into his Nehru jacket, collarless and buttoned up to the throat like a
Beatle jacket, only longer' (282). How are we to read Haroon's jacket
here? Within the swinging 1960s of Kureishi's text, is it a marker of
Indianness (Nehru), or Englishness (the Beatles)? The easy slippage
between the two (Nehru and the Beatles) is more than a marker of
hybridity. It exposes the staged exoticism of Haroon's clothing and signals
its quotation from a vernacular 'English' culture.

When Charlie asks Karim if he meditates and chants every morning,
the protagonist nods his head while revealing the mundane reality of his
everyday life to the reader: 'Dad running around the kitchen looking for
olive oil to put on his hair; my brother and I wrestling over the *Daily
Mirror*; my mother complaining about having to go to work in the shoe
shop' (14). Karim highlights his suburban 'Englishness' via the dull,
ordinary routines that comprise his daily life. Such confessions problem-
atise any easy reading of the protagonist as cosmopolitan or 'transgressive'
(a paradigmatic reading within post-colonial diaspora criticism). Moreover it is precisely Karim's 'average' lifestyle, his *ordinariness*, that *makes*
him transgressive within the critical climate of the late 1990s and early
2000s where detours and deviations from 'normative', 'settled' cultures
inform the reader's dominant horizon of expectations.

## Ordinariness, discrepant cosmopolitanism and the Singhs' suburbia

Alluding to Beckenham ('the place I came into the world') within the
context of Kureishi's novel, Kobena Mercer has noted 'the "ordinariness"
of its [suburbia's] multiculturalism which finds no counterpart in the
different histories of hybridity in the States' (29).[15] This chapter extends
the kind of 'discrepant cosmopolitanism' Mercer identifies between
Britain and America to consider the discrepancies between the 'worldly'
sophistication of the metropolitan centre and that of the everyday suburban locale. The kind of 'ordinariness' Mercer associates with suburbia

is clearly evident in the extraordinary suburban scenes of Liverpool-based artists Amrit and Rabindra Singh in figures 8 and 9. The Singh twins work together on their intricate canvases, producing plural works structured around the syncretic traditions of the Mughal miniature.[16] Their pictures are characterised by an emphasis on 'hybridity': white, Asian and African-Caribbean football supporters are portrayed collectively celebrating the victory of Liverpool United; domestic interiors display Western and Eastern commodities side by side; a portrait of Lady Diana combines the iconography of Britannia with the Hindu goddess Durga.[17] Yet such images offer a version of hybridity that is neither straightforwardly celebratory *nor* cosmopolitan.

'The Last Supper' (1994/5) depicts an Indian family enjoying a Christian feast in a way that playfully evokes Da Vinci's famous image of the same name. Set within the context of the suburban living room, this painting satirises the 'excessive commercialism' of Christmas and by extension the acts of greedy consumption in which the Asian guests engage.[18] The proliferation of consumer products and artefacts within the crammed interior (echoed in the interiors of Kureishi's and Syal's suburban fictions considered below) signal an economic upturn from the working-class inner-city streets of the previous chapter. At the same time, the discount supermarket brands (Tesco value bread and cordial) at the Asian barbecue in 'Indian summer at Dhigpal Nivas' (1994/5) indicate 'the frugal, bulk buying attitude which has become the subject of many a joke shared privately within the Asian community'.[19] The conspicuous presence of these 'mundane', ordinary objects within the Singhs' work also signals a 'provincial' Asian culture, distinct from the sophisticated cosmopolitanism of the city. The potentially nostalgic, idealised imagery of intimate family life within these paintings is constantly being destabilised by their ironic, self-conscious and self-critical look at everyday Asian life in Britain. If the artists are figured *within* these pictures, then the perspective of the artists is usually elevated, distant, aerial.

Although they incorporate the stylistic trademarks and multiple perspectives of the Mughal miniature, the pictures also borrow and incorporate popular images from video, television and film ('The Last Supper' includes *Jason and the Argonauts* on television, as well as film merchandise from *Jurassic Park* and *Aladdin*). There is a photographic quality to these paintings, not just in terms of their verisimilitude but in terms of the subjects looking back at the artists who pose, wave, or smile, as if for the camera. These allusions lend a self-consciousness to the Singhs' work that is emphasised through the proliferation of cameras,

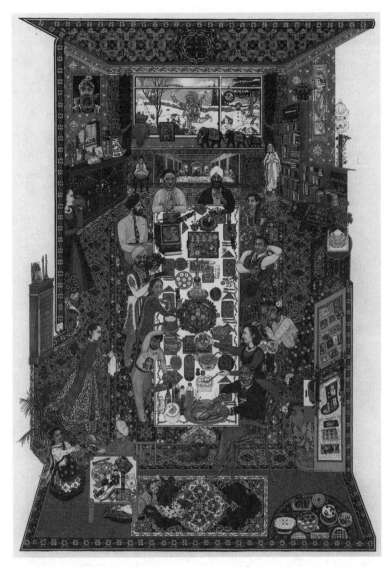

8   Amrit and Rabindra Singh, 'The Last Supper', 1994/5

**9**  Amrit and Rabindra Singh, 'Indian summer at Dhigpal Nivas', 1994/5

camcorders and binoculars *within* them. In 'The Last Supper' one of the artists also records the meal on video. The painstaking attention to detail, which made the traditional miniature dependent on royal patronage, is clearly still in evidence in the work of the Singhs.[20] However the form has become popularised and democratised, not just through the everyday scenes they capture but in terms of the paintings' references to and connotations of mechanical and electronic modes of reproduction. The Singhs' appropriation of the Mughal miniature tradition is by no means a straightforward, apprentice-like mimicry of the Indian 'masters'.[21] It also involves an ironic reinvention of that tradition. Stylised scenes of the sixteenth-century Mughal court (the traditional setting of such paintings) are exchanged here for the English/Asian kitsch of the suburban interior and back garden.

The Singhs' depictions of their day-to-day lives in and around the family home encourage an autobiographical understanding of their work.[22] Focusing on the preparation of food, eating, socialising with friends, watching television, reading books in the living room or going out to a football match, it is the ordinary, the *everyday* upon which the twins focus our attention. Like Kureishi's and Syal's semi-autobiographical novels, these paintings evoke a discrepent cosmopolitanism which celebrates the provincial as much as the transnational; the local as much as the diasporic; working- or lower-middle-class culture rather than elite, 'highbrow' culture. The meals presented in these images are not formal affairs, the barbecue and Christmas dinner deliberately lack sophistica-tion or 'class'. In 'Indian summer at Dhigpal Nivas' the kebabs and samosas are far outnumbered by more humdrum fare: burgers, chicken legs and wings, steaks, ice-cream, supermarket pop, white sliced bread. The immaculate suburban garden in which the family and friends gather houses a hybrid collection of plants (from rhododendrons to weeping willows), all beneath a stylised Indian sky. Yet with its carefully mani-cured border, picket fence, decorative pond, rockery and fountain this is no straightforwardly diasporic setting. This is also a landscape that appears indebted to the aesthetics of the suburban cul-de-sac, with its desire for spatial privatisation and detachment.

The backdrop to this suburban scene also requires more than a knowledge of the diasporic crossovers between the Mughal miniature and the microcosmic rural idyll of the English country garden. An appreciation of 'Indian summer at Dhigpal Nivas' is reliant upon a *local* knowledge of Liverpool. Like many of the Singhs' paintings, it displays an almost cartographic desire to map the city. Directly before the River

Mersey stand Bidston Hill and Windmill, famous landmarks of the Wirral. On the horizon, forming another boundary, runs the cityscape, including Albert Docks, the Anglican and Roman Catholic cathedrals, the 'mushroom tower' and the *Liverpool Daily Post* and *Echo* buildings. The suburban garden in the foreground of this image stands at a distance, not just from the city of Liverpool across the river but, with its burgers, chicken wings and discount cola, from the sophisticated cosmopolitanism of London.

It is suburbia's distance from the racialised venues of the city that also signals something of the difference and distinctiveness of *The Buddha of Suburbia* and *Anita and Me*. Going to watch a football match with his Uncle Ted, and taking the train from Bromley to north London, the narrator of *The Buddha of Suburbia* is transfixed by the site of Brixton and the black inner city outside which he lives:

> Before crossing the river we passed over the slums of Herne Hill and Brixton, places so compelling and unlike anything I was used to seeing that I jumped up, jammed down the window and gazed out at the rows of disintegrating Victorian houses. The gardens were full of rusting junk and sodden overcoats; lines of washing criss-crossed over the debris. Ted explained to me, 'That's where the niggers live. Them blacks.' (43)

Karim's elevated, panoramic view from the commuter train signals something of the narrator's distance from the black inner city he observes. His prolonged fascinated gaze is suggestive of his larger seduction by the 'centre' in this novel. Yet significantly, this is a centre at which he never truly arrives (even when he moves to London he occupies the more sophisticated, middle-class spaces of Chelsea and West Kensington). This inner-city landscape appears alluring precisely because of its difference ('unlike anything I was used to seeing') from the comfortable suburban contexts familiar to him. Karim's distance from Herne Hill and Brixton is underlined by his Uncle Ted who feels the need to annotate the racialised cityscape for the uninitiated narrator ('That's where the niggers live'). Ironically Brixton, arguably the symbolic 'capital' of black Britain in the 1970s appears in Kureishi's 'seventies' novel from the outside. However tantalising, it occupies the horizons of Karim's vision.

Similarly in *Anita and Me* Meena notes that:

> if Tollington was a footnote in the book of the Sixties, then my family and friends were the squashed flies in the spine. According to the newspapers and television, we simply did not exist. If a brown or black face ever did appear on TV, it stopped us in our tracks 'Daljit! Quick!' papa would call, and we would crowd round and coo over the walk-on in some detective

series, some long suffering actor in a gaudy costume with a goodness-gracious-me accent. (165)

For both Meena and Karim 'black Britain' constitutes an exotic site/sight. They are both marginal (footnotes, squashed flies) to the dominant venues of representation pursued in the previous chapters. Such discrepancies need to be understood in terms of the shifting *politics* of representation outlined in the previous chapter. It is the decline of the need to *delegate*, to be representative in black cultural production since the 1980s, that partly informs the 'ordinariness' of Kureishi's and Syal's narrators and that makes them paradoxically *extraordinary* when viewed in terms of the dominant discourses of black representation as they shift over the late twentieth century.

*The Buddha of Suburbia*, in particular, dwells on the politics of black representation and signals an important departure from the realist aesthetics of transparency, authenticity and immediacy privileged in the 1970s and early 1980s. Of course Kureishi's novel is also a realist narrative, but in *The Buddha of Suburbia* the city is above all a *theatrical* space, a locus of performance, display and spectatorship. The novel's focus on the staging of identity allows Kureishi to critique earlier modes of black representation. In suburban Chislehirst, where Haroon (Karim's father) offers sessions as an oriental mystic, or the Kensington stage where Karim, as Mowgli, embarks on his acting career, both father and son are called upon to perform as monolithic black subjects, as authentic Indians. Yet such representations are continually destabilized in a text which is constantly expressing blackness or Indianness in just those terms, as representation, an act, a staged identity.

When Karim is asked by the experimental director Matthew Pyke to invent his own character – ' "we need someone of your own background" … "Someone black" ' – the young actor becomes anxious: 'I didn't know anyone black, though I'd been to school with a Nigerian' (170). Lacking any obvious role models, Karim eventually decides to portray his Uncle Anwar and his recent hunger-strike in protest at his daughter's refusal of arranged marriage. However, Karim's representation is met with hostility from Tracey, the other black actor in the theatre group:

'Anwar's hunger-strike worries me. What you want to say hurts me. It really pains me! And I'm not sure that we should show it
    'Really?'
    'Yes.' She spoke to me as if all I required was a little sense. 'I'm afraid it shows black people –'
    'Indian people –'

'Black and Asian people –'
'One old Indian man –'
'As being irrational, ridiculous, as being hysterical. And as being
fanatical.'...
'... Your picture is what white people already think of us. That we're funny,
with strange habits and weird customs. To the white man we're already
people without humanity.' (180)

At stake in the exchange between Karim and Tracey are those semantic
tensions between representation as delegation and representation as
depiction considered earlier in this book. Tracey's intervention is marked
by the burden of being representative, of presenting a 'positive' black
image in a period when the institutional opportunities for doing so are
limited: a fact gravely underlined in the death of Gene, a less fortunate
West Indian actor who commits suicide because of a lack of parts (201).
Ultimately Karim is asked to abandon his representation of Uncle Anwar;
he is put under pressure to speak for a 'right on' black community. What
'sounds like censorship' (181) to Karim is necessary to Tracey, who urges
the need 'to protect our culture at this time' (181). At the same time
Karim's different agendas of representation (witnessed here in his back
answers to Tracey) work to unsettle and pollute the 'known' designations
of black Britishness in the 1970s. The 'new ethnicity' underpinning
Karim's replies and interruptions opens up alternative positions in the
text, positions that remain conspicuously absent within those fictions
genuinely of the 1970s (the period in which *The Buddha of Suburbia* is
set). Karim's back answers insist on a recognition of difference that gets
concealed in Tracey's use of 'black' as a blanket term. At the same time we
might ask whether Karim's emphasis on alterity, which productively
destabilises essentialist notions of black subjectivity, is also at the expense
of a political position. Tracey's sense of a communal politics is rejected by
Karim, who places an accent on the individual (one old Indian man), an
issue we shall return to at the end of this chapter.

*Anita and Me* is also keen to stage the tensions between alternative
versions of black British history. Just as Karim and Haroon perform an
Indianness that serves to conceal their 'inauthenticity', their ordinariness
as suburbanites, so Meena is asked to perform Indian songs for her family
while hiding her own local imagination. Preparing to sing a romantic
Hindi film song, she states, 'all I could think of was the Poet sniffing at
Anita's hemline like a yard mutt' (114). While Meena mocks her family's
Indian traditions, she is in turn mocked by them for her provincialism:
'Va! She sings Punjabi with a Birmingham accent!' (114).

Where black representations of the 1970s and early 1980s worked to engage their readers with an 'authentic' experience, *The Buddha of Suburbia* and *Anita and Me* ask us to engage with the silences upon which such narratives of authenticity are founded. More specifically, Kureishi's and Syal's texts flaunt the provincial ethnicities of their protagonists within communities that find reassurance in narratives of the exotic.[23] In the opening paragraphs of *Anita and Me* Meena explicitly foregrounds how her past differs from this narrative:

> I do not have many memories of my very early childhood, apart from the obvious ones, of course. You know, my windswept bewildered parents in their dusty Indian village garb standing in the doorway of a 747, blinking back tears of gratitude and heartbreak as the fog cleared to reveal the sign they had been waiting for, dreaming of, the sign planted in the tarmac and emblazoned in triumphant hues of red, blue and white, the sign that said simply, WELCOME TO BRITAIN.
>
> And then there's the early years of struggle and disillusion, living in a shabby boarding house room with another newly arrived immigrant family, Polish, I think would be quite romantic; my father arriving back from his sweatshop at dawn to take his place in the bed being vacated by Havel ...
>
> Of course, this is the alternative history I trot out in job interview situations, or, once or twice, to impress middle-class white boys who come sniffing round. (9)

The history that Meena eventually discards here is worth looking at briefly because it is also a received history of black and Asian settlement. Here, however, that history is retold as mythology, as fabrication: the diasporic journey from homeland to motherland, which is also a journey from expectation to disillusionment; the crowded migrant boarding house and the 'hard' life of manual labour exist only as lies in this context. Like Karim, this is a protagonist who is prepared to exploit her ethnicity to get what she wants. Of course Meena's personal and political history, with which the rest of the novel is concerned, is in no sense the 'true' story of Britain's immigrant communities: at best, the protagonist is an unreliable narrator, a self-confessed liar who also 'turn[s] to mythology to feel complete, to belong' (10). However there are significant differences between the two. The opening paragraph above self-consciously simulates and satirises the generic conditions of post-colonial migrant discourse. It presents the diasporic subject as a journeying subject, a subject who makes global border crossings and who also occupies the border, or threshold (figured here in the airport sign). Meena in stark contrast, has never been anywhere and grounds herself firmly within the enclosed world of Tollington. She is like Karim in this sense: a 'local'.

Meena's and Karim's histories cannot be read straightforwardly in terms of a diasporic past then: a past that is always elsewhere, beyond the landscape it presently inhabits. The immediate landscapes in which *Anita and Me* and *The Buddha of Suburbia* unfold have important things to tell us about the historical conditions of these texts, and the 'newness' of recent ethnicities more generally. Meena's Brummie-accented perform- ances of Hindi songs, like Karim's cockney 'relapses' as Mowgli, are not necessarily transgressive, or subversive acts within the settings in which they appear. In both instances they provoke laughter in their audiences, they are in no sense 'troubling'. It is by bringing the potentially exotic 'down-to-earth' that the humour of these novels is generated. As locals, Meena's Midland-Punjabi and Karim's cockney announce something of their 'ordinariness'.

## The Black Country, Birmingham and *Anita and Me*

From Meena's opening description of Tollington the suburbs emerge as closely bounded locale, a setting that has more in common with the rural landscapes of village England than with the larger industrial conurba- tions of the Midlands:

> I scuttled after papa along the single road ... the main artery which bisected the village. A row of terraced houses clustered around the crossroads, uneven teeth which spread into a gap-toothed smile as the houses gradually became bigger and grander as the road wandered south, undulating into a gentle hill and finally merging into miles of flat green fields, stretching as far as the eye could see. We were heading in the opposite direction, northwards down the hill ... towards the nerve centre of Tollington, where Mr Ormerod's grocery shop, the Working Men's club, the diamond-paned Methodist church and the red brick school jostled for elbow room with the two-up-two-downs, whose outside toilets backed onto untended meadows populated with the carcasses of abandoned agricultural machinery. There was only one working farm now, Dale End farm, bookending the village at the top of the hill, where horses regarded the occasional passers-by with mournful malteser eyes. (11–12)

The village appears here as an isolated community, marooned within a rural, landscape of boundless fields. Its distance and distinctiveness from the modernity and multiculturalism of Birmingham and Wolverhamp- ton, with their *gurudwaras* (94) and 'streets ... full of nosey Indians' (149), is confirmed in this environment of untended meadows and outside toilets, a grocer's shop, Methodist church and working men's club.

'Bookended', and later described as a 'footnote' (165) to the 1960s, Meena's village narrative comprises a marginal, microcosmic textuality that would appear significant for its 'smallness', provincialism, its insignificance.

As the 'carcasses' of farm machinery, scattered around the declining agricultural valley suggest, this is a semi-rural community faced with extinction. It is with Tollington's response to this threat of extinction that I am concerned here. To read the 'face' of this village – with its uneven, gap-toothed smile – is to be confronted with a 'yokel' community that shuns the advances of the city, but that achieves its rusticity through what I will be suggesting is an increasingly cosmetic, and racialised, appeal to the past and pastoral.

Tollington's defence of its landscape emerges in response to plans by the council to develop and urbanise the village. These proposals include the closure of the village school, the construction of a motorway extension alongside the old mine's railway, and the redevelopment of the mine – itself 'a crumbling monument to a halcyon past' (143) – into a leisure or shopping complex. Threatened with this prospect of expansion and modernisation, Tollington increasingly perceives itself as a bucolic village that is, in the words of the Reverend Ince, 'besieged' (191). Meena satirises the villagers' early attempts to mobilise themselves against what the authorities envisage as a Black Country Renaissance and which includes the assistant vicar's unfortunate campaign slogan 'Tollington In Turmoil', or T.I.T., and a protest march that is little more than 'a slow shuffle': 'there were not many participants who could make it up the hill without a motorised zimmer frame' (143).

From beneath this comic green politics, however, emerges a much more sinister and defensive retreat from 'outsiders'. Meena charts the rise of Tollington's environmentalists alongside what is becoming an increasingly enclosed, exclusive and exclusionary village community:

> They [the villagers] had begun whispering in corners whenever a stranger appeared, they had begun dividing themselves up into camps of differing loyalties ... before ... all adults were open and helpful, all children potential playmates, all of us together in this cosy village idyll. This sense of suspicion had begun soon after the news that a new road would soon be running through the village. (142)

Tollington is less a 'borderland' than a site of border control, subject to an unofficial surveillance and policing. The isolation of village life from the cosmopolitanism of Birmingham leaves Meena half-expecting her Indian relatives 'to bring out their passports and get them stamped at the door'

(149) when they come from the city to pay a visit. What Meena calls the villagers' 'polite provincial request' (143) against development is increasingly tempered by a more aggressive, hostile insistence on Tollington's preservation of its past. Mr Pembridge's (a local Conservative politician) speech at the annual Spring Fete is suggestive here:

> 'Beryl [Mrs Pembridge] and I are honoured to be part of Tollington's proud history ... but as you know there are great changes sweeping across our lovely land. A new road is, even as we stand here, burrowing its way into um the land, as I said, and our lovely school is closing down ... this is a time when we must stick together in Tollington to defend ourselves against outside forces, if we are to preserve everything we hold dear ...
>
> '... If I can end by quoting a man I am sure is everybody's hero here, Sir Winston Churchill, who said We Will Fight Them on the Beaches ... Just like our Winnie, we in Tollington must prepare to fight!' (173–5)

Delivered in the grounds of his family's Tudor mansion (open to the public only once a year), Mr Pembridge's stumbling call for unity is itself a comic act, open to ridicule from the working-class audience gathered around him. At the same time his faith in an organic community and distaste for change and outsiders is shared by many of his listeners. The xenophobia underlying Mr Pembridge's green politics is made explicit as he ventriloquises Churchill – 'I am sure ... everybody's hero here' – evoking an homogeneous, singular village community from which Meena's family are excluded. Tollington's patriotic turn to the past here also involves a more worrying process of distillation in which racial difference is placed firmly on the other side of the village frontier. The xenophobia of Churchill's proposed postwar party slogan, 'Keep Britain White', would appear barely concealed behind the rhetoric of Mr Pembridge's speech.[24] As Meena's father explains to the vicar's assistant, Uncle Alan, 'when Mahatma Gandhi came over here to visit, your Mr Churchill described him as "that half-naked little fakir"' (180). Mr Pembridge's nostalgia is symptomatic of a larger desire to recapture a pure, uncontaminated past before the advent of postwar immigration. Tollington's siege mentality, its attempt to barricade itself from development, is very much part of the creation of this patriotic landscape, a 'no-man's land' (135), in which one old lady mistakes the school's demolition crew for soldiers: '"Go on our boys!" she shouted, and began a reedy warble of "It's a long way to Tipperary!"' (269).

The Spring Fete itself is much more than an innocent charity event, bound up as it is within the context of Mr Pembridge's speech. It is decided that the proceeds from the fete stalls will be donated to the church roof fund, not, as in the previous year, to Uncle Alan's Africa charity fund. As such, these stalls are emblematic of a larger turn inwards by the local community:

> Tables groaned under mounds of lovingly presented ... homemade jams, pickles and wines battened down beneath stoppers and corks, seasons of summer fruits and hedgerow flowers compressed into their little glass worlds, bric-a-brac galore, old war medals, Coronation mugs and plates, chamber pots filled with pansies, twenties costume jewellery heavy with chunky paste garnets and emeralds, miner's lamps polished up to become coffee table conversation pieces, crocheted doilies in pastel shades ('Lovely for the dressing table or vanity case'), old gramophone records as big as dinner plates, lacquered powder compacts with pressed flowers petrified under their glass lids. (175–6)

These groaning tables bear witness to what I suggested earlier was Tollington's increasingly 'cosmetic' presentation of itself. This is a museum setting in which the past is presented through the spectacle, display and consumption of an array of objects, artefacts and commodities. These stalls tell us a good deal, not only about Tollington's heritage but, more importantly, about how that heritage is read and consumed. The miner's lamp does not only reveal something about the village's past as a coal-mining community. It is also symptomatic of the current appeal both of and to that past, and its ornamentation in the present. The suburban setting of Tollington has become, like the preserved summer fruits and pressed flowers, a static landscape through its appeal to a 'petrified', pastoral past.

It is through Sam Lowbridge however, a local gang leader, that Tollington's reimagination of its landscape is most explicitly racialised. His transformation from mod to skinhead in the novel coincides precisely with Tollington's increasingly aggressive xenophobia. Interrupting the Fete's charity speech, Sam challenges, with evident support from the crowd, the Reverend Ince's and Uncle Alan's previous donations to Africa, calling for investment in 'our patch', 'Not some wogs' handout' (193). Later, during the demolition of the local school, Sam interrupts a live broadcast for BBC Midlands Today on the demise of 'a picturesque former mining village' (273), shouting into the camera, 'If You Want A Nigger For A Neighbour, Vote Labour' (273). It is not long before Sam and his gang, whose mopeds now sport Union Jack stickers, take up 'Paki bashing' (277), and Mr Rajesh Bhatra becomes the first victim of racial violence in the area.

While these events echo a wider national history of racial intolerance, the village itself continues to turn inwards upon itself. As its protest against the motorway testifies, Tollington increasingly refuses to become a border of negotiation or transaction. The growing suspicion of strangers in Tollington coincides with Meena's own sense of estrangement from a village community with which she begins to recognise her difference along with her similarity. On hearing of the 'Paki bashing' incident, she notes, '[This was too close to home, and for the first time, I wondered if Tollington would ever truly be my home again' (275). At the close of *Anita and Me*, and after witnessing the rising racism of village Tollington, Meena's family prepare to join their Indian friends and relatives in Wolverhampton. During the course of the novel it would seem that Meena gradually detaches herself from her suburban locality, to take up the more familiar 'in-between' position of the cosmopolitan diasporic subject: 'too mouthy, clumsy and scabby to be a real Indian girl, too Indian to be a real Tollington wench ... living in the grey area between all categories felt increasingly like home' (150). The arrival of Namina (Meena's grandmother) from India sees the narrator take a new interest in her South Asian heritage. Towards the end of the novel Meena even lends her friend *To Kill a Mockingbird* and signs the letter to him Meena X.

At the same time Meena's signature is also ultimately ironic, underlining her distance from black urban culture. She confesses to the reader that *To Kill a Mockingbird* was 'a book I had tried to read and found too dense, but which had recently won some big prize in America and was supposedly a great learning experience' (296). Set outside London and on the outskirts of the smaller urban centres of Birmingham and Wolverhampton, *Anita and Me* also asks us to territorialise diasporic cultural production and pay attention to the regional and economic unevenness of the black *British* landscape. At one point Meena describes her middle-class cousins learning 'the capitals of Europe from one of the encyclopedias I had been given at Christmas and had never read' (160). Cosmopolitan criticism fails to illuminate the extent to which *Anita and Me* is also a *working-class* novel informed by a prolonged, 'unsophisticated' attachment to the local.

Set within a mining town that has been in decline since the 1950s, Meena's immediate community comprises the women who work at the neighbouring metal casings factory and their unemployed ex-collier husbands. It is these characters, not her Indian aunties, uncles and cousins in neighbouring Wolverhampton, that constitute Meena's extended family and that inform her attachments to place. Meena grows 'bored' (36), with her families stories of India, 'in these moments they were all far, far away' (72), and regularly escapes family gatherings to go and play with her immediate community: Anita Rutter and the gang who together form the 'Wenches Brigade'. Here Meena escapes from the polite company of her middle-class cousins Pinky and Baby (from the posher side of Wolverhampton) to hold peeing competitions on Sherrie's farm (14), throw cow shit (138), read *Jackie* or steal sweets from Mr Ormerod's shop.

There is an important mismatch in this novel between the 'exotic' migrant history of Meena's parents, with their attachments to the Indian homeland, and Meena's own preference for and preoccupation with her provincial childhood memories of growing up in and around a miner's tithe cottage. The 'smallness' of Meena's village life here could not be further from the dominant symbolic venues of multicultural Britain with which it is contemporary. In contrast to the transgressive, criminalised fecundity and hedonism associated with black life in the 1970s, 'Tollington's version of sexual revolution was Sam Lowbridge's heavy-petting sessions on the park swings … Drugs were what Mr Ormerod kept on the top shelf of his shop, buttercup syrup, aspirin tablets in fat brown bottles … Parties were what grown-ups had … the occasional tea dance organised by Uncle Alan in the church hall' (164).

Meena rarely journeys beyond the confines of this provincial land-scape in the novel: the nearest she gets to London is on her Monopoly board (99), while the occasional trips to Wolverhampton and Birming-ham constitute major adventures for the protagonist. When the fair comes to Tollington, Meena distinguishes herself from and romanticises the itinerant lifestyles of the gypsies: 'I was fascinated by these travelling people, envied their ability to contain their whole home in a moving vehicle … How many countries had they visited, I wondered' (102). While most of the novel unfolds during Meena's six-week school holiday, the family never take a holiday, they do not go away.

The protagonist's 'rootedness' within the valley community is repeat-edly emphasised as she answers her parents in broad Brummie dialect or asks for 'spaghetti hoops' and fish fingers and chips (60) instead of her mother's Indian cooking. That her family's garden is 'the odd one out' in Tollington, seeded as it is with Indian herbs, is a 'constant source of embarrassment' (15) for Meena, who longs for a lawn like the other villagers: 'crammed full with miniature ponds and stone clad wishing wells, tiny porches stuffed with armouries of shiny horse brasses and copper plates' (15). The miniaturised Arcadia (not unlike the suburban lawn in figure 9) around which the Tollington garden is structured here is telling in terms of the village's larger attitude to the countryside in the novel. These gardens are symptomatic of a broader appeal to the pastoral idyll within Tollington, an appeal, moreover, that is shared here by Meena, who suggests to her mother that they get an 'ornamental well' to conceal their 'ugly' (33) front lawn.

Throughout *Anita and Me* Meena shares a nostalgia for and desire to preserve the local village countryside, even as she satirises that nostalgia in her neighbours: 'If I'd have known what was going to happen ... [to the village] ... I would have taken photographs, pressed significant trophies in a scrap book ... kept a diary' (259). Meena, too is keen to preserve the village of her childhood from the impending urban development that signals the end of the local community. Returning to the village after a stay in hospital at the end of the novel, Meena's smile fades as she sees how the familiar landscape of her childhood has been 'carved up' by the motorway (293). She notices 'more strangers hanging around Tollington' and compares earlier memories of the village bounded by fields to the shrinking cornfields, now 'the only stretch of land separating us from the "townies" we so often mocked, the day trippers, the girls in their high heels' (299). Meena's nostalgia is a complex, challenging one. Even within the context of her neighbours' racialised desire to exclude outsiders, her narrative reveals a strikingly similar suspicion of those who do not apparently 'belong'. Towards the end of the novel her sentimental attachment to the village grows stronger:

> those days when hordes of children hung around the dirt arena [the Yard] looking for companionship and diversion were effectively ended by the closing of the village school ... With the children otherwise engaged in this commuter hell, the village turned into the Pied Piper's Hamelin; without the children around wreaking havoc with bikes and balls and skipping ropes, playing 'Tick' between our corner and Mr Ormerod's shop, the streets were empty and unloved ...
>
> It was not, however, any quieter; before the motorway opened, the village had its own soothing background noise ... full of birdsong and women's voices and the odd car rumbling through, sometimes the wind in the trees around the Big House played percussion and in summer, there was always the somnolent undertone of meandering bees. But all these notes became indistinct and fuzzy when pitched against the constant low roar of the motorway traffic. (297–8)

Meena's recollections here signal a new kind of nostalgia, different from those of earlier postwar black British writing and from her parents, for a homeland left behind. In contrast, *Anita and Me*'s reminiscences direct us 'inwards', to the propagation of memories 'here', in England. At the same time as she exposes and distances herself from Tollington's racialised retreat and revisioning of itself as a bucolic village idyll, Meena also embraces a regressive provincialism that is carefully rebuked elsewhere. To the end Meena remains attached to a largely utopian, idealised, benign village fiction: a Tollington of street games, bird song and meandering bees. Her nostalgia is for a friendly, close-knit, working-class neighbourhood, whose day-to-day existence unfolds around the Yard, the heart of the community. As Tollington is gradually redeveloped, Meena displays a similar sense of loss, a desire to return to the older community remembered by her neighbours. Even as she grows increasingly critical of suburban Tollington's racialised exclusions, Meena nostalgically turns away from the modernity of the multicultural metropolis in favour of an older, village England. This is not a criticism of the novel, or its protagonist. As Gilroy asks in the epigraph to this chapter, is not there a danger in always being identified as transgressive? It is precisely the 'ordinariness' of Meena that signals her novelty as a protagonist and that makes her so compelling as a character.

### Refurbishing suburbia: commuter poetics in Kureishi's *The Buddha of Suburbia*

There could be nothing more suburban than suburbanites repudiating themselves. (Hanif Kureishi)[25]

a lot of English 'art' ... dwells, gloats on and relives nostalgic scenarios of wealth and superiority. It's easy therefore for Americans to see Britain as an old country, as a kind of museum, as a factory for producing versions of lost greatness ... Even the recent past, the Beatles, punks, the numerous Royal Weddings, are converted into quaintness, into tourist mugs and postcards, into saleable myths. If imperialism is the highest form of capitalism, then tourism is its ghostly afterlife in this form of commercial nostalgia which is sold as 'art' or 'culture'. (Hanif Kureishi)[26]

At the beginning of *The Buddha of Suburbia* Karim's mother is described wiping 'her hands repeatedly on a tea towel, a souvenir from Woburn Abbey' (4). The allusion goes almost unnoticed within the context of a novel where commodities, and commodity fetish are exposed through the constant referencing of household objects. Karim's narrative is notable for the extent to which it is patterned around an inventory of domestic accessories and decorations, a scattering of brands and trademarks. In the opening pages of the novel the souvenir tea towel is joined by a whole range of other products and proper names: *New Statesman*,

*Daily Mirror,* Dvorak, Catherine Cookson, *Melody Maker,* Old Spice, *Fantasia on Greensleeves,* Krishnamurti, *On the Road, Sergeant Pepper, Live at Leeds, Candid Camera, Ummagumma,* 'A saucerful of secrets', Levi's, Marks and Spencer, books on Buddhism, Sufism, Confucianism and Zen, Walnut Whip, Monkey Brand tooth powder, 'Come together', *Vogue, Harper's and Queen, Steptoe and Son,* Debenhams, *The Dharma Bums,* Marc Bolan, *Candide.*

Through Karim's digressive inventories, the suburban interior appears (like the Singhs' living room in 'The Last Supper') crammed with material goods, a fact that distinguishes the semi-detached from the stark basements and bedsits of early postwar fiction where acts of production (work and the search for it) overshadowed rituals of consumption. The extent to which this list is concerned with *narrative* commodities: musical (*Sergeant Pepper, Melody Maker*); literary (Catherine Cookson, *The Dharma Bums*); journalistic (*New Statesman, Vogue*); visual (*Steptoe and Son, Candid Camera*) suggests a more self-conscious inter*textuality* than their random proliferation at first implies. There is an assured, middle-class sophistication associated with many of the items gathered here, which is evocative of the upwardly mobile south London suburbs and their proximity to the metropolitan centre. We are a long way here from the working-class kitsch of the Tollington Fete where Coronation mugs, crocheted doilies and chamber pots filled with pansies are the order of the day. At the same time the consumables on display in Kureishi's novel signal not a dominant cultural elite but the radical cultural *diversity* of the city. Combining 'high' (Dvorak) and 'popular' (Walnut Whips), 'Indian' (Monkey Brand tooth powder) and 'English' (Marks and Spencer) objects and brand names, Kureishi's hybrid eclecticism disrupts those nostalgic, imperial scenarios of which he is critical in the opening quotation.

However, the process of indexing, recording and remembering these everyday objects, tastes and fashions of the 1960s and 1970s, makes *The Buddha of Suburbia* more susceptible to the kind of 'superficial' narrative tourism he denounces than first seems. Karim's narrative elaborations, in which the recent past is told via a proliferation of commodities, many of which recall the historical moment in which the novel is set, are not merely parodic. They also effectively 'periodise' the novel. Intriguingly here, *The Buddha of Suburbia* would appear to be putting into operation a form of nostalgia that the novel, and its author, have otherwise distanced themselves from. Read as a narrative recovery of the recent past, and with its references to both punk and the Beatles, *The Buddha of Suburbia* raises a number of interesting questions in relation to the second epigraph above. On the one hand, Kureishi's novel reinvents, mongrelises and decolonises the 'old country' through his inventories. At the same time, *The Buddha of Suburbia* might be said to place a certain cultural investment in that country. Itself a cultural commodity, a saleable myth of bygone Britain, the novel shares a complex relationship to those forms of commercial nostalgia that Kureishi criticises.

The tea towel from Woburn Abbey appears to be an ironic reference to the 'quaintness' with which Karim's suburbia is more generally obsessed. This is a suburbia that offers a willing market to those products of 'lost greatness' identified by Kureishi. On display here is the tourist memento, a souvenir that records a journey within heritage England. This within the context of a novel where commodity fetish regularly reveals a preoccupation with the past. Of course this tea towel is more than a decorative surface commemorating heritage England, an implied retreat from the urban spaces of central London. It is also, more immediately, an accessory in the domestic rituals of cleaning. In the hands of Karim's mum, the towel is part of a more general attention to and cultivation of interiors in a suburbia, 'of which it was said that when people drowned they saw not their lives but their double-glazing flashing before them' (23).

There is a lingering attention in *The Buddha of Suburbia* to acts of renovation, decoration and restoration. The narrator's journeys across suburbia are punctuated by fleeting scenes of home-improvement: 'I rode slowly [from Bromley to Chistlehurst] and watched the men hoovering, hose piping, washing, polishing, shining, scraping, repainting' (39). Karim's Uncle Ted runs Peter's Heaters (a successful central heating installation business), insulating his customers from the outdoors in order that he and his wife Jean can afford their new home in Chislehurst. Eva and Margaret (Karim's mum) become increasingly preoccupied with interior design and decoration during the course of the novel. Meanwhile the only physical work in which Karim engages is the gutting of Eva's new property in London. Accumulatively, these apparently insignificant, everyday activities become symptomatic of a white, suburban ethnicity, and a more pervasive 'English passion ... for DIY, Do It Yourself, for bigger and better houses with more mod cons' (75).

At stake in this seemingly benign English passion for refurbishment is a larger retirement from the public or political realm. Walking through the streets of Bromley one day, Karim observes that:

> All the houses had been 'done up'. One had a new porch, another double-glazing, 'Georgian' windows or a new door with brass fittings. Kitchens had been extended, lofts converted, walls removed, garages inserted ... Display

was the game. How many times on a visit to families in the neighbourhood, before being offered a cup of tea, had we been taken around a house – 'The grand tour again,' sighed Dad – to admire knocked through rooms, cunning cupboards and bunk-beds, showers, coal bunkers and greenhouses. (74–5)

Here the decorative thresholds of the home draw attention to themselves less as entrances than as façades. The doors and windows of these dwellings are to be looked at, rather than through; they announce a postmodern privileging of surface, of a commodity culture bent on 'the painstaking accumulation of comfort and, with it, status – the concrete display of earned cash' (75). Moreover the porches and double-glazing reveal a culture keen to insulate itself from the outside. The extended kitchens, loft conversions and knocked-through rooms are part of an investment in interiority, an ever-expanding private world. These sub-urban homes constitute important spectacles within the novel, stage sets, even 'heritage' sites in which 'period' themes: Georgian windows, brass fittings and porches form part of a retrospective architecture. The detached interior is turned into a theatrical setting in this context, a locus of 'display' and 'exhibition' available for a neighbourly tourism, or what Karim's dad ironically refers to as 'the grand tour'.

Eva's progress in the novel is exemplary of this retreat into the domestic interior. Her rise from do-it-yourself enthusiast to professional interior designer in the novel is clearly not unconnected to her eye for restoration at a time in the 1970s when, 'Victorian or Edwardian houses were generally smashed open and stripped bare' (112). Exposing wooden floors, building a conservatory and reinstalling period fireplaces in Chistle-hurst (112), or renovating the West Kensington flat to simulate the 'soft' interior of the country house, are, like the tea towel earlier, markers of a larger cultural nostalgia being expressed in the text. Eva's interiors restage the 'indoors' less as functional spaces than as settings anticipating a pleasurable, leisurely gaze. Interviewed by *Furnishings* magazine at the end of the novel, Eva offers an apparently unrehearsed guided 'tour' (261) of her newly revamped London property to the photographer and journalist:

'As you can see, it's very feminine in the English manner,' she said to the journalist as we looked over the cream carpets, gardenia paintwork, wooden shutters, English country-house armchairs and cane tables. There were baskets of dried flowers in the kitchen and coconut matting on the floor. (261)

Eva's flat presents a carefully organised, manicured environment that borrows heavily from a village rhetoric and it is no coincidence that she goes on to win a contract 'doing, designing and decorating a country house' (282) in the closing pages of the novel. Interestingly, Eva's move to the city is accompanied by a return, through the renovation of property, to the countryside and the suburban ideal she has apparently left behind. Moreover, the interior she shows off here is distinct from her suburban home in Beckenham at the start of the text, a home decorated with 'ethnic' and 'oriental' paraphernalia that signalled her desire for the city and the multiculturalism associated with it.[27] The longer she spends in the city the more bored she grows with Haroon, whom she once desired as the performing buddha of suburbia. Although Eva has left semi-rural Chistlehurst in favour of the city, she appears increasingly during the course of the novel to be organising her life around its values. As Karim remarks at one point, 'she wanted to scour that suburban stigma right off her body. She didn't realise it was in the blood and not on the skin' (134). Karim's visceral image of the repudiation of suburbia is central to the argument of this chapter. Suburbia constitutes the abject within Kureishi's novel. It is that which both Karim and Eva (his adopted 'mother' and mentor) seek to scour, or shed, like dead skin from their bodies, but which lingers as a residual trace within them.

Kureishi's protagonist is motivated by an anxious desire to purify himself of a provincial suburbanism that continues to haunt him. Even as he rejects Bromley in order to embrace the worldly cosmopolitanism of the city, he remains profoundly attached to the suburbs he has sought to leave behind. This section will pursue the extent to which *The Buddha of Suburbia* is contaminated by the suburban culture it would appear to repudiate, a culture that localises itself even as it tries to move beyond the local.

If interiority and a retreat from the public realm are symptoms of the suburban condition in *The Buddha of Suburbia*, then indoors induces feelings of claustrophobia in Karim, who is constantly struggling to escape its confines. As Haroon practises his meditation, half-naked on the floor of their semi-detached in Bromley, Margaret asks Karim to draw the curtains, thereby screening her husband from the neighbours:

'It's not necessary, Mum. There isn't another house that can see us for a hundred yards -unless they're watching through binoculars.'

'That's exactly what they are doing,' she said.

I pulled the curtains on the back garden. The room immediately seemed to contract. Tension rose. I couldn't wait to get out of the house now. I always wanted to be somewhere else, I don't know why. (4–5)

The semi-detached in Kureishi's novel becomes a metonym of suburbia's smallness and parochialism, its confinement from the worldly inter-nationalism of the city that Karim is so keen to inhabit. At night in his

suburban bedroom that is decorated from top to bottom with newspapers (6), Karim drinks exotic teas, listens to music, reads political
journalism and installs a television so he can watch programmes on
London, Europe and America. His 'little room' in which he imagines the
'whole world converging' (62) is a physical rebuke to the inwardness of
the suburban landscape.

It is within this context that Karim decides early on in life that the
enclosed, claustrophobic spaces of south London can provide only temporary accommodation: 'a leaving place, the start of a life' (117). Abandoning Bromley in favour of the metropolitan centre, Karim presents
suburbia as a point of departure in the novel, a 'route' on the way to the
city. The narrator's move, approximately half-way through the text, is, in
this sense, 'a one-way journey, a permanent location in a new and
stimulating urban space'.[28] As if to reinforce this journey, *The Buddha of
Suburbia* is formally composed around two roughly equal sections
headed 'Part One: In the suburbs' and 'Part Two: In the city'. The text's
structure imposes a linear, 'straightforward' logic on Karim's journey
from periphery to centre.

However, the contents of these two sections are not as stable as they
first seem. Karim, in fact, never settles permanently in either the suburbs
or the city, but perpetually journeys between the two. His arrival in
London is not a sustained act of resettlement: 'home' is a sofa in the front
room of Eva's flat. Karim's bohemian lifestyle, fashioned on his hero,
Charlie (Eva's son), is itself a reaction against the conservative values of
suburbia. Arrival is endlessly deferred by this 'itinerant' (94) narrator as
he 'wander[s] among different houses and flats carrying [his] life-
equipment in a big canvas bag' (94) and never washing his hair. Even
when he lives in Bromley, Karim can be seen criss-crossing between the
suburban settings of Penge and Chislehurst and between suburbia and
the city: 'there were five places for me to stay: with Mum at Auntie Jean's
[Chislehurst]; at our now empty house [Bromley]; with Dad and Eva
[Beckenham]; with Anwar and Jeeta [Penge]; or with Changez and Jamila
[the city]' (93). Karim's nomadism is symptomatic of his desire to uproot
himself, to escape from the parochialism of the suburbs and to embrace a
cosmopolitan position within his narrative, a position which he explicitly
attributes to the metropolitan centre of London.

Yet for all his posturing as a bohemian, Karim's zig-zag journeys
throughout *The Buddha of Suburbia* have as much in common with the
back and forth trips of the suburban commuter. Travelling on the train
from suburbia to the city in Part One of the novel, Karim draws a parallel

between his own journey and the daily commute made by his father (a clerk in the city), carrying 'keema and roti and pea curry wrapped in greasy paper in his briefcase' (43). Of course Karim's travels are distinct from his father's routine journeys to and from work that are 'regulated to the minute' (46). Commuting for Karim appears less a regime of control than a strategy of evasion, escape and liberation: 'I was not too unhappy, criss-crossing South London and the suburbs by bus, no one knowing where I was. Whenever someone – Mum, Dad, Ted – tried to locate me, I was always somewhere else' (94). Like the commuter's, though, Karim's journeys are not characterised by a linear, teleological passage from A to B (as the sequential sections of the novel suggest), but a potentially interminable complex of to and from trips between destinations. To commute, in this sense, is to inaugurate a series of *returns*.

Even when he leaves the suburbs for the city, Karim is repeatedly witnessed going back home to Bromley. As Bart-Moore Gilbert notes, 'despite his disavowals of suburbia, it is remarkable how often Karim is drawn back to his roots'.[29] Departure in this text is never final or con-clusive. When he moves back to his mother's house in the suburbs, Karim longs to return to the city that he has recently escaped to: 'Although I was only a few miles away over the river, I missed the London I was getting to know and played games with myself like: if the secret police ordered you to live in the suburbs for the rest of your life, what would you do? Kill yourself?' (145). However, on returning to the city a few pages later, he displays a paradoxical desire to return to the suburbs: 'I wanted to run out of the room, back to South London, where I belonged, out of which I had wrongly and arrogantly stepped.' (148). These return journeys are symptoms of the narrator's (suburban?) hesitancy, of his inability to move on. Travel in this sense is as much a sign of directionlessness as it is dynamism. Despite his claim in the opening lines of the novel (and in implicit contrast to the suburbanite) that he is 'going somewhere' (3) the narrator of this novel is repeatedly figured peering back over his shoulder. Indeed, as an intertextual reference to H.G. Wells (who said suburban 'roads go nowhere'), Karim exposes himself as parasitic upon the suburban discourses he is so keen to leave behind. A potentially adventurous, worldly itinerancy is constantly being curbed during Karim's travels, by a contrary, suburban desire to return, to go back where he has come from: in short, to commute.

For all its privileging of travel, *The Buddha of Suburbia* ventures beyond London only once, and even this is a negative experience, sending Karim scurrying back to the suburbs. The journey takes place towards the end of the novel, when Karim's theatre company tours the United States (an event Karim has been eagerly anticipating for weeks). At the end of the trip and for the first time in the novel Karim decides not to make the return journey, to stay on in New York:

> When the others went back to London I ripped up my ticket and stayed in New York. There was nothing for me to do in London, and my aimlessness would be eyeballed by my father, who would use it as evidence that I should have become a doctor; or, at least, that I should visit a doctor. In New York I could be a walking stagnancy without restraint. (249)

The paradoxical dynamic of Karim's journeying (as simultaneously moving on *and* dwelling, or staying put), is clearly evoked here in Karim's account of himself as a 'walking stagnancy'. The narrator's self-diagnosis is shared by his father, who reads his son's itinerant wanderings (his 'aimlessness') around London as a failure to progress (become a doctor). Karim appears to stay put, even as he moves on. It is perhaps no surprise then that despite his best efforts to go somewhere, to leave the suburbs behind (he destroys his return ticket), Karim soon becomes homesick, flying back to London prematurely: 'I was glad to be doing it: I missed my parents and Eva' (258).

Karim's return to London is not prompted by a boredom with New York, on the contrary, it is the sheer extravagance of big-city life that threatens to overwhelm him. In relation to the modernity and permissive attitudes of the North American metropolis, Karim appears to feel increasingly 'suburban'. Cajoled into watching an experimental bondage session in New York between his rock star friend Charlie and a prostitute, Frankie, Karim soon begins to feel out of his depth:

> I stood there, and then I cleared my throat. 'Are you both sure you want me here and everything?'
> 'Why not?' said Frankie, looking at me over her shoulder. 'What d'you mean?'
> 'Are you sure you want spectators at this thing?'
> 'It's only sex,' she [Frankie] said. 'He's not having an operation.
> 'Oh yes, OK, but –'
> 'Sit down, Karim, for God's sake,' said Charlie. 'Stop farting about. You're not in Beckenham now.'
> 'I know that.'
> 'Well then, can't you stop standing there and looking so English?'
> 'What d'you mean, English?'
> 'So shocked, so self-righteous and moral, so loveless and incapable of dancing. They are narrow, the English. It is a Kingdom of Prejudice over there. Don't be like it!' (253–4)

There is a significant slippage in this passage between Karim's suburban-ism and his ethnicity: his 'Englishness'. Karim's mannerisms (the way he clears his throat), along with his broken, hesitant speech and inability to 'dance' all signal an awkwardness that at once signifies Englishness. Karim does not appear capable of leaving England behind in the way that his friend Charlie (who is of course no less 'suburban' than Karim) seems to have done. Directly after his unsettling experience in Charlie's bedroom, Karim flies home. This passage is interesting because Karim is interpel-lated as provincial, prudish and prejudiced: all those qualities that Karim has (critically) associated with suburbia elsewhere in the novel. Charlie's point that Karim is not in Beckenham now encourages a consideration of the extent to which he remains *of* the suburbs, even as he attempts to leave them behind.

## Conclusion: 'here and there ...'

'Perhaps it is the odd mixture of continents and blood, of here and there, of belonging and not, that makes me restless and easily bored. Or perhaps it was being brought up in the suburbs that did it' (3). In this frequently quoted sentence from the opening paragraph of *The Buddha of Suburbia* Karim makes a telling, tentative suggestion. His unstable, hybrid identity is not simply a product of ethnicity (of being Indian and English), but of *locality* ('perhaps it was being brought up in the suburbs that did it'). If Karim is 'easily bored' in the suburbs, then paradoxically the 'restlessness' this boredom generates is at least partly responsible for the dynamic, inventive and unsettling identity politics of the novel.

Earlier in this chapter we considered Tracey's and Karim's different positions on the politics of black representation. Unlike Tracey's fixed 'black-and-white' stance, the protagonist's perspective is constantly 'moving on' in the novel, a factor which makes him difficult to 'pin down', but which also makes him very much a part of an unstable contemporary black British experience.[30] Karim is a chameleon. Like Meena in Syal's novel, he reinvents and repositions himself as black or white, Asian or cockney as the situation suits him. As such Karim and Meena are not simply victims of their ethnicity, they also actively exploit and manipulate that ethnicity (as does Haroon during the novel's buddha performances).

Karim deploys strategies of evasion and uncertainty in his day-to-day communications, through strategic shifts 'back-and-forth'. This kind of 'to-and-fro' dynamic is reiterated within the larger pedestrian rhetoric of *The Buddha of Suburbia* and what I have termed the text's commuter poetics. The protagonist's back and forth commuter journeys are mirrored in his identity politics in that they involve a doubling and displacing identity, 'here and there' (also a key 'move' within post-colonial diasporic discourse).[31]

However, if such back and forth movements allow Karim (and Kureishi) to question and complicate earlier, monolithic notions of black subjectivity, then this is at the cost of a communal black politics. Karim shuttles between identities, positions and politics without ever firmly committing or attaching himself to any. Moreover, Karim's implied critique of suburbia as a depoliticised sphere is complicated by his own inability to take the kind of political stance made within literatures of the 1970s and early 1980s.

Karim is notable for the extent to which he avoids politics. His failure to attend the anti-Nazi protest march against the National Front (loosely based on the Southall riots of 1978), after Changez gets attacked in the vicinity, is typical of his detachment in the novel. In many ways Karim is the opposite of his childhood friend, Jamila, who joins a commune (the one domestic space in the novel that rejects the semi-detached's insularity) populated by queers, socialists and environmentalists. While Karim reads high European literature, Jamila reads black American writing and joins the black women's centre. At the end of the novel Karim takes a part as the son of an Indian shopkeeper in a soap opera 'which would tangle with the latest contemporary issues ... abortions and racist attacks, the stuff that people lived through but that never got on TV' (259). However his motivations for taking the job are personal rather than political: 'Millions watched those things. I would have a lot of money. I would be recognized all over the country. My life would change overnight' (259). The closing stages of *The Buddha of Suburbia* unfold during the run-up to a General Election and a Conservative Party victory, and Karim's politics display a Thatcherite accent on the individual that the novel is at once a critique of. Karim's move away from and scepticism towards a 'right on' culture does not necessarily signal progress in this context.

Writing on the symptoms of suburban living some two years before the publication of *The Buddha of Suburbia* Kureishi notes that in such locations:

> there is a refusal to admit humanity beyond the family, beyond the household walls and garden fence. Each family as an autonomous, self-sufficient unit faces a hostile world of other self-contained families. This neurotic and materialistic privacy, the keystone of British suburban life, ensures that the 'collective' or even the 'public' will mean little to these people.[32]

While on one level *The Buddha of Suburbia* is a satirical attack on suburbia's retreat from the communal and the public, Karim, often despite
himself, displays strikingly similar symptoms. As Terry, a communist
colleague of Karim's, states, 'You're not attached to anything, not even to
the Party' (241). The narrator is, from beginning to end, marked by a
locality he seeks to expel.

The suburban street is a depoliticised space offering little opportunity
for meeting, or communal action. The 'tree-lined' suburban avenues of
*The Buddha of Suburbia* are low density spaces, whose 'echoing streets'
(74) are 'quiet and uninhabited ... as if the area had been evacuated. The
silence was ominous' (101). The commuter journeys of *The Buddha of
Suburbia*, appear wholly different from those modes of pedestrian
rhetoric put into operation within literatures of the 1970s and early
1980s. Here a committed 'stand' in the streets has been exchanged for a
more evasive, non-confrontational wandering.

Nevertheless, and as this chapter has argued, Karim's journeys are not
simply a sign of his detachment from the local landscape, or his ability to
somehow transcend it: his commuter trips also anchor, or situate, him
within suburban Bromley. The dynamic of return that characterises
Karim's travel is crucial to an understanding of the localized nature of his
journeys between the city and the suburbs. In *The Buddha of Suburbia*
commuting is more than a potential strategy of evasion. As a geographically specific mode of transport associated with the suburbs, such
journeys situate Karim even as he appears to be leaving these situations
behind. The narrator positions himself in spite of and because of his
attempts to move on.

If suburbia indicates the waning of an earlier politics of black representation in the 1970s and early 1980s, then it also signposts the emergence
of the new politics of representation that began to gain ground in the mid-
1980s. Where the street provided access to a realist aesthetics of immediacy,
directness and authenticity (witnessed already in the work of Johnson
and Dhondy), the geography of suburbia outlined above foregrounds the
privileging of an aesthetics of distance, artifice, self-consciousness and
irony (witnessed already in *The Satanic Verses*). However, in contrast to
Rushdie's novel where Brickhall was notable as a nomadic, transnational
space of East/West crossings, the suburbias of Syal and Kureishi, this
chapter has argued, also display a staid provincialism, a shrinkage from
the (post)modernity and multiculturalism of the metropolis.

The work of Hanif Kureishi and Meera Syal shares a complex relationship to current debates on black representation. While both novels occupy

the geographical margins of much larger metropolitan centres, they have also been notably 'centred' within and beyond the academy. *Anita and Me* and *The Buddha of Suburbia* were adapted respectively for radio, film and television, while Kureishi's early screenplays were cited as exemplary narratives by those critics who first articulated the new politics of representation: Stuart Hall, Judith Williamson, Mercer and Julien.[33] The canonical and cult status of these two novels has, ironically, furnished them with a representative authority that both texts work to disrupt.

By situating themselves in suburbia, at a remove from the city, *Anita and Me* and *The Buddha of Suburbia* place themselves at a distance from the inner city that had been the 'representative' venue of black cultural production during the 1970s and early 1980s. This 'distance' is underlined by the fact that both novels turn away from the cultural present in order to reoccupy and reinvent the recent past. By removing themselves from the inner city and from the present, these novels are part of a much larger body of black cultural production since the mid-1980s to attend to the historicity of the black British experience.[34] This archive of artistic production contrasts with that of the 1970s and early 1980s, where it was immediacy and 'nowness' that characterised black cultural expression.

The emergence of an historical consciousness within recent literature has gone critically unregistered within what I have argued elsewhere is a severely underhistoricised body of writing.[35] Nevertheless, its appearance represents an important break with earlier postwar literatures. From the 1950s to the early 1980s the past nearly always appears in the form of nostalgias for a landscape left behind. Over that period memory is a 'diasporic' narrative, recollecting a range of 'imaginary homelands' beyond Britain's shores. From the mid-1980s however, there has been an increasingly tangible shift away from, even 'boredom' with, those nostalgic scenarios of the homeland, as a new generation of 'born-and-bred' (a phrase evoked within Kureishi's novel) black Britons have begun to narrate something of the 'hereness' of their pasts.

Part of the novelty and distinctiveness of *The Buddha of Suburbia* and *Anita and Me* is that both texts explore narrative histories of protagonists who are insiders. The pasts within these two novels are important for their production of an 'internal' history, a history that exposes a prolonged period of dwelling in Britain. Set in the late 1960s and 1970s, *Anita and Me* and *The Buddha of Suburbia* return to a key phase in black British history. These youthful coming-of-age novels unfold over a period itself known as the 'coming of age' of a politicised black community in Britain.[36] If this was the period in which 'black' had begun to operate as a governing, unifying category for the first time, then their protagonists clearly contribute to a dismantling of the frameworks of representation upon which that category was sustained. In this sense both novels display a confrontation between what Hall referred to as the first and second moments of black cultural politics. It is in terms of this historical context that these novels need to be read if their politics of representation are to be understood. Both texts exist beyond the narratable boundaries of a politicised black literature in the 1970s. In terms of that decade Meena and Karim represent seriously 'flawed' narrators. They are 'extraordinary' as opposed to 'representative' characters. Meena's disregard for *izzat* (family pride or honour), such as Karim's homosexuality and mixed parentage, situate them outside the discursive orthodoxies policing available versions of black Britishness at that time. It is in this context that *Anita and Me* and *The Buddha of Suburbia* might be said to produce a set of interpretative anxieties, problems and frustrations in terms of the received history of the 1970s. How, for example, would we discuss the 'middle-classness' of Karim (whose father is a clerk in the city) and Meena (whose mother is a school teacher), in terms of the kind of polemic attack on 'Di black petty-booshwah' (1980) by Linton Kwesi Johnson? Both fail as authentically 'right on' ethnic subjects within the periods they narrate.

## Notes

1 Hanif Kureishi, *Birds of Passage* (1983), in *Outskirts and Other Plays*, London: Faber & Faber, 1992, p. 188.
2 Hanif Kureishi, *The Buddha of Suburbia*, London: Faber & Faber, 1990, p. 3.
3 Paul Gilroy, *Small Acts*, London: Serpent's Tail, 1993, p. 169.
4 F.M.L. Thompson, *The Rise of Suburbia*, Leicester: Leicester University Press, 1982, p. 6.
5 At the time of writing Gurinder Chadha's latest film, *Bend it Like Beckham* (2002), has just been released. The film tells the story of a suburban teenager's dreams of becoming a professional footballer.
6 Kureishi, *The Buddha of Suburbia*, and Meera Syal, *Anita and Me*, London: Flamingo, 1996. All further references are to these editions and are included in the text.
7 Anthony D. King, '"Excavating the multicultural suburb": hidden histories of the bungalow', in R. Silverstone (ed.) *Visions of Suburbia*, London: Routledge, 1997, pp. 55–85.
8 John Clement Ball, 'The semi-detached metropolis: Hanif Kureishi's London', *Ariel*, 27:4 (1996), pp. 7–27 (p. 20). This essay offers an excellent overview of suburbia in relation to Kureishi's work.

9  Silverstone (ed.) *Visions of Suburbia*, p. 8.
10 Michael Brackwell, *England Is Mine: Pop Life in Albion from Wilde to Goldie*, London: HarperCollins, 1997, p. 109. For a full account of *The Buddha of Suburbia*'s vexed relationship to the *bildungsroman* see Berthold Schoene, 'Herald of hybridity: the emancipation of difference in Hanif Kureishi's *The Buddha of Suburbia*', *International Journal of Cultural Studies*, 1:1 (1998), pp. 109–27. For a more wide-ranging discussion of the *bildungsroman* in relation to black British writing see Mark Stein, 'The black British *Bildungsroman* and the transformation of Britain: connectedness across difference', in B. Korte and K.P. Muller (eds) *Unity and Diversity Revisited? British Literature and Culture in the 1990s*, Tübingen: Günter Narr, 1998, pp. 89–105.
11 Robert Fishman, *Bourgeois Utopias: The Rise and Fall of Suburbia*, New York: Basil Books, 1987.
12 Hanif Kureishi, 'Some time with Stephen: a diary', in *Sammy and Rosie Get Laid – The Script and the Diary*, London: Faber & Faber, 1988, p. 100.
13 Stuart Hall, 'Song of Handsworth praise', in *Black Film/British Cinema*, ICA Document 7, London: ICA, 1988, p. 17.
14 David Sibley, *Geographies of Exclusion*, London: Routledge, 1995.
15 Kobena Mercer, *Welcome to the Jungle*, London: Routledge, 1994, p. 29.
16 The Mughal miniature is a 'Muslim' genre that incorporates Hindu and European art forms. At a recent conference held at the National Museum in Edinburgh ('Subcontinental Scatterings', 2001) the twins showed a video-documentary of their artistic careers and spoke eloquently about the struggles they had encountered in working jointly and in drawing on what were seen as constraining Indian traditions. During their formal training the artists resisted attempts to make them cultivate 'individual', 'original' styles, styles which the Singhs associate with European artistic aesthetics.
17 See 'Painting the town red' and 'O come all ye re-eds!', 'Daddy in the sitting room I, II & III' and 'Diana: the improved version', in *Twin Perspectives: Paintings by Amrit and Rabindra KD Kaur Singh*, Liverpool: Twin Studio, 1999.
18 *Twin Perspectives*, p. 48.
19 *Twin Perspectives*, p. 58.
20 The Singhs also rely on commissions to continue their work because of the length of time each image takes to complete.
21 This was a complaint of their early teachers at art school.
22 In the notes accompanying 'The Last Supper', for example, we are told, 'Even the Christmas cards hanging from the door … are faithful copies of exact ones received by the artist' (*Twin Perspectives*, p. 48).
23 As Kureishi has commented in terms of his own childhood: 'We were frequently referred to as "second-generation immigrants" just so there was no mistake about our really belonging in Britain' (Kureishi, 'Bradford', in *My Beautiful Laundrette and Other Writings*, London: Faber & Faber, 1996, pp. 134–5.

24 Paul Gilroy, *There Ain't no Black in the Union Jack*, London: Routledge, 1987, p. 46: 'It has been revealed that, at the suggestion of Churchill, a Conservative cabinet discussed the possibility of using "Keep Britain White" as an electoral slogan as early as 1955.'

25 Kureishi, *The Buddha of Suburbia*, p. 134.

26 Kureishi, 'Some time with Stephen', p. 82.

27 Although as Bart Moore-Gilbert notes in *Hanif Kureishi*, Manchester: Manchester University Press, 2001: 'The cane tables, coconut matting and shutters all reflect the incorporation of foreign, more specifically eastern items within "English" décor' (p. 129).

28 Ball, 'The semi-detached metropolis', p. 21.

29 Moore-Gilbert, *Hanif Kureishi*, p. 126.

30 For instance, Karim's satirisation of Tracey in the quotation above soon shifts to sympathy: 'It was difficult to disagree with someone whose mother you'd found kneeling in front of a middle-class house with a bucket and mop' (181).

31 The back-and-forth movements of Karim the commuter display classic symptoms of the kind of diaspora poetics evoked by Homi Bhabha: 'we find ourselves in the moment of transit where space and time cross to produce complex figures of difference and identity, past and present, inside and outside, inclusion and exclusion. For there is a sense of disorientation, a disturbance of direction, in the "beyond": an exploratory restless movement caught so well in the French rendition of the words *au-délà* – here and there, on all sides, *fort/da*, hither and thither, back and forth' (Homi Bhabha, *The Location of Culture*, London: Routledge, 1994, p. 1).

32 Kureishi, 'Some time with Stephen', p. 101.

33 *My Beautiful Laundrette* (1986) and *Sammy and Rosie Get Laid* (1988) were identified by these critics as critical to the shift of that period.

34 The earliest examples of this trend include Elyse Dobson's play *Motherland* (1984), which records the lives of Caribbean women in 1950s Britain, and Caryl Phillips's accounts of early postwar black London in *The Final Passage* (1985) and of 1940s Yorkshire in *Crossing the River* (1993). See also Isaac Julien's and Colin MacCabe's re-presentation of the Silver Jubilee in their screenplay *Diary of a Young Soul Rebel* (1991); Andrea Levy's recollection of the 1960s in *Every Light in the House Burnin'* (1994); Alex Wheatle's fiction of 1980s south London in *Brixton Rock* (1999); David Dabydeen's account of 1970s Balham in *The Intended* (1991); V.S. Naipaul's return to 1950s London in *The Enigma of Arrival* (1987); 1970s Salford in *East Is East*, or the inter- and postwar years of Zadie Smith's bestseller *White Teeth* (2000).

35 James Procter, *Writing Black Britain 1948–1998*, Manchester: Manchester University Press, 2000, pp. 1–12.

36 Mercer *Welcome to the Jungle*, p. 12.

# 5

# The north

## Introduction: 'another country ...'

> When I got to Bradford I took a taxi. It was simple: Bradford is full of taxis. Raise an arm and three taxis rush at you. Like most taxi drivers in Bradford, the driver was Asian and his car had furry, bright purple seats, covered with the kind of material people in the suburbs sometimes put on the lids of their toilets ... The taxi driver had a Bradford-Pakistani accent, a cross between the north of England and Lahore, which sounds odd the first few times you hear it. Mentioning the accent irritates people in Bradford. How else do you expect people to talk? they say. And they are right. But hearing it for the first time disconcerted me because I found that I associated northern accents with white faces, with people who eat puddings, with Geoffrey Boycott and Roy Hattersley. (Hanif Kureishi)[1]

In the previous chapter suburbia was explored as an excentric site of representation at which a discrepant cosmopolitanism could be identified. Bromley and Tollington, it was suggested, are not simply border spaces across and beyond which their protagonists range, but provincial locales in which they are embedded. As 'locals' Meena and Karim display an 'ordinariness' and 'hereness' at odds with the diversity and sophistication of the multicultural metropolis. They reveal the extent to which black Britain might be marked by regional differences. As they explore the provincial limits of the city, these protagonists do not simply share an oppositional relationship to the metropolitan centre, they also have the effect of *provincialising* London. The city is no longer the 'centre' within these texts, it exists as an exotic setting, beyond the everyday (as a space on Meena's monopoly board or a view from Karim's carriage). This chapter extends the issues of local difference, which are also bound up with issues of class difference, to explore the construction of northern England (and Bradford in particular) within black British and racial discourses

Hanif Kureishi's sense of 'culture-shock' on travelling north from London to the city of Bradford in 1986 is instructive here. Mentioned in a non-fictional essay entitled 'Bradford', the Yorkshire-Pakistani accent that troubles the writer is worth pursuing because of the ways in which it hints at the emergence of a vernacular Asian British culture. But why does Kureishi find the local accent so *disconcerting*?

Kureishi's account is telling for the ways in which it at once confronts and confirms, while silencing and simplifying a set of local and regional affiliations, affiliations that in this quotation become markers of difference: between the taxi driver and the artist, north and south, Yorkshire and Kent, Bradford and London. A shared diasporic heritage is secondary in this description, to a series of regional stereotypes and distinctions. The north is synonymous with a (caricatured) white, provincial ethnicity (with people who eat pies, with Boycott and Hattersley) that the taxi driver appears both to share and be incompatible with.

London does not seem to raise the same kind of contradictions for Kureishi: the metropolitan centre is allowed to transcend its own locality as it becomes the yardstick against which he measures the north. 'I hadn't become accustomed to Bradford and found myself making simple comparisons with London. The clothes people wore were shabby and old; they looked as if they'd been bought in jumble sales or second-hand shops. And their faces had an unhealthy aspect: some were malnourished' (126). The regional differences that emerge through Kureishi's essay do not carry equal weight. There is a sense in which it is Kureishi's worldly cosmopolitanism, his 'Londonness', that authorises his ethnography of the north. In it, Bradford tends to appear (like the taxi-driver, Boycott and Hattersley) not just parochial, but a 'race apart': 'I could have been in another country' states Kureishi at one point, 'This was not anything like the south of England' (43).

The disjunctions that emerge here between Kureishi's intellectual, middle-class metropolitan perspective and that which he evokes within working-class Bradford return us to the problematic issues surrounding representation (as a dual process of depiction and delegation) considered in the previous chapters. It was argued in these debates that the need to portray 'black' as a unified, coherent, 'right on' subject had rapidly decreased as black cultural production increased, thereby reducing the burden of needing to speak on behalf of a larger black constituency.

Kureishi's narrative questions the extent to which the 'enunciative modalities' of black representation have been freed through its demarginalisation. It suggests that certain expressions of ethnicity still remain more central than others. The distance between the 'centred', cosmopolitan representative (Kureishi) and 'marginal', subaltern representation

(Bradford) is emblematic of this persistence ·of a hegemonic black or Asian Britishness that threatens to silence and other those communities it claims to speak for.

Kureishi's 'disconcertedness', his unease with the Bradford he encounters, is confirmed when he is physically and verbally attacked in a pub by a South Asian youth (one of the Bradford Twelve, Kureishi tells us) for his 'reactionary' (130) representation of their community in *My Beautiful Laundrette* (1986). The writer's encounter in Bradford uncannily prefigures the more organised violence that erupted there after the publication of *The Satanic Verses,* three years later. In its Bradford form the 'Rushdie Affair' signalled a critical intervention in the politics of black representation in the late 1980s. Muslim protests on the streets of Bradford formed part of a refusal to be spoken for by the elite (mis)representation (*The Satanic Verses*) of an avant-garde, cosmopolitan intellectual speaking from the metropolitan centre. This rejection not only confirmed a crisis in the representational apparatus of British 'blackness' or Asianness, and the death of the author's role as delegate. It was also exemplary in terms of its illumination of a crisis in the coherence of Asian or black 'Britishness', a crisis that was already tangible in Kureishi's uneasy encounter with the 'provincial' north.

*The Satanic Verses* exposed a series of discontinuities between literary and 'literal' geographies that were compounded in Bradford. The novel celebrates post-colonial migrant hybridity, 'we all are, black and brown and white, leaking into one another', and yet its author induced a fracture in the city's 'race relations'.[2] The text 'cling[s], obstinately' to the notion that something is 'gained' through 'translation' and yet it failed to translate on to the streets of Bradford where Rushdie's diasporic epic was graphically destroyed by Britain's largest South Asian community, and where the author's name became an empowering signifier in racist graffiti and taunts.[3] The furore over *The Satanic Verses* also exposed certain regional differences between an Asian British north and south. Protests over the book were not evenly spread across the country, nor were they centred on London, but were largely confined to the north of England and towns such as Bradford and Burnley. In 1990 journalist and travel writer Malise Ruthven described a Rushdie demonstration in London in which northern Muslims travelled south to lend their support:

> They came in their thousands from Bradford and Dewsbury, Bolton and Macclesfield the old industrial centres; from the outer suburbs like Southall and Woking ... from the cities of Wolverhampton, Birmingham, Manchester and Liverpool. They wore white hats and long baggy trousers. Most of them

were bearded; the older men looked wild and scraggy ... mountain men from
Punjab, farmers from the Ganges delta, peasants from the hills of Mirpur ...
After decades of living in Britain, they still seemed utterly *foreign*: even in
Hyde Park, a most cosmopolitan part of a very cosmopolitan city, where
Arab families foregather in summer, where French, Spanish and Dutch are
spoken sooner than English, they were aliens. They were not sophisticated,
sauve metropolitans ... they were aliens ... men from the sticks, irredeemably
provincial.[4]

What is striking about Ruthven's account is the extent to which Bradford,
and the north, appear to displace Mirpur as the utterly foreign, alien, the
irredeemably provincial. Gathering at a protest in London, these outsiders within the cosmopolitan city are presented as men from the sticks,
uncontaminated by the modernity and sophistication of the metropolitan
centre: they are wild and scraggy, unchanged since their arrival in
England. To what degree such 'wildness' is informed by the regional
ethnicities of rural northern India (the Punjab) or of regional (and particularly northern) England remains unclear in this account. Speaking in
the aftermath of the book-burnings, Salman Rushdie's own descriptions
of the protestors reveal a similar discrepancy between cosmopolitan and
'provincial' modes of representation. The crowd, a key figure of plurality
and diversity in Rushdie's fiction ('by its very nature superabundant,
heterogeneous, many things at once'), became, in its Bradford form, a
blood-baying 'mob'.[5]

## Black Britain beyond the centre

Before turning to consider the implications of Bradford's regional landscape in more detail (a landscape which since Kureishi's visit has become
symbolically 'central' to racial politics in Britain), this chapter will consider the larger implications of a regional reading of black British culture.
To date there has been little critical discussion of black Britain as a
culturally and economically uneven landscape. If black British culture
has become, in Hall's terms, increasingly 'centred' since the late 1980s,
then that centre is all too often taken to be London, a venue that
simultaneously speaks for a much wider black British constituency.[6]

Yet black 'Britain' constitutes a socially varied landscape that, as the
literature considered below suggests, is marked by local, vernacular affiliations and differences.[7] The 'centralization' of blackness identified by Hall
needs to be read alongside this devolving cultural production. This chapter
'grounds' the kind of internal contestations, tensions and differences that

Hall sees as productively 'unsettling' the discursive unities of black identity in the 1980s to show how they correspond to a number of shifts taking place within the cultural geography of black settlement over the same period.

Across the postwar period the relationship between Britain's black communities and the urban environments in which most of them live has become dangerously axiomatic. In a whole range of narratives concerning 'race' (artistic, socio-political, racist, historical, geographical) the black body and the built landscape share a common location that is at once fixed, naturalised and non-negotiable. On one level such a logic merely reproduces the limits of a 'lived' postwar black settlement whose boundaries are almost exclusively that of the city. On the other hand, it fails to acknowledge the presence of an increasingly regional, locally accented black British literature in the late twentieth and early twenty-first centuries, outside London and beyond the urban.

Certainly London persists as the cultural capital of black Britain.[8] What remains worrying however, is that regular slippage, evident in much critical debate, between the metropolitan centre and a larger, more nebulous national landscape. Within such commentary it would seem that the city (and London in particular) provides the only sustaining setting for an excavation and interrogation of black culture, the only available archive and inventory. In this disavowal of (spatial) difference, particularly surprising given the centrality of 'difference' to notions of the 'new ethnicity', London is allowed to stand for and speak on behalf of what is in fact a geographically varied, unstable and national community. Where does what Rob Shields terms the 'spatial mythology' of the north/south divide come into black British discourse, for example?[9] Or what is the difference between the black English and the black Scottish experience? The neglect of such cultural markers in the differentiation 'black Britishness' would appear to reflect the kind of unquestioned sense of that community's dislocatedness from (British) 'locality', and locale's provenance as a purely white, working-class setting.

The assumption of a stable, fixed, coherent location from which one can begin to narrate black Britain as a whole informs this chapter's turn away from London towards the kind of 'foreign', 'provincial' landscapes of the north identified by Kureishi. The word 'provincial', which tradi-tionally carries negative connotations, is used as an affirmative signifier within the context of this chapter, allowing a consideration of the limits of elite metropolitan discourses and the experiences they exclude. To take a 'provincial' focus is not to imply that the consequences of these debates are in turn local or confined. On the contrary, such localities share a complex attachment to black diasporic formations, transnational trajectories and travels. Indeed, black British *locale* is arguably as significant as the more fashionable space of the 'black Atlantic' in terms of its potential to question and critique notions of an homogeneous, unified national community.

The currency of Paul Gilroy's recent work on the transnational black Atlantic has been accompanied by a forgetting of that critic's earlier insights into the implications regional geography and his assertion that 'local factors may all play a decisive part in shaping precisely what it means to be black'.[10] In an essay published in *The Empire Strikes Back* (1982) Gilroy noted that 'localised struggles ... continually reveal how black people have made use of notions of community to provide an axis along which to organise themselves'. The concept of 'community' is important, he argues, because 'it links distinct cultural and political traditions with a *territorial* dimension, to collective actions and consciousness' (my emphasis).[11]

In *There Ain't no Black in the Union Jack* (1987) Gilroy elaborates on this association between identity and territory to suggest that the defence of black locale in the riots of the late 1970s and early 1980s was in part a struggle to gain autonomy in overseeing the local environment. Making links between the miners' strike of 1984 and black insurrection over the same period, Gilroy questions the unifying rhetoric of Thatcher's 'one nation' asserting the significance of '*regional* or *local*' affiliations over national ones:

> No coherent argument is provided as to why, for example, socialists should answer the voices of Wales, Yorkshire or Tyneside – all places where regional traditions are a key axis of political organisation – with a language of the British national interest. 'Geordie', 'Hinny', 'Brummie' or 'Scouse' may all be political identities which are more in harmony with the advancement of socialist politics in this country than those conjured into being by the phrase 'fellow Britons' or even by the word citizen, given the way in which citizenship is allocated and withheld on racial grounds. These regional or local subjectivities simply do not articulate with 'race' in quite the same way as their national equivalent. (54)

We need to be wary at this point of romanticising regionality as a 'genuine' site of black cultural expression, a setting that is distinct from and more 'right on' than the synthetic, hybrid spaces of the metropolitan centre. Such a logic not only encourages a return (albeit within a new context) to the kind of strategic black essentialism dominant in the 1970s and early 1980s. To romanticise the regional is to risk complicity with a much longer tradition of English cultural criticism (both conservative and Marxist) in which locale is allowed to generate a certain nostalgia, for an older, organic, untroubled England that is *itself* deeply racialised. As Gilroy himself is well aware, if the local offers a means of disrupting the notion of an homogeneous national community, then it also represents one of the most seductive sites for its reproduction.

Gilroy does not elaborate on how regional and local subjectivities articulate with 'race'. Nevertheless his recognition of the possibilities of regional subjectivity for disrupting monolithic conceptions of nation-hood and citizenship provides an illuminating context for the consider-ation of local identities in recent black British cultural production. One of the most successful British plays or films of recent years, Ayub Khan-Din's *East Is East*, is a striking example of how locale (in this case Salford) is increasingly coming into focus within the Asian and black arts. *East Is East* was not marketed only as a northern comedy, and Khan has ques-tioned the easy alignment of the film in relation to mainstream Asian cultural production emerging from London: 'The play and the film, they're both as much Northern pieces as they are Asian pieces. The two run parallel and should be seen as such.'[12] Meanwhile, the new accents (from Karim's cockney and Meena's brummie to Jackie Kay's Scots) emer-ging in contemporary writing register the diaspora experience as simul-taneously a sedentary, provincial experience. If increased social mobility has been seen as contributing to a 'dilution' of dialects and a desedimen-tation of locale, then the presence of such accents within contemporary diasporic writing challenges any easy opposition between 'travelling' and 'regional' cultures.

Such accents are part of a much wider proliferation of regional dialects within 'everyday' black British culture. The variety of these vernaculars is increasingly apparent on British national television, from the 'Standard English' of Trevor McDonald on *News at Ten* to the second series of Channel 4's *Big Brother* which included a black 'brummie' and an Asian 'Geordie'. Scripting Indian actors with scouse and Birmingham accents, Homepride's 1990s television advertisements for Indian cook-in sauces worked to identify something of the 'provincialism' of diaspora culture. Unfolding within kitsch the suburban interiors of Birmingham and Liverpool, rather than the exotic Indian outdoors these adverts presented South Asian experience as a local, 'English' experience. Further, these local black and Asian Englishes need distinguishing from the kind of metropolitan standard, "English' English accent' spoken by cosmopolitan

writers such as Salman Rushdie, whose work has been seen as exemplary
in the 'worlding' of the English language in the late twentieth century.[13]

The appearance of poetry anthologies such as *The Sun Rises in the
North* (1991), a collection of poems published in Huddersfield with
funding from Yorkshire Arts, Kirklees Council and North West Arts, is
suggestive of some of the new regional connections made available
within black British writing. Bringing together four 'Northern writers'
from Sheffield and Manchester, it is a regional framework that is used
here to bring together a group of black poets with otherwise very
different cultural affiliations: Indian, American, Caribbean and African.[14]
Of course to cite or site these poets as 'northern' is not to exhaust their
ethnicities: this is not their only position. Nevertheless, it is a position
that is too often erased in the scramble for the migrant subject's 'diasporicity', and is therefore worthy of further interrogation here.

At stake here is more than an issue of literary aesthetics. What the
media referred to as the 'northern riots' in 2001 are suggestive of a larger
shift in the location of racial politics over the past twenty years. If Brixton
was perceived as the epicentre of racial tensions in 1981, then by 2001 it
was Burnley, Oldham and Bradford. Of course the Brixton 'disorders'
were by no means an isolated 'metropolitan' incident during that long
hot summer, which also saw racial conflicts in:

> Handsworth in Birmingham, Chapeltown in Leeds, Bolton, Luton, Leicester,
> Nottingham, Birkenhead, Hackney, Wood Green, Walthamstow, Hull, High
> Wycombe, Southampton, Halifax, Bedford, Gloucester, Sheffield, Coventry,
> Portsmouth, Bristol, Edinburgh, Reading, Huddersfield, Blackburn, Preston,
> Ellesmere Port, Chester, Stoke, Shrewsbury, Wolverhampton, Newcastle,
> Knaresborough, Derby, Stockport, Maidstone, Aldershot ...[15]

On the one hand, these dispersed acts of rebellion, the high-tide mark of
a politicised black resistance in Britain in 1981, tell the story of an
increasingly articulate, regional black British community of the kind that
Gilroy alluded to above. At the same time their virtual absence in
accounts of what became known as the 'Brixton riots' speaks of a certain
cultural amnesia surrounding these locally-accented events, which have
since been 'reallocated' to the hegemonic centre of London.

If the labelling of the riots of 2001 as 'northern' was an acknowledgement of their distance from London and the south, then accounts of
the conflicts in Bradford, Burnley and Oldham also relied upon a series
of silences around the role that locality and locale played within them.
The disorders were blamed by the police and the media on the presence

of 'outsiders', groups of youths who didn't live locally, but who came into the community to cause trouble. Similarly, the participation of local white communities in the riots was persistently underplayed in the disorders which were documented as 'race riots'. Such explanations have the effect of deterritorialising insurrection. The government's recent attack on 'inward-looking Asian communities' and its call for 'faith' schools to ensure that a quarter of their intake comes from outside the local neighbourhood was prompted by the 'northern riots' of 2001.[16] These debates reveal a political anxiety over regional black and Asian British communities and a desire to supplant them with an increased sense of citizenship and national identity or belonging. They fail to acknowledge the extent to which the riots were primarily a struggle over locale, as the targeting of specific buildings in Manningham, and the repeated riots within that area, from the 'uprisings' of 1995 to the 'Rushdie' demonstrations of the late 1980s, suggest.

## Bradford, the 'Rushdie Affair' and the reimagination of landscape

To date, dominant accounts of the events surrounding the publication of Rushdie's book have focused on its larger, global dimensions: the divisions and differences between a 'secular' West and a 'fundamentalist' East, between Islam and Christianity, intolerance and tolerance, censorship and free speech. In addition to the problem that such binaristic categories raise is the issue of the role that micropolitics played in the affair. In the Middle East Khomeini used the fatwa as a means of asserting political hegemony in the light of a cease-fire with Iraq and the election of a woman prime minister in Pakistan. In India and Pakistan party politics were a major motivation in the anti-Rushdie campaign.[17]

Similarly, in Bradford, *The Satanic Verses* did not initiate protest and counter-protest within a political vacuum, it acted as a catalyst to local and pre-existing cross-cultural tensions. In August 1981 twelve Asian youths were put on trial after being found in possession of explosive devices. The arrest of the 'Bradford Twelve' initiated a wide-scale response and campaign by the local Asian community. Their plea of 'self-defence' in the light of increased National Front activity and lack of police support was accepted by the court in 1982.[18] In 1984 the local South Asian community organised and won a fight for the provision of halal meat in Bradford's schools. In the same year the city became the centre of national media attention as Ray Honeyford, head teacher of a predominantly Muslim school in Bradford, was pressured to resign in heated demonstrations after his racist remarks about Pakistanis were published. The inter-communal tensions surrounding these different campaigns at a local level partly inform the intensity of response to Rushdie's novel in Bradford.

What follows is not an account of how Rushdie's elite cosmopolitan narrative was delegitimised by the more 'real', authentic demonstrations of Bradford's working-class Muslim community. Rather it concentrates on how that city reimagined itself as locale in the aftermath of the book-burnings, an event that threw the city's image into crisis. Bradford was projected to an international audience in January 1989 as the flashpoint of Rushdie-related tensions. Those now iconic images of *The Satanic Verses* being set alight by Bradford's South Asian community against the backdrop of City Hall were repeatedly transmitted, replayed and reprinted for a national audience in the late 1980s and early 1990s. During this period the city became synonymous with the kind of 'racial troubles' for which Brixton had become famous a decade earlier. Following the global dissemination of footage of the book-burnings, this northern town began to reinvent itself in terms of a distilled village landscape built upon a racialised rhetoric of the past and the pastoral.

Published in 1991, Tom Clinton's *Laugh? I Nearly Went to Bradford* was written and released during the critical phase of tensions surrounding the 'Rushdie Affair'. The book is a 'look at certain dramatic and challenging events in Bradford's recent history and their impact on Bradford's image' as well as an attempt 'to recover its dignity and self esteem'.[19] A local politician, Clinton dwells on series of 'positive' images of the city. He lingers, for example, on City Hall, 'a monument to the Victorian Fathers' (15) of Bradford. Excavating the building's architectural history (based on the Palazzo Vecchio in Florence), he elaborates on its solid structure (stone staircases, oak-panelled rooms, Yorkshire stone). Clinton goes on to contrast Bradford's early riches and the 'natural' splendour of City Hall ('reflecting the geophysical bowl-like shape of the City outside its walls' (15)) with the 1970s concrete architecture that dominates the city's postwar skyline. This nostalgic digression on City Hall involves more than the recuperation of an architectural history; it also reveals a forgetting of the recent past that is conspicuously absent from it.[20] During the book-burnings, the solid Victorian masonry of City Hall was temporarily dislocated from its firm foundations. As protesters congregated in front of the building, it floated on a crowd of Muslim protesters and protesting banners. The need to dwell upon City Hall's Victorian past in the aftermath of the 'Rushdie Affair', is, it will be argued, part of larger desire within the city to re-establish continuity with an earlier, less troubled period of history.

Clinton's book opens with a vision of Bradford far removed from the urban environment and the Asian communities synonymous with it, a place that is paradoxically 'nowhere':

> Imagine. You're driving along a moorside road, seemingly in the middle of nowhere and surrounded by rough wild landscape. Below you, to your left and in the valley bottom, a distant road curves alongside the river before it climbs the sloping crag on the other side of the valley. It seems to be heading for a cluster of buildings which look like a remote farm ... Your attention is drawn towards a large official looking sign on the roadside ... The sheep scatter as you walk through the springy heather in order to read what the sign says. The sign, topped by a colourful heraldic coat of arms reads. *City of Bradford Metropolitan Council – Baildon Moor.*
>
> You are rather surprised.
>
> It's not at all what you expected of a place called Bradford. (1)

The panoramic, distant border setting described above affords no view of the city: the only settlement in sight is a remote farm. Exchanging Bradford for Baildon Moor, the city for the country, the narrative makes an appeal for Bradford through an appeal to rural territory and landscape. The scene is carefully localised and determinedly 'Yorkshire' with its 'wild' weather, 'craggy' landscape, 'a dry stone wall', 'a curlew' (1), and yet it is a setting we are 'surprised' by. What we 'expect' to see in Clinton's account is absent. His opening description conjures a depopulated, exclusionary landscape, a purified, provincial setting in which the metropolitan centre is rendered invisible.

There is nothing necessarily unique about Bradford's turn to the past in the 1980s and 1990s. Heritage critics such as Robert Hewison and Patrick Wright have identified Britain's wider national investment in itself as an 'old country' over the same period.[21] As John Urry explains, 'Instead of manufacturing goods, Britain is manufacturing heritage', a process that 'not only involves the reassertion of [traditional] values' but also propagates 'a stifling of the culture of the present':[22]

> We are all aware of problems and trouble, of changes within the structure of society, of the dissolution of old values and standards ... The heritage represents some kind of security, a point of reference, a refuge perhaps, something visible and unchanged. Our environmental heritage ... is a deeply stabilising and unifying element within our society.[23]

The continuities offered by Bradford's heritage to its white population create an imaginary solidarity, a unified community against or outside which the 'multicultural' present is defined, dislocated and 'stifled'. Not only does it distort and conceal social and spatial inequalities within the city, it defers an acknowledgement of the multicultural present which poses a threat to Bradford's 'old values and standards'. The drive to present Bradford as a 'living past', a phrase that recurs in the imagery of the city in the late 1980s and 1990s, is more than a nostalgic retreat from industrial decline in the region. Bradford's re-imagination of itself in the post-'Rushdie-Affair' period has involved a construction of local history in which the city's largest migrant community is not just selectively acknowledged, but actively forgotten through the recollection of an older, whiter Bradford.

The processes of recollection documented below are by no means consistent or wholesale. Following the 'Rushdie Affair', public images of the city like those made available in Clinton's book rarely display a distaste for the city's South Asian community or a desire to exclude them. At points Clinton even celebrates the 'diversity' of the city, 'a fascinating patchwork of language, art, music, food, and entertainment, much of it based on village cultures from other continents. Given that the indigenous culture stemmed largely from the existence of 17th/18th century villages the concept of Bradford as one huge 'village' is hardly surprising' (7). However, Clinton's 'global village' has more in common with an idealised 'village England' in which the organic community lives on in neighbourly harmony. His account has the effect of erasing difference in order to present an homogenous, unified locale: 'the success of Bradford's future, was, and will be, due to the people who are proud to call themselves "Bradfordians"' (44). Those who are proud to call themselves Hindu, Sikh, Muslim, Pakistani, Indian, Bangladeshi apparently have little role in this account of the city's future.[24]

Clinton's account displays many of the symptoms of the new racism that I will be suggesting informs Bradford's re-imagination of itself more generally. New racism emerged in Britain in the late 1960s and takes a radically different standpoint to the older racisms of empire.[25] Imperial racism constructed an inferior/superior dichotomy centred on 'biological' difference. The new racism functions more subtly: it does not discriminate in terms of biology, or believe in an inherent superiority over other races. New racism is centred on cultural differences that are delineated by national boundaries and that incur a division between insiders and outsiders, indigenes and foreigners. This shift in racist discourse is essentially one from the body to the national landscape. As Anna Marie Smith describes it in her eloquent account of New Right discourse:

> The structures which are common to both Powellian/Thatcherite racism
> are spatial structures. Powell constructed the entry of ... peoples from the
> former colonies ... as a 'black invasion' ... After decolonisation British borders
> were re-invented through racially biased immigration laws ... [this] ...
> redefined the limits of the British nation. The ... immigration laws of the
> 1960s and 1970s should be regarded as spatial strategies which firmly placed
> the unwanted 'black invader' on the other side of the national frontier.[26]

Smith's interpretation of how new racism functions in terms of the
nation's borders enlightens a reading of Bradford's local boundaries. On
1 April 1974, less than a year after the 1971 Immigration Act came into
effect, Bradford was expanded to include 'village' neighbourhoods such
as Ilkley, Keighley and Baildon. A tightening of the nation's limits was
echoed in a broadening of Bradford's margins. Both pieces of government
legislation involved a renegotiation of borders; both legitimated the tactics
of exclusion. The opening-up of Bradford's metropolitan boundaries was
used in the 1980s and 1990s to reimagine Bradford as a pastoral threshold,
the 'gateway to the Yorkshire Dales'. As this border landscape, typified in
Clinton's 'peripheral' vision of the city, came to replace the urban landscape of the city itself, the white countryside was allowed to replace the
multicultural metropolis as the essential image of Bradford. These racialised
border tactics were not just spatial but historical structures, facilitating a
return to an older village England, exemplified in what tourist maps of
the city signpost as Brontë Country. As Anna Marie Smith convincingly
argues, new racism can be diagnosed in terms of trauma whose main
symptom is forgetting (132–3). The distilled village scene in terms of which
Bradford remembers itself is therapeutic in this sense, a means of forgetting the racial disturbances that have come to characterise the present.

## Bradford and the tourist landscape

The drive following the 'Rushdie Affair' to portray Bradford as a 'living
past', a phrase that recurs in tourist literature of the city in the early 1990s,
reveals Bradford as a nostalgic city, a city that is concerned with the past
and where the past is an ongoing concern (figure 10). The desire to locate
Bradford outside its urban borders, to position it within a natural or
'pure' setting, offers a means of rarefying the multicultural city. It also
exposes a tendency to recuperate a past before Asian settlement, and to
re-present itself beyond the limits of the city and its contemporary
'troubles'. Paul Gilroy's observations on the relationship between ethnicity
and urban space are particularly revealing in this context:

LIVING IN THE PAST

10   Bradford, 'Living in the past', 1994

The black presence in cities is novel and symptomatic of their post-war decline but it is somehow appropriate. Contemporary racism has identified black settlers with the cities in which most of them live and their cultural distinctiveness with its urban setting. Black life discovered amidst urban chaos and squalor has contributed new images of dangerousness and hedonism to the anti-urbanism of much English cultural commentary. How much less congruent is a black presence with the natural landscapes within which historically authentic English sensibility has been formed?[27]

According to Gilroy, the continuity between the black population and the city speaks also of a discontinuity between the black subject and the country. As urban Bradford is exchanged for a city defined in terms of its rurality, or what Clinton calls 'the largest village in the country', a gap is opened between Bradford as 'Little Pakistan' and Bradford as 'Little England'. The broadening of Bradford's borders has been exploited in order to present a city beyond its negative associations with industrial decline, poverty and the Pakistani communities with which this urban 'squalor' has become synonymous.

I will now turn to consider in more detail how Bradford reimagined itself by focusing on the city's construction of a tourist landscape. Tourist space is illuminating in the context of this chapter's debates because of the particular appeal it makes, within a British context, to the past and the pastoral. Moreover, tourist space is one of the most self-consciously imagined and reflected upon settings within contemporary popular culture. If the rural landscape is no longer a site of reverie and contemplation in everyday life then, as John Urry has argued, the tourist remains as a kind of semiotician 'reading the landscape for signifiers of certain pre-established notions or signs derived from various discourses of travel and tourism' (12).[28]

Long before tourism got under way in Bradford, the city's most famous son, J.B. Priestley, set out on a very different tour of England. Returning to his home town in autumn 1933, Priestley nostalgically recalls the imperial might associated with Bradford's wool industry in the late nineteenth century:

there is nothing that can be spun and woven that does not come to Bradford. I remember myself, as a boy, seeing there samples of human hair that had been sent from China: they were pigtails that had been cut off by Imperial command … Take down some of those … samples and you bring the ends of the earth together … These wools and hairs will … be sent all over the place.[29]

The poverty and squalor that Kureishi associates with Bradford in his journey of 1985 was still some way off in the *English Journey* of 1933, when the city's status as imperial Worstedopolis was still secure. 'Millions of yards of fine fabrics had gone streaming out, from their [Bradford mill workers'] hands, to almost every part of the world ... these folk may be said to have lent a hand in the great process of civilisation. (194). Before the Second World War, when this was written, the empire upon which much of Bradford's wealth was built had not yet returned to 'haunt' it in the form of large-scale post-colonial immigration. Yet migration was nothing new to Bradford, a city whose growth was founded upon waves of settlers coming to the city during the nineteenth and twentieth century.

As an isolated and sparsely populated market town in the north of England became the worsted textile capital of the world in the 1800s, significant numbers travelled from elsewhere in Britain and Ireland to live and work in Bradford. By the time of *English Journey*, Bradford already had a substantial Eastern and Central European migrant community. Priestley recalls the 'odd mixture in pre-war Bradford. A dash of the Rhine and the Oder found its way into ... 't'mucky beck'. Bradford was determinedly Yorkshire and provincial, yet some of its suburbs reached as far as Frankfurt and Leipzig' (160). The book describes the European in Bradford as 'odd', 'alien' and 'outlandish'. At the same time it celebrates their presence in the city, which paralleled European progression. Their rivers, the Rhine and t'mucky beck, polluted by industry, are allowed to flow as one in Priestley's imagination. Bradford's suburbs open up to encompass and include Frankfurt and Leipzig, they work together in the name of 'the great process of civilisation'.

During the 1980s and 1990s these diverse communities and histories were flagged up within Bradford's tourist landscape. National Heritage signs across the city now direct the visitor to Victorian Bradford and its renovated mills, the 'rugged' landscape of the Brontës, its museums, monuments, galleries and cemeteries. A section of Bradford known as 'Little Germany' pays architectural homage to the ornate buildings left behind by wealthy German wool merchants. Streets and squares such as Heidelberg Road and Bavaria Place signpost a European presence in the city.

Unlike 'Little Germany', which points to a community within a larger community, Bradford's more recent South Asian settlers have produced names that lexically carry the sense of been overtaken or subsumed: 'Bradistan', 'Pakiford', 'Curry Capital' (6).[30] These names, for which there are no heritage signs, convey something of the threat of being eclipsed by a South Asian settler community of around seventy thousand, fifty

mosques and seventy Indian restaurants. In comparison with the industrial pollution of Priestley's Rhine, the more recent post-colonial
'contamination' of Bradford has not been so easily incorporated within
the city's imaginary.[31] Where the imaginative border shift of Priestley's
essay sees the suburbs open up to include the migrant community, the
desires and motivations exposed within the city's recent heritage maps
form part of a return to a pure, authentic past, beyond or outside which
the Muslim community exists. South Asian Bradford's absence from the
tourist landscape speaks of a wider cultural amnesia that this section will
now elaborate upon.

In *The Tourist Gaze* John Urry cites Bradford as one of 'the most
unlikely ... centres of a heritage-based tourist development' (105). Yet
following the onset of the city's tourist initiative in 1980, it won awards in
1982 and 1983 as England's fastest-growing tourist destination. This
rapid growth in Bradford's tourist industry during the 1980s needs to be
considered alongside the growth of an increasingly vocal and politicised
South Asian community. Bradford's reimagining of itself began as this
community was beginning, more strenuously then ever before, to redefine
and assert its identity and rights within the city. By seeing the rise of
heritage-based tourism and issues concerning 'race' in Bradford dialogically,
a more insidious drive behind the city's re-presentation of itself emerges.

Memory and its visual representation in tourist literature offered a
means of imaginatively forgetting Bradford's South Asian communities.
Writing in a more general context, Urry notes that:

> The advertising material produced by holiday companies shows that the
> tourist is white; there are simply no black faces. The countryside particularly
> is constructed as 'white' ... [and] ... heritage is overwhelmingly populated by
> white faces ... One might also wonder whether part of the attraction of
> heritage for many white visitors is precisely the fact that it is seen as
> predominantly white – while many larger cities are disapprovingly viewed
> as having become 'multicultural'. (142–3)

Urry's observations are borne out in the advertising leaflet for Bradford
shown in figure 11, where the only 'ethnic' face is that of the dubiously
racialised puppet, Sooty. The relaxing tourists at Five Rise Locks and the
onlookers at the Industrial Museum are all white. They set up an
uninterrupted dialogue with the equally 'English' human exhibits: the
Victorian man atop horse and cart, the Brontës and the locomotive
driver. The drinkers inside the Woolpack, although unseen, are also
white, the actors in what was, at the time, an all-English cast in the only
British television soap opera set in the countryside: *Emmerdale*.[32]

**11** Bradford, 'We've got the lot', 1994

Rendered in the quintessential medium of the countryside, water-colour, the prevailing blue, green and brown washes evoke the familiar palette of the pastoral scene. The advert invites visitors to explore a bucolic

**12** *Bradford Travel Manual, 1995*

Bradford: the rugged moors of Baildon and Ilkley, the bleak beauty of
Haworth, the tranquil waters of Five Rise Locks, the picturesque scenery
of Eshot, alias Emmerdale. Bradford is over-layered with a series of rural
landscapes that multiply to effectively conceal the city. This is reinforced

by the tourist literature that goes with the leaflet, describing tours to 'Summer Wine Country', 'Brass Band Country', 'Brontë Country'. Alongside this countrified city are images of Bradford's 'Living Past' signposting the city's Victorian heritage: Salt's Mill ('world famous treasure from the golden age of Empire'), the Industrial Museum, steam locomotives and working horses. At the centre of these images, inscribed in a scrolling font, are the words 'We've got the lot': its very claim to total inclusion here emphasises something of the exclusion and dislocation of Bradford's South Asian communities from it. Ironically, even the Alhambra Theatre signals an older Bradford, built as it was before the Second World War and the arrival of the city's South Asian communities.

At the bottom of the advert is a picture of 'Bradford: the city in the countryside'. Here the city is invisible. Within the valley bottom where we expect to find Bradford is a meandering river: the Broad ford from which the city derived its name. As Bradford returns to its etymological and geographical roots, as Broad ford supersedes Pakiford, the threat of a Powellian river of blood is erased, it becomes as distant as the racially contaminated city.

Where South Asian Bradford does feature in Bradford's tourist landscape it is depicted in very different ways to the localised imagery evoked in figure 11. Figure 12 shows the cover of Bradford's 1995 Travel Manual and contains, among other things, details of the 'Flavours of Asia tours'. The cover image is emblematic of the city's internationalism, evoking a world city that can not only celebrate its hybrid geography, the product of global migration but can make it commercially viable. However the South Asian in Bradford is as invisible here as it was in figure 11. The image cleverly signifies a multicultural Bradford without having to present it. Where white Bradford is presented through an appeal to the countryside and the lay of the land, Bradford's South Asians appear emphatically dislocated from the landscape: something out-of-space.

From these observations a series of disjunctions emerge between Bradford's living past and its multicultural present, between the firm foundations and solid stability of history exhibited in the Victorian architecture of Salt's Mill and the transient tastes of Bradford's 'Flavours of Asia' tours. Between the official signs that point to Little Germany and unofficial signs like 'Little Pakistan'. Between the natural beauty inscribed within the wild crags of Ilkley Moor and Brontë country, and the exotic beauty of Bombay Stores with its 'Aladdin's cave of sarees, silks, fabrics and gifts'.[33]

These disjunctions all exist outside the frame of figure 12. This photograph flirts with the iconography of postmodernism. Mass communications (as exemplified in mass migrations) has resulted in a 'time-space compression' and the advent of the 'global village' with which Bradford appears contiguous. Eating in the city is an international experience: its 'flavours' include 'Asian ... Greek, American, Mexican, French, Italian, Chinese and, of course, fine Yorkshire baking'.[34] The travel tours allow visitors to entwine the 'global' within a local environment: one can follow 'In the footsteps of the Brontës', visit Little Germany and 'Spend an evening in India' at Mumtaz's Paan House as part of the 'Flavours of Asia' tour scheme.[35] These itineraries focus solely on the city's continuities. They encourage the visitor to elide and forget the tensions and inequalities within contemporary Bradford.

More worryingly, there is a sense in which the inclusion of Bradford's South Asian community within the city's tourist scheme represents a form of colonisation from within the metropolitan centre. Unlike the man who drives the working horses and who is a simulacrum of Victorian industry, Bradford's South Asians represent the only 'live exhibit' in the city's tourist manifesto, the only 'real' workers. The economic potential of this community has been realised and exploited by the tourist industry.[36] As jobs in the textile industry declined, Bradford's South Asians came up against racial discrimination in looking for other work in the city: they were given little alternative but unemployment or self-employment.[37] This partly informs the preponderance of Asian restaurants that Bradford now generates tourism from. The lack of mainstream work beyond the family and immediate community has inhibited Muslim integration within the local economy and environment, a fact that the tourist industry capitalises on by encouraging Bradford's Asians to market their otherness. Where heritage Bradford works to market a Victorian culture that is unequivocally 'here', it is 'The idea of sampling the rich exotic culture of the Indian subcontinent' that represents the tourist appeal of Bradford's Asians, a community coerced into selling its difference or distance from the city.[38] The attraction of this community rests on its 'failure' to integrate and the extent to which it can display 'exoticness'. The appeal of the 'Flavours of Asia' tours lays partly in the cathartic effects of its segregative subtext: the Asian's cohesion with his or her 'own kind' and his or her invisibility within other areas of Bradford's industry. How much less congruent would the Pakistani be on the Victorian working horses, or indeed on *any* of the heritage-based projects listed in figure 11. Moreover, *who* is being invited to visit and sample Bradford's tourist landscape is crucial to an understanding of the power relations concealed within these images of the city. It is the white tourist, not the Indian waiter, who is eating 'exotic' cuisine here. If Bradford does offer a cosmopolitan environment, then its South Asian communities are not the ones 'experiencing' it. They are clearly the exhibits, not the tourists in this landscape. The city's tourist literature following the 'Rushdie Affair', evokes a 'familiar', white regional landscape in which the foreign is reproduced as the exotic rather than the 'local'.

## Travelling north: an 'English' journey?

So far this chapter has focused on white representations of tourist space in Bradford. In this final section I will turn to consider tourism more generally as a trope within black British cultural production. Ingrid Pollard's photographs of rural England and Scotland are arguably the most frequently cited black British tourist representations. During the 1980s Pollard worked to expose and disrupt the presumed whiteness of the tourist landscape. Her series of photographs 'Pastoral interludes' (1984) consist of five pictures.[39] The title of the sequence automatically locates the images within a larger English literary and artistic tradition of the 'Pastoral'. The references in the captions to the Lake District and the quotations from Wordsworth's 'I wandered lonely as a cloud' and Blake's 'Jerusalem' signal an (unromantic) play with Romantic poetry. (These are also quotations that have come to carry a particular resonance within different post-colonial contexts, from Wordsworth's daffodils in Caribbean literature to Blake's green and pleasant land: a central metaphor in Enoch Powell's 'Rivers of blood' speech.)

The use of the word 'interludes' in the title of this sequence is also intriguing. 'Interlude' suggests a 'break', interval, or change of activity between longer periods; it signals, perhaps, that the black figure does not 'belong' within these landscapes, that her location is only temporary. Interlude is also a theatrical term suggesting a brief dramatic *performance*. Stylised and 'artificial', these images are 'posed' in a way that de-naturalises both the English countryside, and the black subject's relationship to it.

Part of a larger photographic project entitled *D-Max* ('the range of blacks that a photographic emulsion can offer'), Pollard's work explores blackness 'as a social and political construction rather than a cultural absolute'.[40] The images reject the clarity of the realist documentary photograph: they have been hand-tinted in order to give the impression of watercolours and to create 'nostalgia by referring to a genre of hand-tinted postcards'.[41] These self-reflexive images are not simply photographs of tourists, they comment ironically upon the discursive practice of photography itself (note the cameras *within* these photographs) and

13   Ingrid Pollard, 'Pastoral interludes', 1984

the dominant modes of representation (watercolours, postcards) adopted within rural English landscapes and English tourism.

Any nostalgia generated by these photographs is immediately disrupted by the captions that appear alongside them. The captions in figures 13–17 underline the ambivalence of the black subject in these settings. These are 'sublime' landscapes of terror, unease and dread in which the subjects are seen as unbelonging. At the same time there is a disjunction between image and caption in these photographs, the text tells a different narrative to that of the picture. In figure 14 where are the 'waves', or the 'baseball bat' of figure 16? Similarly, the 'Lake District' alluded to in figure 13 does not feature in any of the images, which were taken in Sussex, Derbyshire and St Andrews. Speaking on Pollard's work, John Taylor has observed these captions destroy 'what remains of the cohesion of the picture'.[42] The ellipses either side of the statements suggest that they are excerpts from a larger narrative. The sense of unity, continuity and

... **Searching for sea-shells; waves lap my wellington boots, carrying lost souls of brothers & sisters released over the ship side** ...

**14** Ingrid Pollard, 'Pastoral interludes', 1984

coherence that the English countryside is meant to supply is returned here as fragment, quotation, *interlude.* The use of ellipsis signals absence and loss within a landscape that has conventionally offered nostalgic return to a lost presence.

The figures within Pollard's landscapes are out of place; their uneasy, self-conscious postures, their clothing (headwraps, baseball caps) and accessories (baseball bats replace walking sticks) signal a black urban culture much more at home in the city rather than the country. Pictured against a series of boundaries (dry-stone walls, fences, barbed wire), these are landscapes that appear to bar the entry of the photographer. Yet Pollard's stance is not straightforwardly 'oppositional' as John Taylor puts it. She is depicted as both the passive object of the camera's gaze and an active onlooker whose gaze exceeds the limits of the picture's frame. By lingering to observe the scene around her, Pollard colludes with dominant ways of seeing the English landscape, even as she haunts it through her presence and captions.

... death is the bottom line. The owners of these fields; these trees and sheep want me off their GREEN AND PLEASANT LAND. No Trespass, they want me DEAD. A slow death through eyes that slide away from me ...

**15** Ingrid Pollard, 'Pastoral interludes', 1984

Pollard's pictures signal the availability of an alternative discourse of travel to that which dominates contemporary black British literature. If the success of writers such as V.S. Naipaul, Salman Rushdie and Caryl Phillips can be at least partly explained in terms of their sustained figuration of travel then they evoke very different journeys to the kind to be found in 'Pastoral interludes'. Naipaul, Rushdie and Phillips are prize-winning novelists for whom journeying is an extended metaphor of the migrant condition.[43] Alongside their fictional work all three writers have produced successful non-fictional travel narratives. Naipaul's journeys in India and the Caribbean, Phillips's accounts of travel in Europe and the United States and Rushdie's adventures in Central America have all attracted a substantial readership.[44]

Compared with Pollard, these worldly, well-travelled writers have much more in common with what Timothy Brennan has identified as the 'cosmopolitan celebrity'. Cosmopolitan celebrities are writers who share

... **feeling I don't belong. Walks through leafy glades with a baseball bat by my side** ...

**16**  Ingrid Pollard, 'Pastoral interludes', 1984

a preoccupation with 'a *world* literature whose traditional national boundaries are (for them) meaningless', who privilege 'international' debates over 'internal' ones, and who are, in short, 'not so much an elite at *home*, as ... spokespersons for a kind of perennial immigration, valorised by a rhetoric of wandering, and rife with allusions to the all-seeing eye of the nomadic sensibility'.[45] Now based in either London, New York or both, these three very different writers all deal with a knowing, sophisticated, independent mode of travel that has appealed to an equally knowing, educated, middle-class audience.

In keeping with this chapter's focus on non-metropolitan, provincial discourse, I am less interested here in the particular meanings of such cosmopolitan (and canonical) male travel writing than in the more 'vulgar', working-class, or popular, modes of mass tourism it implicitly or explicitly seems to exclude. Naipaul, Phillips and Rushdie construct themselves as travellers, not tourists. Moreover their attitude to the latter tends to be lofty

... a lot of what **MADE ENGLAND GREAT** is founded on the blood of slavery, the sweat of working people ... an industrial **REVOLUTION** without the Atlantic Triangle ...

**17**   Ingrid Pollard, 'Pastoral interludes', 1984

and disdainful. In Naipaul's *The Enigma of Arrival*, for instance, the narrator is described looking down from the crest of a Wiltshire valley on to Stonehenge and the gaudily dressed tourists who congregate below. The visitors are viewed with disapproval by the journeying narrator whose lingering, melancholy ramblings contrast with the 'light' day trips of the holiday maker. What follows is not a critique of these individual writers and their 'failure' to be somehow 'authentically working-class'. Rather it is an attempt to elaborate on a critical blind spot in which the class connotations of such travel writings and the locations they speak from go unseen.

In her debut novel, *Every Light in the House Burning* (1994), Andrea Levy offers a fictional recollection of the *Windrush* generation through the memories of Winston Jacob. However the text begins not with an account of the transatlantic crossing but with a family holiday, and a coach journey from a council estate in Highbury to Pontin's holiday camp in Brixham. It is the eleven-year-old narrator's (Angela Jacob) first holiday, and the family travel 'by coach because it is cheaper than the train'.[46] The celebration of the cosmopolitan traveller has been at the expense of such 'minor' journeys. I have in mind here a series of fictional travels across and within northern England, Scotland and Wales, journeys that depart from, terminate at or unfold within locations such as Glasgow, Blackpool, Whitley Bay, the Lake District, Haworth, south Wales, the Pennine Way, and Manchester.[47] These tourist narratives share a difficult, uncomfortable relationship to the more 'sophisticated' itineraries of the cosmopolitan travel writing that resonates from the south of England and the metropolitan centre. They evoke the dominant figure of diaspora literature, the journey, in order to parody or poke fun at it. They also point to a devolving literary landscape in which class and locality need to be considered alongside ethnicity.

In order to elaborate on the implications of these 'provincial' journeys and their difference from cosmopolitan travel now, I want to concentrate on three particular day trips depicted within recent black and Asian cultural production: Jackie Kay's 'Sassenachs', Gurinder Chadha's *Bhaji on the Beach* and Tariq Latif's 'On the 43 to the terminus'. Describing, respectively, a train journey from Glasgow to London, a coach trip from Birmingham to Blackpool and a visit, by a Mancunian Asian, to Valletta, Malta's capital, these various journeys are made by public transport and openly flaunt their subjects' 'unworldly', tourist status. If each of these texts evokes the familiar diaspora trope of the journey, then their brevity (as day trips) and scale (as 'local' rather than transnational travels) estranges that trope and asks the reader to consider their difference from the international itineraries of cosmopolitan travel. Unlike the independent, solitary journeys of Naipaul, Rushdie and Phillips, Chadha, Kay and Latif in different ways present a 'provincial', popular tourism, *en masse*.

Of the three texts, Tariq Latif's is the only one to take place overseas. Where Kay and Chadha's narratives unfold within the British landscape, Latif's poem 'On the 43 to the terminus' is set in Malta. Yet if the scene implies a departure from locale, the poem appears more concerned with the speaker's articulation (and *silencing*) of a local, northern English identity. A Pakistani poet living in Manchester, Latif's 'On the 43 to the terminus' invites us to read its speaker autobiographically. The reasons for his visit to this popular British tourist destination remain unclear, however.[48] If Malta's Mediterranean geography, its close proximity to both Europe and North Africa and its Moorish, migrant history appear to encourage a symbolic reading of this landscape as a gateway to the East, then it is a reading that the text itself certainly never invites. On the contrary, the opening of 'On the 43 to the terminus' supplies the speaker with a 'local', northern identity (confirmed again later on in the poem) that resists a 'common-sense' understanding of him as transnational traveller:

> It's Manchester weather in Malta.
> The rickety bus, packed with tourists,
> Thunders towards Valletta.
> Just above the driver is written,
> 'Think God,' and the way he took
> That last corner we all did.[49]

The opening line, 'It's Manchester weather in Malta', foregrounds dwelling within travel as 'home' (Latif lives in Manchester) is allowed to translate 'away'. The use of 'Manchester' (as opposed to, say, 'monsoon') works to 'frame' and position the speaker while simultaneously disrupting a reading of the scene/speaker as foreign or exotic. If the poem describes a 'pilgrimage' then it is a profane, rather than sacred, journey (note the blasphemy of lines 5 and 6). To make sense of the poem's opening, the reader is required to make a series of regional and national identifications; the lines depend upon a local knowledge of north-west England and its (wet) climate. Moreover the reference to climate reproduces a larger discourse of 'Englishness' in which the weather constitutes a ritual topic of conversation.

Focusing on the trip itself, rather than the points of departure and arrival either side of it (the 'terminus' remains unseen in this poem), 'On the 43 to the terminus' appears to place a particular emphasis on journeying. Yet the poem employs such 'diasporic' imagery only to abandon it as the narrative and the journey progress and a more 'mundane', everyday tourism emerges:

> Our combined breathing
> Has steamed up the windows.
> I keep nodding off and each time
> I surface, for some reason, I know
> The exact nature of the conversation
> The Germans, behind me are having.
> I stop myself short from speaking
> To them in my Mancunian English. (14)

The condensation on the windows (a result of the cramped conditions on the coach and the weather outside) means that the passing Maltese landscape remains unseen and unannounced within this poem. The speaker refuses to aestheticise or offer commentary on the tourist setting. This is a speaker who seems unmoved or unmotivated by travel abroad, as he drifts in and out of sleep. The poem has nothing to say about Malta, or the experience of being 'elsewhere'. In many ways 'On the 43 to the terminus' is a poem describing a provincial 'English' journey that reproduces some of the stock ingredients and stereotypes of the hackneyed British tourist narrative (it reveals a suspicion of foreign drivers, before going on to describe an encounter with German tourists).

The speaker's relationship to the other tourists remains ambiguous, however. Both the German conversation and the speaker's response to it are announced within the poem and withheld by the speaker. What are the Germans talking about? What was the speaker going to say to them, and why does he not want them to hear his Mancunian accent? If he is uncomfortable with his northern Englishness, why does he speak of it *here*, within the poem? Are the German tourists being racist? Or is the speaker himself revealing a certain 'English' xenophobia?

These are all questions that are raised but remain unanswered within this poem. Nevertheless, they are questions that suggest an alternative travel narrative. Malta is not simply a diasporic contact zone between East and West, it is also a provincial package-holiday resort. With its English cuisine and red telephone boxes, Malta constitutes a very different kind of destination to those that appear within cosmopolitan literatures. Indeed there is something intriguingly unadventurous and staid about Latif's trip, which substitutes an account of a cramped tourist coach for descriptions of the cultural riches of Valletta. This is not in any way a criticism of a 'vulgar' black British tourism. On the contrary it is the mundane nature of the journey described in 'On the 43 to the terminus' that signals its distinctiveness from the more 'cultured' forms of travel announced earlier in this section.

As with Latif's Malta (and Chadha's Blackpool), Jackie Kay's 'Sassenachs' announces a tension between the well-travelled, cosmopolitan migrant (the kind of 'sophisticated' traveller that the speaker of the poem tries, but fails, to mimic) and that of the 'local', working-class subject, for whom journeying is in itself a rare occasion. The poem describes the train journey of two young girls from Glasgow to London:

> Me and my best pal (well, she was
> Till a minute ago) are off to London.
> First trip on an InterCity alone.
> When we got on we were the same

Kind of excited – jigging on our seats,
Staring at everyone. But then,
I remembered I was to be sophisticated

Describing a first trip to London, 'Sassenachs' asks us to engage with the ironic situation of a speaker who is a child of the African diaspora, but who, along with her friend Jenny, does not appear to have been *anywhere*. Whether 'jigging' excitedly in their seats, shouting and singing loudly ('Sassenachs, sassenachs here we come / Sassenachs sassenachs Rum Tum Tum Tum') within the confined space of the carriages, or eating egg mayonnaise sandwiches washed down with Irn Bru (a Scottish soft drink), the poem asks us to engage with a travel narrative that is playfully, disruptively 'unsophisticated':

So when Jenny starts shouting,
'Look at that, the land's flat already,'
when we are just outside Glasgow
(Motherwell actually) I feel myself flush.
Or even worse, 'Sassenach country.
Wey Hey Hey.' The tartan tammy
Sitting proudly on the top of her pony;
The tartan scarf swinging like a tail.
The nose pressed to the window.
'England's not so beautiful, is it?'
And we haven't even crossed the border

The speaker's (flawed) performance as the 'sophisticated' traveller (which is overturned in the closing lines as the best friends burst into laughter at Euston Station after identifying a 'sassenach') ultimately betrays the innocence of their journey. The mis-reading of local geography, in which the suburbs of Glasgow are mistaken for England, reveals the extent to which their lives have been confined to that city. Even Motherwell is a foreign landscape for Jenny. Yet the poem does evoke a border crossing, even if that border is misidentified. Unlike the border crossings of the diaspora artist, however, this boundary is an 'internal' one and appears more difficult to locate. Scotland becomes England within Jenny's 'parochial' imagination. The poem signals a tension not between the black 'outsider' and the British landscape (the kind of tension we might expect) but between the black Scottish speaker and the English south towards which she and her friend travel. 'Sassenachs' does not deal with transatlantic links but with internal, regional and national differences. As such it draws attention to what this book has suggested is the 'unevenness' of the British landscape. The girls display nothing but dissent towards the hegemonic centre, London. Through their journey to the metropolis, the city becomes something foreign and exotic. In 'Sassenachs' it is white London and England that are rendered 'ethnic'.

> Finally, we get there: London, Euston;
> And the very first person on the platform
> Gets asked – 'Are you a genuine sassenach?'
> I want to die, but instead I say, Jenny.
> He replies in that English way –
> 'I beg your pardon,' and Jenny screams
> 'Did you hear that Voice?'
> And we both die laughing, clutching
> Our stomachs at Euston station.

The comic name calling – 'Sassenachs' – reverses a characteristic convention of Kay's poetry, which more often works to challenge the taxonomy of blackness. Poems such as 'So you think I am a mule?' and 'In my country' describe black speakers being labelled and misidentified as others or outsiders in ways that the poems then go on to contest. By reversing this convention Kay avoids reducing the narrative to an account of the journey of two provincial Scots girls. 'Sassenachs' also has the effect of *provincialising* Englishness, which in this poem is not a transcendental or universal signifier of Britishness but is forced to display its difference.

The carnivalesque elements that erupt within Kay's 'Sassenachs' are more fully on display in Gurinder Chadha's, *Bhaji on the Beach* (1993), a film that incorporates many of the 'stock' images of white working-class tourism. Written by Meera Syal, it tells the story of an organised day trip by a South Asian women's collective from the suburbs of Birmingham. The film takes us on a ponderous journey by minibus, up the motorway, via the service station to a declining seaside resort in the north of England, a trip that is accompanied by a Punjabi version of Cliff Richard's 'Summer holiday'.[50] As with 'Sassanachs' and 'On the 43 to the terminus', *Bhaji on the Beach* puts into operation a 'minor', provincial English journey distinct from the typical cosmopolitan itinerary.

On the one hand, Blackpool operates as an unlikely diasporic or border space within *Bhaji on the Beach*. Likened by one the characters to Bombay, and with its own festival of lights (the Blackpool illuminations, not *Diwali*), the opening shots of Blackpool beach are accompanied by a Hindi soundtrack, while later the film features a stylised 'Bollywood' scene in which pantomime darling Ambrose Waddington pursues Asha across the Winter Gardens during a rainstorm.[51] If the effect of such scenes is comic and ironic, then there is also a certain logic to the film's 'translation' of Blackpool's symbolic landscapes. This northern seaside resort, Tony Bennett observes, has historically constructed itself as an imperial space, 'at the centre of the nation and, even more grandiosely, of the Empire' (135). At various times the Winter Gardens has hosted 'Nigger minstrel' shows; the South Pier was given an 'Indian' façade; and the entrance to the Pleasure Beach designed as a Maharaja's palace. '[T]he thematics and architecture of pleasure' that traditionally 'inveigled the pleasure-seeker in relations of complicity with imperialist values and sentiments' (141) in Blackpool certainly motivates the desire of Ambrose (a local white gentleman who is also a representative of old England or Englishness) for Asha.[52]

Blackpool (like the 'black country' of *Anita and Me*) is an overwhelmingly white space, yet the Asian characters are more than exotic 'exhibits' within it. The second-generation characters, in particular, participate in a provincial, working-class tourism, from fish and chips and candy floss to deck chairs and donkeys, in a manner that also articulates a discrepant mode of tourism within the broader context of cosmopolitan travel. By placing Asian figures within this white landscape – on the beach, in the sea, up Blackpool Tower – Chadha deliberately defamiliarises and disrupts its ethnicity, its presumed whiteness. Much of the humour of *Bhaji on the Beach* is generated through the characters' engagement with an older, traditional, white working-class England. With its ubiquitous kiss-me-quick hats and Union Jacks, it recalls a version of Englishness before postwar immigration that the film both flirts with and destabilises. If the film is about a journey away from home (Birmingham), then the characters' participation in the cultural offerings of the traditional seaside resort display a certain 'at-homeness' within the English landscape.

Blackpool is ultimately a liberatory site of play and excess for the characters in *Bhaji on the Beach*. As Roger Bromley notes, the film:

> takes its characters out of the time and space of the everyday and into the 'timeless' and boundless realm of the excursion, the world of 'play' in which the crises and stalemates of the quotidian are magnified, distorted and seen as contingent. It is a trip taken for pleasure and, importantly, for 'cultural' health; it is a journey away from the site of contestation and conflict but always with the intention of returning to it, recreated and activated. (161)

Organised by Simi of the Sahili Women's Centre, the outing offers a means of escape from the pressures and constraints of everyday life in Birmingham. For Asha the trip provides a welcome break from her mundane life behind a corner-shop counter. Hashida decides to join the day trippers on the spur of the moment after finding out she is pregnant and breaking up with her black boyfriend. Ginder uses the trip to escape from her violent husband and spend some 'quality time' with her five-year-old son. Meanwhile teenage sisters Madhu and Ladhu use the trip as an opportunity to disentangle themselves from the constraining influence of their parents. In Blackpool they pursue the possibilities of romance with two local white boys, before sampling the pleasures of a pub.

Blackpool, Bennett observes, is a carnivalesque location, and certainly the northern seaside resort performs this function within *Bhaji on the Beach*. The usually restrained, middle-class, conservative Asian women that comprise the Sahili group find themselves within an unfamiliar tourist venue in which carnival elements, 'excessive eating and drinking, the suspension of sexual prohibitions, the subversion and transgression of normal rules of behaviour, the symbolic inversion of dominant ideological values', proliferate.[53] Significantly, as the film progresses, the women find themselves increasingly participating in and enjoying this culture. The elderly, moralising Pushpa is most radically transformed by the outing. On the minibus ride to Blackpool she appears horrified by the sight of men pulling 'moonies' at them in the outside lane. By the end of trip though she is pictured cavorting with (and clearly enjoying) the male strippers in the pub, and on the trip back to Birmingham she bursts into laughter at the sight of a souvenir piece of rock, in the shape of a pair of breasts. Elsewhere in the film we see Madhu and Ladhu getting drunk (and later throwing up on the Ferris wheel); Asha briefly flirting with Ambrose; Hashida telling her elders to 'fuck off' before seeking out an abortion. In different ways these women's 'excesses' allow liberation from the restraints and conventions of Asian female life in suburban Birmingham. Blackpool allows the women to transgress or invert the hegemonic ideological values of their culture.

Of course carnival is not necessarily positive, progressive or transgressive in itself. Bakhtin was more interested in the cultural and ideological transformations that carnival could produce rather than the intrinsic value of carnival.[54] Pleasure is a complex, ambivalent issue in this film, where, for example, the male stripper's removal of an item of Ginder's clothing reveals a bruise and exposes to the other women in the group the violence she has suffered at the hands of her husband. The result of this revelation is that Pushpa and the other older members of the group support Ginder's choice to leave her husband where previously they had been critical.

*Bhaji on the Beach* describes an outing to the Blackpool 'illuminations', and it is also a film about illumination. As Roger Bromley points out:

Sex, pleasure, food and family, are all subject to transcoding within the film which transfers its cast of characters from a recognisably 'Asian' enclave in Birmingham to Blackpool, the quintessentially white, working-class seaside resort, which becomes a metaphorical site for exploring the transformations of 'Asianness' brought about by the pressure of migration and intergenerational conflicts'. (158)

The carnivalesque tourism in which the Asian day trippers partake also exposes tensions and discrepancies, internal to that community. These tensions centre on differences between black and Asian ethnicities (the 'problem' of Hashida's boyfriend being black, or Pushpa's suspicious side glances at other black tourists on the beach), generation, gender and class. The carnivalesque excesses of this film result in a proliferation of difference that Stuart Hall identifies as central to new ethnicities. Moreover, as a location that is locally and regionally distinct from Birmingham and the Midlands, Blackpool is central to this illumination of difference.

Of course Blackpool is no utopian, or unproblematic venue within *Bhaji on the Beach*, as the racism experienced by the Asian women, both at the service station and at the seaside, testifies. For all the correspondences established within the film, the holiday resort remains in many ways 'foreign' to the Asian visitor. Yet at the same time the northern working-class destination, because of its difference from the middle-class suburbs, offers a productive, if unexpected site at which to interrogate the internal divisions of a community.

## Conclusion: 'a surprising place'

I want to close now by returning to the outskirts of Bradford with which this chapter began. Merle Collins's poem 'Visit to Yorkshire – again' is instructive here, structured as it is around a series of return visits to Haworth, a village on the borders of Bradford that features prominently in tourist literature following the 'Rushdie Affair'. Like Ingrid Pollard's photographs, Collins's poem describes a black subject following in the footsteps of certain canonical literary figures:[55]

Yorkshire was not really as I remembered it
But then, the last time I visited
The Brontes had created for me a world
Not so much of Black or white
As of indeterminate shades
Of art
That had no colour
Of pleasure that existed for its artistic self[56]

The poem writes back to the imperial canon of nineteenth-century literature, specifically *Jane Eyre* and *Wuthering Heights*, in order to record a growing disillusionment with Brontë country as it shifts from being a place of 'indeterminate shades that had no colour' to a chequered landscape of blacks and whites. The heritage setting of Haworth is steadily racialised and politicised by the return visits of the speaker, and the act of return is, I think, central to this poem.

> Then I loved the cobbled streets
> Sometimes I even walked
> the mystic moors
>
> Yorkshire when I visited, later,
> Was not exactly as I remembered it
> From then (17)

Return is figured in this poem as both a ghostly act of revisitation (note the lingering 'again' of the title and the fact that she doesn't visit the Brontës' but visits 'with' the Brontës) and as a memorial process, an act of 'remembrance' (a word that is repeated throughout). The speaker is not simply haunted by this landscape, with its staring crowds; she also haunts it. 'Sometimes I even walked / the mystic moors' says the speaker, playfully suggesting a ghostly reclamation of that other ghostly text: *Wuthering Heights*. The speaker of this poem is a revenant who defines herself in terms of return and revisitation.

Evoking Haworth as a memorial space, the poem *also* flirts with a dominant national investment in such heritage settings in terms of nostalgia. In the closing lines the speaker elaborates on her memories of Yorkshire to note that 'England is not as I remember it, either, / from the times when my dad smiled and sang / put on his ex-serviceman's uniform / went off whistling to celebrate the day that / WE / had victory in the war' (18). The reference to the speaker's father in these lines suggests a sentimentality that the rest of the poem has worked to critique. Yet crucially the speaker's nostalgia also disrupts a racially distilled return to a pure organic village England. The closing lines of Collins's poem, particularly the emphatic 'WE', draw attention to an inside history conventionally situated outside the national landscape. The speaker is an outsider, inside this setting and 'we' here offers difference in place of consensus.

The poster reproduced in figure 18 presents the parsonage visited by Collins in 'Visiting Yorkshire – again' and was part of a series evoking Bradford as 'A surprising place'. The image works to question 'false' impressions of the city following the book-burnings in Bradford, at a

**18**  Bradford, 'A surprising place', 1990s

time when the city's image might be said to have been in crisis. At the top of the advert, above the border it reads Bradford Economic Development Unit – 'myth breakers'. And yet this assertive little statement is immediately drawn into question by the image of Bradford that appears below it. Here the city is exchanged for the outlying village of Haworth, and Brontë country. Like Tom Clinton's distant vision of Bradford (which was also presented as a 'surprising' place), this is a metropolitan district without a metropolis. The borders between myth deconstruction and myth construction dissolve within this poster. What we have here, in black and white, is the *purely white*, distilled national landscape of heritage England. The static, wintry image of the parsonage and graveyard announce a location frozen in time, stuck in the past. Presented here is a burial ground that is buried beneath virgin white snow, untouched and unblemished by the crowds of the city. An unpopulated setting, this dead, deathly landscape is nevertheless resurrected and returned to us here as the real Bradford, a Bradford that is here and now, a Bradford which has broken with the myths of the past, and yet struggles to re-animate that past. This ghostly image in which, like something out of *Wuthering Heights*, the dead live on, is most profoundly haunted by the slogan at the very bottom of the poster: 'A surprising place'. What are we meant to see that's so surprising here? Why is *this* Bradford surprising? Viewed within the context of post-Rushdie-affair Bradford, it is the urban disorders, of the multicultural city and the local South Asian community that ultimately haunt this scene, that are at once living and dead in this image, absent from the picture, but hauntingly present in the poster. This image depends for its meaning on the very community that is conspicuously, *surprisingly*, nowhere within it.

## Notes

1 Hanif Kureishi, *My Beautiful Laundrette and Other Writings*, London: Faber & Faber, 1996, pp. 124–5. All further references are to this edition and are included in the text.

2 Salman Rushdie, *Imaginary Homelands*, London: Granta, 1991, p. 394.

3 Rushdie, *Imaginary Homelands*, p. 17.

4 Malise Ruthven, *A Satanic Affair: Salman Rushdie and the Rage of Islam* (London: Chatto & Windus, 1990.

5 Rushdie, *Imaginary Homelands*, p. 32.

6 Stuart Hall, 'Minimal selves', in *Identity: The Real Me*, ICA Document 6, London: ICA, 1987, p. 44.

7 The emergence of a body of artistic production that can include, for example,

Meera Syal's Birmingham and Blackpool, Tariq Latif's Manchester, David Dabydeen's Hastings, Abdulrazak Gurnah's Canterbury, Jackie Kay's Glasgow, Karline Smith's Moss Side, E.A. Markham's Ulster, Ingrid Pollard's photographs of the Lake District, Amit Chaudhuri's Oxford, Moniza Alvi's Pennines, Fred D'Aguiar's Whitley Bay and Bristol, Rukshana Ahmad's Peak District, Almas Khan's Bradford, Caryl Phillips's Sneddington and Yorkshire, Merle Collins's Yorkshire and Naipaul's Wiltshire points to the break-up of a monolithic black British literary landscape. Even Kureishi's suburbs, it was argued in Chapter 4, negotiate a provincial landscape beyond the 'centre'.

8  There is some excellent work being done at the moment on 'post-colonial London', a title which it seems to me is helpful for the ways in which it refuses that easy slippage between London and Britain being discussed elsewhere in this chapter. See for example John McLeod's (ed.) special issue of *Kunapipi* on Postcolonial London (vol. 21:2, 1999). Both John McLeod and John Ball have (separate) forthcoming publications in this area.

9  R. Shields, *Places on the Margin*, London: Routledge, 1991. Although Shields does not explore the question of ethnicity in relation to this divide himself, his chapter on 'The north–south divide in England' (pp. 207–51) is a useful starting point for thinking about such questions.

10  Paul Gilroy, *There Ain't no black in the Union Jack*, London: Routledge, 1987, p. 231.

11  Paul Gilroy, 'Steppin' out of Babylon – race, class and autonomy', in Centre for Contemporary Cultural Studies (ed.) *The Empire Strikes Back*, London: Routledge, 1982, p. 286.

12  'I speak English, not Urdu', *The Guardian*, 31 October 1999. I am extremely grateful to Hannah Young for drawing my attention to this article.

13  Rushdie, 'Imaginary homelands', in *Imaginary Homelands*, p. 18.

14  Dejani Chatterjee, John Lyons, Cheryl Martin and Lemn Sissay, *The Sun Rises in the North*, Huddersfield: Smith/Doorstep Books, 1991, p. 5.

15  Peter Fryer, *Staying Power: The History of Black People in Britain*, London: Pluto Press, 1984, p. 399.

16  *The Guardian*, 11 December 2001, p. 1. Also see www.guardian.co.uk/race for access to full official reports on the 'northern riots', including *The Bradford District Race Review* and the Home Office report: *Community Cohesion: A Report of the Independent Review Team* chaired by Ted Cantle.

17  Y. Samad, 'Book burning and race relations: political mobilisation of Bradford Muslims', *New Community*, 18:4 (1992), p. 517.

18  Raminder Singh, 'Destination Bradford: Bradford's South Asian community', *South Asian Review*, 7:1 (1987), p. 18.

19  Tom Clinton, *Laugh? I Nearly Went to Bradford*, Bradford: Bradford Library Service, 1991, back sleeve.

20  Although Clinton does not mention the demonstrations in his lengthy description of City Hall, the postscript to his text acknowledges that 'City

Hall ... formed the backcloth against which millions of television viewers saw a copy of *The Satanic Verses* burnt by angry Muslims' (53).

21  R. Hewison, *The Heritage Industry*, London: Methuen, 1987. P. Wright, *On Living in an Old Country: The National Past in Contemporary Britain*, London: Verso, 1985.

22  J. Urry, *The Tourist Gaze: Leisure and Travel in Contemporary Societies*, London: Sage, 1990, p. 109.

23  Strong in Urry, *The Tourist Gaze*, p. 56.

24  Similarly Clinton records jokes directed at white holidaymakers from Bradford – '"Where's your passport?", "Why haven't you got your turbans on then?", "Get a bloody job"' – (p. 4) to argue that: 'admitting that you actually CAME from Bradford was somehow difficult ... I mean the place was a scruffy, dying town ... wasn't it? Surely it was full of empty crumbling mills and dirty cobbled streets? And wasn't the place full of "foreigners" who had come to steal all our jobs?' (p. 3). Although Clinton appears concerned with the impact of South Asian settlement on the image of Bradford, his interest is not in challenging racist perceptions of that settlement, nor with offering an alternative presentation of their communities. Instead Clinton prefers a return to Bradford's prewar and pre-immigration past, its natural beauty and imperial wealth, to construct a more positive image of the city.

25  The classic account of 'new racism' is Martin Barker's *The New Racism*, London: Junction Books, 1981.

26  Anna Marie Smith, *New Right Discourse on Race and Sexuality: Britain 1968–1990*, Cambridge: Cambridge University Press, 1994.

27  Paul Gilroy, *Small Acts*, London: Serpent's Tail, 1993, p. 80.

28  Urry, *The Tourist Gaze*, p. 12.

29  J.B. Priestley, *English Journey*, London: Heinemann, 1934, pp. 157–8. All further references are included in the text.

30  Dervla Murphy, *Tales from Two Cities: Travel of Another Sort*, London: John Murray, 1987, p. 6.

31  In her popular anthropological study of Bradford Dervla Murphy records the reaction of an elderly man in Manningham, swinging his arms to encompass his surroundings: 'five years fighting for my country? Only to come back to my own city over-run with dirty vermin! Here they're all around us, every street like a sewer full of rats!'

32  The cast was all-English at the time the advertisements were produced. Following other British soap operas, *Emmerdale* has created roles for black actors in recent years.

33  *Bradford Travel Manual – 1995*, Bradford: Bradford Economic Development Unit, 1994, p. 30.

34  *Bradford Travel Manual – 1995*, p. 5.

35  *Bradford Travel Manual – 1995*, pp. 26–7.

36  These wider socio-ecomomic issues are neglected within tourist literature which claims to have given 'a major boost to the Asian business sector',

*Developing Bradford's Tourist Industry,* Bradford: Bradford Economic Development Unit, 1994, p. 2.

37  Singh, 'Destination Bradford', p. 20.

38  *Developing Bradford's Tourist Industry,* p. 2.

39  Three depict the photographer, alone, walking, sitting and standing within rural or heritage environments. The other two are of a man standing in a river, fishing. I am extremely grateful to Ingrid Pollard for drawing my attention to several inaccuracies within an earlier draft of this section.

40  Gilroy, 'D-Max' in *Small Acts,* p. 117.

41  P. Kinsman 'Landscape, race and national identity', *Area,* 27:4 (1995), p. 303.

42  J. Taylor, *A Dream of England: Landscape, Photography and the Tourist's Imagination,* Manchester: Manchester University Press, 1994, p. 257.

43  We have the transatlantic crossings of texts such as *The Final Passage* and *Crossing the River,* the repetitious allusions to trips by plane, train and foot in Rushdie's fiction, and the wandering, itinerant protagonists for whom Naipaul is famous, from Ralph Singh of *The Mimic Men* to the restless 'I' narrator of *The Enigma of Arrival* published almost thirty years later.

44  See *The Middle Passage* (1962); *An Area of Darkness* (1964); *India: A Wounded Civilization* (1977); *Among the Believers: An Islamic Journey* (1981); *A Turn in the South* (1989); and *India: A Million Mutinies Now* (1990) by Naipaul. See *The Jaguar Smile: A Nicaraguan Journey* (1987) and *The Riddle of Midnight* (1987) by Salman Rushdie. See *The European Tribe* (1987), *The Atlantic Sound* (2000) and *A New World Order* (2001) by Caryl Phillips.

45  Tim Brennan, 'Cosmopolitans and celebrities', *Race and Class,* 31:1 (1989), pp. 1–19.

46  Levy, *Every Light in the House Burnin',* London: Headline Review Publishing, p. 69.

47  See Moniza Alvi's poems, from the Pennine Way to the hills of south Wales; the Blackpool of Gurinder Chadha's film *Bhaji on the Beach;* Merle Collins's trips to Yorkshire; Fred D'Aguiar's 'Sonnets from Whitley Bay'; Chila Burman's images of the seaside; the Lake District of Ingrid Pollard's photographic series 'Pastoral interludes'; the remote Scottish coastal village of Torr in Jackie Kay's *Trumpet,* not to mention Tariq Latif's account of a coach trip to Malta in 'On the 43 to the terminus'.

48  Latif lives in Manchester, where he has worked in a cash and carry, in clothes shops and as a part-time roadie.

49  Latif, *The Minister's Garden,* Todmorden: Arc Publications, 1996, p. 14.

50  A similar kind of journey takes place in the film *East Is East* where the search for brides for the sons of an Asian family in Salford, Manchester, takes us on a trip, not to Pakistan but up the road to Bradford.

51  Music, particularly Hindi music, plays an important role in *Bhaji on the Beach.* If music conventionally contributes to the 'realism' of film, then, it often has different, disjunctive role within *Bhaji.* Simon Frith's point that the reality that music 'describes/refers to is a different sort of reality than that described/

referred to by visual images' (Frith, 'Hearing secret harmonies', in Colin MacCabe (ed.) *High Theory/Low Culture: Analysing Popular Television and Film*, Manchester: Manchester University Press, 1986, p. 65) is an instructive one within this context.

52 T. Bennett 'Hegemony, ideology, pleasure: Blackpool', in T. Bennett *et al.* (eds) *Popular Culture and Social Relations*, Milton Keynes: Open University Press, 1986, p. 141. Bennett also enlists 'the mock invasion (successfully repulsed!) of the town by Afghan hordes' and ' penny slot machines which, when activated, depicted white men shooting 'natives' (p. 141).

53 Bennett, 'Hegemony', p. 147.

54 As Tony Bennett points out, 'It was the … new meanings which accrued to the carnivalesque as a consequence, rather than the mere brute fact of carnival, that Bakhtin regarded as valuable' ('Hegemony', p. 148). I would like to thank Hannah Young, one of my dissertation students in 2002, for helping me re-think many of the issues raised in this section.

55 For another interesting example of a poem offering a critique of English 'literary' heritage see Dejani Chatterjee's 'Visiting E.M. Forster', in *The Redback Anthology of British South Asian Poetry*, Bradford: Redback Press, 2000.

56 Merle Collins, 'Visiting Yorkshire – again', in *Rotten Pomerack*, London: Virago Press, 1992, p. 17.

# 6

# Conclusion
## train stations and travel bags

In May and June 1998 the Museum of London held an exhibition entitled *Windrush – Sea Change* as part of the *Windrush* anniversary celebrations. Displayed on the walls were enlarged, grainy, black-and-white photographs of the *SS Empire Windrush*, its passengers disembarking. On one wall were blown-up extracts from the log detailing the passengers that docked in Tilbury in the summer of 1948. In another (this time blank) log-book, visitors who had arrived on the ship fifty years before were invited to record their memories and/or leave contact details. In its attempt to map a genealogy of post-war black Britain and to memorialise a part of its past, this exhibition, like so much of the *Windrush* celebrations, highlighted a diaspora community that was also a dwelling community, a community that had stayed put. Next to the log-book, 'preserved' within a glass case, was a pile of travelling bags. Whether or not this old, battered, brown leather luggage (now at least fifty years old) was supposed to be that carried by the black arrivants in the boat-train photographs displayed on the walls was unclear. Yet the way in which the cases (now, it would seem, 'excess baggage', surplus to requirements) memorialised the 'pastness' of black Britain was striking. Luggage that in the early postwar years had signified a community moving on/ moving in, became, on entering the museum, an 'historical' marker of dwelling.

*Dwelling Places* ends with this 'beginning'. In the aftermath of July 1998 and the fiftieth anniversary of the so-called 'Windrush Generation', a new archive of narratives and images depicting black arrival have come to light.[1] Among the most popular images to have been recirculated by the media, those most frequently exposed have been the early photographs of loaded contact zones such as Tilbury Docks and railway stations such as Victoria and Waterloo.[2] These images present the 'just-arrived' black subject of the 1950s 'landing up' in England. Many have been reassembled, retouched and retinted in ways that encourage a certain nostalgia, highlighting the 'historicity' of the migrants, supplying them with an

**19**  'New arrivals at Victoria Station', 1956

iconic status that has helped make them part of the dominant imagery of black Britain in the late twentieth and early twenty-first centuries.[3] One of the effects of this recent iconography has been to disarticulate the images from the realist documentary frameworks within which they originally appeared in newspapers and magazines such as *Picture Post*.

Of course, to look back at the original contexts of these early images, before their recent recirculation, is not to gain privileged access to a more real, unmediated version of the black British past. As Stuart Hall has argued in an early essay on images of black settlement, 'No such previously natural moment of true meaning, untouched by the codes and social relations of production and reading, exists'.[4] Writing in 1984, Hall

**20**  'New arrivals at Victoria Station', 1956

was more concerned not with what these images *really* mean but with what they might *come* to mean in the present as they risk being exposed to apolitical, avant-garde contemporary critical practices and the 'theoretical purism' of the 'post-marxist, post-Lacanian, post-*Screen*, post-Foucault, post-modernist deluge'.

This book has argued that the tendency towards abstraction and dislocation in avant-garde diaspora discourse risks exposing postwar black British cultural production, as a whole, to the kind of 'purism' identified by Hall. Diaspora theory, which derives and generates a substantial part of its meaning and its cache from the post-theories enlisted above, has increasingly provided the dominant 'language' through which to view and make sense of black British culture, and post-colonial migrant cultures more generally. The railway station photographs reproduced below seem particularly susceptible to such vocabularies. Like the chronotope of the motel or hotel in James Clifford's 'Traveling cultures', or the ship in Paul Gilroy's *The Black Atlantic*, the railway station appears notable as a figure of mobility and migration. The platforms in figures 19 and 20 are itinerant spaces, transitory locations of ceaseless back and forth movements. Within these photographs the station appears as a kind of borderland, a liminal space between past and future, between homeland and motherland, the Caribbean and England. The eyes of the crowds are difficult to read: are they looking forward, or back? Their gaze appears stereoscopic.[5] The sheer abundance of baggage performs a hyperbolic function within the images. The black crowds are figured floating among a sea of suitcases, sacks and boxes which are themselves signifiers of a community adrift, on the move, homeless. Lined up or piled anonymously together (who owns what here?), the belongings captured within these photos are unequivocally markers of *unbelonging*.

And yet if this kind of 'diasporic reading' helps us to follow something of what is going on in these images, it remains silent about those aspects of the pictures that cannot be reduced to a poetics of journeying, home-lessness and detachment. What the dominant agendas of diasporic discourse risk erasing from the historical narrative of the 'boat-train' arrivants is their cultural significance as a *dwelling crowd*. Standing around at London's major stations, these figures effectively congest, or 'jam' the national landscape. The station does not simply signify as a transitory borderland in this context. To a large extent the anxieties that these images announce are to do with the peculiarly *stationary* nature of the crowds gathered there. What are they waiting for? Why don't they move on? By the 1970s images of black crowds loitering on the street were to contribute to a range of similar panics relating to the sedentary black body (see Chapter 3). However, in the 1950s the lingering arrivants were seen to present a very particular kind of 'problem'.

'Thirty thousand colour problems' was the headline of an article on the boat-train crowds published in *Picture Post* on 9 June 1956.[6] The 'problem' concerned a seven-hundred-strong West Indian crowd gathered at Victoria Station: how are they to be dispersed, shifted, 'moved on' from this landscape? 'No return ticket', ran a subheading. The crowd 'cannot get back', they had made a 'one-way passage', not only that, but 'Many have landed at a port without even money to get to the town where they have friends and hope to find a job' (38).

These crowds have nowhere to go back to and no clear route forward: 'One girl who arrived on this boat tipped open the handkerchief she was using as a purse, and poured a few pathetic pieces of silver in her lap. 'Enough, enough to Convet Station?' She meant Coventry' (38). The worldly 'back-and-forth' dynamic of diaspora travel is complicated here by the uncertain stasis of the stranded, directionless crowd, a crowd that appears to be going *nowhere*.

It is not just the immediate problem of getting this static, immobile crowd to move on, but the more general potential of these arrivants to settle, to dwell, to accommodate themselves, that fuels the principal anxieties of

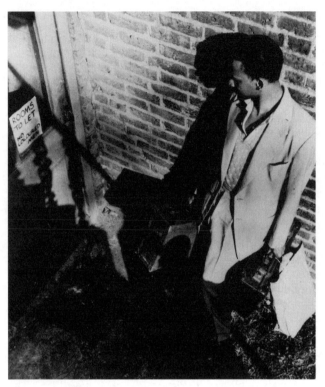

**21** 'Travel bags: "Rooms to let"'

the *Picture Post* article. Most of these immigrants, we are told, are:

> decent, useful citizens who will create only one major social problem –
> housing them. The end of their journey is a comparatively highly-rented
> room, frequently owned by one of their own colour, in an over-crowded,
> broken-down house in an old Victorian slum. Not understanding the taut-
> ness of the housing situation, this creates resentment by the coloured
> people, who feel they are being treated as outcasts. It builds up friction with
> the white population and at this rate, will create a colour bar. There is a
> whiff of it already. It must be stopped in the West Indies but how? (38)

The language used to evoke black housing here – over-crowding, decay,
dilapidation, the colour bar, the 'smell' (there's a whiff of it already) –
recalls the racialised rhetorics of housing explored in Chapter 2. Here,
though, I am more interested in the way that dwelling forms the dominant anxieties and tensions within an article on *travel* (the boat-train

**22**  'Travel bags: unpacking suitcases at Clapham Shelter'

crowds). These tensions between settlement and migration are perhaps
most visible in the as yet unpacked semiotics of the travel bags as they
appeared in the early railway station photographs.

A centre piece of the Museum of London's display, travel bags are a
dominant figure of displacement in narratives of diaspora more generally. Yet while such baggage signals movement and migration, it also
anticipates arrival, settlement, home.[7] The bulging suitcases and sacks,
boxes and baskets that accompany the early West Indian settlers are
abundant, loaded signifiers within the *Picture Post* images above. However,
if this collective 'baggage' would appear to signify, unambiguously, as part
of a diasporic iconography, of a travelling culture, then I want to suggest
that, viewed historically, it is a contradictory emblem, a sign that is also
caught up in an apparently absent politics of dwelling.[8] 'Bewildered,
hopeful, their possessions at their feet', states the caption for one of the

**23** 'Travel bags: in search of accommodation'

photographs: a picture of the Customs hall, Southampton, in which the West Indian crowd, sitting and standing, appears almost anchored, immobilised by the weight of bags, suitcases and baskets grouped around it. The crowds here are certainly not travelling light. In relation to the account of the housing predicament that concludes the *Picture Post* article, the sheer volume of luggage within these photographs comes to signify something of the 'problem' they represent: who will house them? The crammed bags, full to bursting, anticipate the conditions of the teeming, 'over-crowded' dwelling places that would later become signifiers of black settlement and accommodation (see Chapter 2). However, although these travel bags in certain ways anticipate the conditions of the dwelling place, they are not, in themselves, residencies. If the migrants literally 'lived out of' their suitcases during the boat journey to England, then it would be a mistake to interpret them solely as signifiers of a nomadic sensibility.[9] Much of the heavy, cumbersome, fragile luggage displayed in these photographs is not that of the itinerant traveller, nor is it somehow that of the 'innocent rural peasant'.[10] These bags betray an intention to settle, to put down roots: much of it appears capable only of making a one-way trip. Situated within the cultural history that surrounds the 'in between' journeys of these pioneering black settlers, the travel bag is not simply a marker of travel, it also carries with it the burden of dwelling. The bags are metonyms of the 'one major social problem' that the West Indian Settlers evoke in the *Picture Post* article: housing. Where will all these intimate, personal, possessions and belongings be unpacked, where will they be *housed*?

These issues are clearly at stake in figures 21, 22 and 23. Presenting the now well-known narrative of the housing problem in early postwar Britain, these images appear much more self-consciously staged than the railway station photographs, where many of the crowd appear unconscious of the photographer's presence. What they do provide however, is a particularly concentrated, *symbolic* narrative of the black settler's encounter with the white domestic threshold. Figure 18 unambiguously illuminates the 'problem' identified within the *Picture Post* article earlier. The cracking walls of the property's exterior, the basement setting (the stairwell's shadow falls diagonally across this scene) and, perhaps most of all, the sign pasted on the grubby doorway: 'Rooms to Let – No coloured Men', quote heavily from the racial imaginary of the black housing predicament in the 1950s. Within this context the black man's travelling bags are potent signifiers of homelessness. Suspended from his arms, there appears to be no place to put down these bags, no place to rest. Again though, the baggage is not simply a marker of restlessness and mobility, it also signposts a search for home, a dwelling place. Like the suitcases, boxes and bags of the station crowds earlier, these cases are less signs of a community *moving on,* than of a community *moving in*: next door, upstairs, along the corridor, down the street.

## Notes

1 The General Introduction to J. Procter (ed.) *Writing Black Britain: 1948–1998*, Manchester: Manchester University Press, 2000, lists some of the sites at which this important archive has been displayed. It also elaborates on the problems involved in privileging this event as a beginning, hence its appearance in inverted commas above.

2 Tilbury was where the *SS Empire Windrush* docked in 1948.

3 This nostalgic iconography is exemplified in the BBC's excellent *Windrush* website (www.bbc.co.uk/education/archive/windrush/). Here the *SS Empire Windrush* appears in various backdrops, notably in a sepia montage alongside profiles of pioneer settlers, a sunset and an ancient compass and helm. This faded, blurry image is presented upon a virtual boarding ticket that has been electronically aged and retouched in order to appear soiled and heavily crumpled.

4 Stuart Hall, 'Reconstruction work: images of post-war black settlement', *Ten 8*, 16 (1984), pp. 2–9.

5 'Stereoscopic' here refers to a dominant mode of seeing within diaspora texts. Rushdie refers to 'stereoscopic vision' as a 'double perspective' (*Imaginary Homelands*, London: Granta, 1991, p. 19). Alternatively, Paul Gilroy has foregrounded the importance of 'bifocal cultural forms' (p. 3) in his *The Black Atlantic: Modernity and Double Conscious*, London: Routledge, 1993.

6 *Picture Post*, 9 June 1956, p. 28. All further references are to·this issue and are included in the text.

7 This was underlined in an exhibition held at the Museum of London in May and June 1998: *Windrush – Sea Change*. One of the displays at the exhibition was a pile of old leather suitcases. If this exhibit signalled a travelling community on the one hand, then the battered old baggage also *memorialised* that community, highlighting the length of its stay.

8 Travelling bags constitute a repetitious referent within diaspora discourse. See, for example, the image of the travel bag in Salman Rushdie's highly influential migrant novel *Midnight's Children* (1981). At the start of that text Tai the boatman refers to Aadam Aziz's portable 'doctori attache' as a 'sister-sleeping pigskin bag from Abroad full of foreigners' (p. 20). Aadam, who has just returned from Europe, represents the opposite of Tai the local who has lived in the enclosed Kasmiri valley as long as anybody can remember. This bag opens up a series of travelling metaphors that are unpacked during the course of the novel. In contrast, the travel bags of the 'just-arrived' West Indians operate in the images above as markers of accommodation and settlement.

9 Caryl Phillips imagines houses as suitcases and suitcases as houses in his excellent novel set in this period: *The Final Passage* (1985).

10 As Hall argues, these 'are not country bumpkins' ('Reconstruction work', p. 4).

# Select bibliography

Anon. *Bradford Travel Manual – 1995*, Bradford: Economic Development Unit, 1994

Anon. Developing *Bradford's Tourist Industry*, Bradford: Economic Development Unit, 1994

Anon. *Here to Stay: Bradford's South Asian Communities*, Bradford: Bradford Heritage Recording Unit, 1994

Baker, H.A. Jr, Diawara, M. and Lindeborg, R.H. (eds) *Black British Cultural Studies: A Reader*, Chicago, University of Chicago Press, 1996

Ball, J. 'The semi-detached metropolis: Hanif Kureishi's London', *Ariel*, 27:4 (1996), pp. 7–27

Barker, M. *The New Racism*, London: Junction Books, 1981

Baucom, I. *Out of Place: Englishness, Empire and the Locations of Identity*, Princeton: Princeton University Press, 1999

Baugh, E. 'Friday in Crusoe's city: the question of language in two West Indian novels of exile', *ACLALS Bulletin*, Fifth Series, 3, in S. Nasta (ed.) *Critical Perspectives on Sam Selvon*, Washington, DC: Three Continents Press, 1988, pp. 240–9

Benjamin, W. *Charles Baudelaire: A Lyric Poet in the Era of High Capitalism*, translated by Harry Zohn, London, Verso, [1969] 1999

Bennett, L. *Jamaica Labrish*, Kingston: Sangsters, 1966

Bennett, T. 'Hegemony, ideology, pleasure: Blackpool', in T. Bennett *et al.* (eds) *Popular Culture and Social Relations*, Milton Keynes: Open University Press, 1986

Berry, J. *Bluefoot Traveller: An Anthology of West Indian Poets in Britain*, London: Limestone, 1976

Berry, J. *Fractured Circles*, London: New Beacon Books, 1979

Berry, J. *Lucy's Letters and Loving*, London: New Beacon Books 1982

Bhabha, H. 'The third space', in J. Rutherford (ed.) *Identity: Community, Culture, Difference*, London: Lawrence & Wishart, 1990

Bhabha, H. *The Location of Culture*, London: Routledge, 1994

Bhabha, H. 'Culture's in-between', in S. Hall and P. du Gay (eds) *Questions of Cultural Identity*, London: Sage Publications, 1996

Bhabha, H. 'The world and the home', in A. McClintock and E. Shohat (eds) *Dangerous Liaisons: Gender, Nation and Postcolonial Perspectives*, Minneapolis: University of Minnesota Press, 1997

Birbalsingh, F. 'Samuel Selvon and the West Indian literary renaissance', *Ariel*, 8:3, in S. Nasta (ed.) *Critical Perspectives on Sam Selvon*, Washington, DC: Three Continents Press, 1988.

Bird, J. *et al.* (eds) *Mapping the Futures*, London: Routledge, 1993

Boehmer, E. *Colonial and Postcolonial Literature: Migrant Metaphors*, Oxford: Oxford University Press, 1996

Brackwell, M. *England Is Mine: Pop Life in Albion from Wilde to Goldie*, London: HarperCollins, 1997

Brah, A. *Cartographies of Diaspora*, London: Routledge, 1996

Brathwaite, K. 'Sir Galahad and the islands', *Bim*, 25 (1957), pp. 8–16

Brathwaite, K. 'The new West Indian novelists – I', *Bim*, 8:31 (1960), pp. 199–210

Brathwaite, K. *History of the Voice*, London: New Beacon Books, 1984

Braziel, J. and Mannur, A. (eds), *Theorizing Diaspora*, Oxford: Blackwell Publishers, 2002

Brennan, T. 'Cosmopolitans and Celebrities', *Race & Class*, 31:1 (1989) pp. 1–19

Brennan, T. *Salman Rushdie and the Third World: Myths of a Nation*, London: Macmillan, 1989

Brennan, T. *At Home in the World: Cosmopolitanism Now*, Cambridge, Mass.: Harvard University Press, 1997

Bromley, R. *Narratives for a New Belonging: Diasporic Cultural Fictions*, Edinburgh: Edinburgh University Press, 2000

Carby, H. 'White woman listen! Black feminism and the boundaries of sisterhood', in Centre for Contemporary Cultural Studies (ed.) *The Empire Strikes Back: Race and Racism in 70s Britain*, London: Routledge, 1982, pp. 212–36

Carter, Paul. *Living in a New Country: History, Travelling and Language*, London: Faber & Faber, 1992

Centre for Contemporary Cultural Studies (ed.). *The Empire Strikes Back: Race and Racism in 70s Britain*, London: Routledge, 1982

Chatterjee, D. *et al. The Sun Rises in the North*, Huddersfield: Smith/Doorstep Books, 1991

Chatterjee, D. (ed.) *The Redback Anthology of British South Asian Poetry*, Bradford: Redback Press, 2000

Cheyette, B. '"Ineffable and usable": towards a diasporic British-Jewish writing', *Textual Practice*, 10:2 (1996), pp. 295–313

Chow, R. *Writing Diaspora: Tactics of Intervention in Contemporary Cultural Studies*, Bloomington: Indiana University Press, 1993

Clifford, J. 'Traveling cultures', in L. Grossberg, G. Nelson and R. Treicher (eds) *Cultural Studies*, New York: Routledge, 1992, pp. 96–116

Clifford, J. *Routes: Travel and Translation in the Late Twentieth Century*, Cambridge, Mass.: Harvard University Press, 1997

Clinton, T. *Laugh? I Nearly Went to Bradford*, Bradford: Bradford Library Services, 1991

Cohen, R. *Global Diasporas: An Introduction*, Seattle: University of Washington Press, 1997

Cohen, S. *Folk Devils and Moral Panic: The Creation of the Mods and the Rockers*, Suffolk: MacGibbon & Kee, 1972

Collins, M. *Rotten Pomerack*, London: Virago Press, 1992

Crawford, R. *Devolving English Literature*, Edinburgh: Edinburgh University Press, [1992] 2000

D'Aguiar, F. 'Against black British literature', in M. Butcher (ed.) *Tibisiri: Caribbean Writers and Critics*, Sydney: Dangeroo Press, 1989

D'Aguiar, F. *British Subjects*, Newcastle-upon-Tyne: Bloodaxe Books, 1993

Davies, C.B. *Black Women, Writing and Identity: Migrations of the Subject*, London: Routledge, 1994

Davies, H. (ed.) *The New London Spy: An Intimate Guide to the City's Pleasures*, London: Corgi Books, 1966

Davies, M. *City of Quartz: Excavating the Future of Los Angeles*, London: Verso, 1990

Deleuze, G. and Guattari, F., translated by B. Massumi. *A Thousand Plateaus: Capitalism and Schizophrenia*, London: The Athlone Press, 1988

Emecheta, B. *In the Ditch*, London: Allison and Busby, 1972

Emecheta, B. *Second Class Citizen*, London: Allison and Busby, 1976

Fabre, M. 'Samuel Selvon: interviews and conversations', in S. Nasta (ed.) *Critical Perspectives on Sam Selvon*, Washington, DC: Three Continents Press, 1988, pp. 64–76

Fishman, R. *Bourgeois Utopias: The Rise and Fall of Suburbia*, New York: Basil Books, 1987

Foucault, M. 'Of other spaces', *Diacritics* (1996), pp. 22–7.

Frith, S. 'Hearing secret harmonies', in C. MacCabe (ed.) *High Theory/Low Culture: Analysing Popular Television and Film*, Manchester: Manchester University Press, 1986

Frow, J. 'Literature as regime (meditations on an emergence)', in E. Beaumont Bissell (ed.) *The Question of Literature*, Manchester: Manchester University Press, 2001

Fryer, P. *Staying Power: The History of Black People in Britain*, London: Pluto Press, 1984

Fyfe, N. (ed.) *Images of the Street: Planning, Identity and Control in Public Space*, London, Routledge, 1998

Gilroy, P. 'Steppin' out of Babylon – race, class and autonomy', in Centre for Contemporary Cultural Studies (ed.) *The Empire Strikes Back*, London: Routledge, 1982

Gilroy, P. 'Police and thieves', in Centre for Contemporary Cultural Studies (ed.) *The Empire Strikes Back*, London: Routledge, 1982, pp. 143–82

Gilroy, P. *There Ain't no Black in the Union Jack: The Cultural Politics of Race and Nation*, London: Routledge, 1987

Gilroy, P. 'Nothing but sweat inside my hand: diaspora aesthetics and black arts in Britain', in *Black Film/British Cinema*, ICA Document 7, London: ICA, 1988, pp. 44–6

Gilroy, P. *Small Acts: Thoughts on the Politics of Black Cultures*, London: Serpent's Tail, 1993

Gilroy, P. 'Diaspora and the detours of identity', in K. Woodward (ed.) *Identity and Difference*, London: Sage Publications, 1997, pp. 301–43

Glass, R. *Newcomers: The West Indians in London*, London: Centre for Urban Studies and Allen & Unwin, 1960

Grewal, G., Kay, J., Landor, L., Lewis G. and Palmer, P. *Charting the Journey: Writings by Black and Third World Women*, London: Sheba Feminist Publishers, 1988

Griffiths, P. *A Question of Colour?*, London: Leslie Frewin, 1966

Gutzmore, C. 'Carnival, the state and the black masses in the United Kingdom' (1978), in W. James and C. Harris (eds) *Inside Babylon: The Caribbean Diaspora in Britain*, London: Verso, 1993, pp. 207–30

Hall, S. 'Lamming, Selvon and some trends in the West Indian Novel', *Bim*, 6:23 (1955), pp. 172–8

Hall, S. 'Racism and reaction', in *Five Views of Multi-cultural Britain*, London: Commission for Racial Equality, 1978

Hall, S. 'Reconstruction work: images of post-war black settlement', *Ten 8*, 16 (1984), pp. 106–13

Hall, S. 'Minimal selves', in *Identity: The Real Me*, ICA Document 6, London: ICA, 1986

Hall, S. 'Song of Handsworth praise', in *Black Film/British Cinema*, ICA Document 7, London: ICA, 1988, p. 17

Hall, S. 'New ethnicities', in *Black Film/British Cinema*, ICA Document 7, London: ICA, 1988

Hall, S. 'The local and the global: globalisation and ethnicity', in A.D. King (ed.) *Culture, Globalisation and the Third World System: Contemporary Conditions for the Representation of Identity*, Basingstoke: Macmillan, 1991, pp. 19–39

Hall, S. 'Old and new identities old and new ethnicities', in A.D. King (ed.), *Culture, Globalisation and the Third World System: Contemporary Conditions for the Representation of Identity*, Basingstoke: Macmillan, 1991, pp. 41–68

Hall, S. 'Cultural identity and diaspora', in P. Williams and L. Chrisman (eds) *Colonial Discourse and Post-colonial Theory: A Reader*, London: Harvester, 1994, pp. 392–403

Hall, S., Critcher, C., Jefferson, T., Clarke, J. and Roberts, B. *Policing the Crisis – Mugging, the State, and Law and Order*, London: Macmillan, 1978

Hallward, P. *Absolutely Postcolonial: Writing Between the Singular and the Specific*, Manchester: Manchester University Press, 2001

Hamilton, B. '*The Lonely Londoners*', *Bim*, 7:25 (1956), pp. 61–2

Harvey, D. *The Condition of Postmodernity: An Enquiry into the Origins of Cultural Change*, Oxford: Blackwell, 1990

Hebdige, D. *Subculture: The Meaning of Style*, London: Routledge, 1979

Hebdige, D. *Cut 'n' Mix: Culture, Identity and Caribbean Music*, London, Routledge, [1987] 1994

Helmreich, S. 'Kinship, nation, and Paul Gilroy's concept of diaspora', *Diaspora*, 2:2 (199s), pp. 243–50

Hewison, R. *The Heritage Industry*, London: Methuen, 1987

Hinds, D. *Journey to an Illusion: The West Indian in Britain*, London: Heinemann, 1966

Hooper, R. (ed.) *Colour in Britain*, London: British Broadcasting Corporation, 1965

Huxley, E. *Back Streets New Worlds*, London: Chatto, 1964

Islam, S.M. *The Map-makers of Spitalfields*, Leeds: Peepal Tree Press, 1997

Jacobs, J. *The Death and Life of Great American Cities*, London: Routledge, 1961

Jacobs, J. *Edge of Empire: Postcolonialism and the City*, London: Routledge, 1996

James, W. and Harris, C. (eds) *Inside Babylon: The Caribbean Diaspora in Britain*, London: Verso, 1993

Jameson, F. *Postmodernism, or The Cultural Logic of Late Capitalism*, Durham: Duke University Press, 1991

Johnson, L.K. *Dread Beat and Blood*, London: Bogle L'Ouverture, 1975

Johnson, L.K. *Inglan Is a Bitch*, London: Race Today Publications, 1980

Johnson, L.K. 'Interview: Linton Kwesi Johnson talks to Burt Caesar', *Critical Quarterly*, 38:4 (1996)

Kaplan, C., *Questions of Travel*, Durham: Duke University Press, 1996

Kay, J. *Other Lovers*, Newcastle-upon-Tyne: Bloodaxe Books, 1993

King, A.D. '"Excavating the multicultural suburb": hidden histories of the bungalow', in R. Silverstone (ed.) *Visions of Suburbia*, London: Routledge, 1997, pp. 55–85

Kinsman, P. 'Landscape, race and national identity', *Area*, 27:4 (1995), pp. 300–10

Krishnaswamy, R., 'Mythologies of migrancy: postcolonialism, postmodernism and the politics of (dis)location' *Ariel* 26:1 (1995)

Kureishi, H. *Sammy and Rosie Get Laid: The Script and the Diary*, London: Faber and Faber, 1988

Kureishi, H. *The Buddha of Suburbia*, London: Faber & Faber, 1990

Kureishi, H. *Outskirts and Other Plays*, London: Faber & Faber, 1992

Kureishi, H. *The Black Album*, London: Faber & Faber, 1995

Kureishi, H. *My Beautiful Laundrette and Other Writings*, London: Faber & Faber, 1996

Kureishi, H. *My Son the Fanatic*, London: BBC Films, 1999

Lamming, G. *The Emigrants*, London: Michael Joseph, 1954

Lamming, G. *The Pleasures of Exile*, London: Michael Joseph, 1960

Latif, T. *The Minister's Garden*, Todmorden: Arc Publications, 1996

Leech, K. *Brick Lane 1978*, Birmingham: AFFOR, 1980

Levy, A. *Every Light in the House Burnin'*, London: Headline Review Publishing, 1994

Lewis, P. *Islamic Britain: Religion, Politics and Identity among British Muslims*, London: I.B.Tauris, 1994

Looker, M. *Atlantic Passages: History, Community and Language in the Fiction of Sam Selvon*, New York: Peter Laing Publishing, 1996

MacDonald, I. 'The law student (extract from a novel in progress)', *Bim*, 9:34 (1962), pp. 119–32

McLeod, J. (ed.) special issue of *Kunapipi* on Postcolonial London, 21: 2 (1999)

Mehmood, T. *Hand on the Sun*, Harmondsworth: Penguin, 1993

Mercer, K. (ed.) *Black Film/British Cinema*, ICA Document 7, London: ICA, 1988

Mercer, K. *Welcome to the Jungle: New Positions in Black Cultural Studies*, London: Routledge, 1994

Mercer, K. and Julien, I. 'Introduction: de margin and de centre', *Screen*, 29:4 (1988). pp. 2–11

Miles, R. and Phizacklea, A. *White Man's Country*, London: Pluto Press, 1984

Mirza, H. *Black British Feminism: A Reader*, London: Routledge, 1997

Mishra, V. '(B)ordering Naipaul: indenture history and diaspora poetics', *Diaspora*, 5:2 (1996), 189–239

Mishra, V. 'The diasporic imaginary', *Textual Practice*, 10:3 (1996), pp. 421–47

Moore-Gilbert, B. *Hanif Kureishi*, Manchester: Manchester University Press, 2001

Morley, D. and Chen, H. *Stuart Hall: Critical Dialogues in Cultural Studies*, London: Routledge, 1996

Morley, D. and Robins, K. *British Cultural Studies*, Oxford: Oxford University Press, 2001

Morris, M. 'Interview with Linton Kwesi Johnson', *Jamaica Journal*, 20:1 (1989), pp. 17–26

Moughtin, C. *Urban Design: Street and Square*, Oxford: Architectural Press, 1992

Murphy, D. *Tales of Two Cities: Travel of Another Sort*, London: John Murray, 1987

Naipaul, V.S. *The Mimic Men*, London: André Deutsch, 1967

Naipaul, V.S. 'Without a place, Naipaul interviewed by Ian Hamilton', *Savacou*, 9:10 (1974), pp. 120–6

Naipaul, V.S. *The Enigma of Arrival*, London: Penguin, 1987

Nasta, S. (ed.) *Critical Perspectives on Sam Selvon*, Washington, DC: Three Continents Press, 1988

Nasta, S. and Rutherford, A. (eds) *Tiger's Triumph: Celebrating Sam Selvon*, Hebden Bridge: Dangeroo Press, 1995

Nasta, S. *Home Truths: Fictions of the South Asian Diaspora in Britain*, Basingstoke: Palgrave, 2002

Nazareth, P. 'Interview with Sam Selvon', *WLWE*, 18:2 (1979), in S. Nasta (ed.) *Critical Perspectives on Sam Selvon*, Washington, DC: Three Continents Press, 1988, pp. 74–94

Nazareth, P. 'The clown in the slave ship', *Caribbean Quarterly*, 23:2/3, in S. Nasta (ed.) *Critical Perspectives on Sam Selvon*, Washington, DC: Three Continents Press, 1988, pp. 234–9

Owusu, K. *The Struggle for the Black Arts in Britain*, London: Comedia, 1986

Paquet, S. *The Novels of George Lamming*, London: Heinemann, 1982

Patterson, S. *Dark Strangers: A Sociological Study of the Absorption of a Recent West Indian Group in Brixton, South London*, London: Tavistock Publications, 1963

Phillips, C. *The Final Passage*, London: Picador, 1985

Phillips, C. *A New World Order: Selected Essays*, London: Secker & Warburg, 2001

Phillips, M. and Phillips, T. (eds) *Windrush: The Irresistible Rise of Multi-racial Britain*, London: HarperCollins, 1998

Pilkington, E *Beyond the Mother Country: West Indians and Notting Hill White Riots*, London: I.B. Tauris, 1988

Pines, J. 'Representations of black Britishness', in D. Morley and K. Robins (eds) *British Cultural Studies: Geography, Nationality, Identity*, Oxford: Oxford University Press, 2001, pp. 57–66

Piper, K. *Step into the Arena: Notes on Black Masculinity and the Contest of Territory*, Rochdale: Rochdale Art Gallery, 1991

Powell, E. *Reflections: Selected Writings and Speeches by Enoch Powell*, edited by Rex Collins, London: Bellew Publishing, 1992

Priestley, J. *English Journey*, London: Heinemann, 1934

Prescod, M. *Land of Rope and Tory*, London: Akira Press, 1985

Procter, J. 'Descending the stairwell', *Kunapipi*, 20:1 (1998), pp. 21–31

Procter, J. *Writing Black Britain 1948–1998: An Interdisciplinary Anthology*, Manchester: Manchester University Press, 2000

Ramchand, K. 'The West Indies', *Journal of Commonwealth Literature*, 12:3 (1978) pp. 43–51

Ramchand, K. 'Songs of innocence, songs of experience: Samuel Selvon's *The Lonely Londoners* as a literary work', *WLWE*, 21:3 (1982), pp. 644–54

Ramchand, K. and Nasta, S. (eds) *Foreday Morning: Selected Prose 1946–1986*, Harlow: Longman, 1989

Richardson, C. *A Geography of Bradford*, Bradford: Bradford University Press, 1976

Richmond, A. *Colour Prejudice in Britain: A Study of West Indian Workers in Liverpool, 1941–1951*, London: Routledge, 1954

Rohlehr, G. 'The folk in Caribbean literature', *Tapia*, December 1972, in S. Nasta (ed.) *Critical Perspectives on Sam Selvon*, Washington, DC: Three Continents Press, 1988, pp. 29–43

Rojeck. C. and Urry, J (eds) *Touring Cultures: Transformations of Travel and Theory*, London: Routledge, 1997

Rose, E. *Colour and Citizenship: A Report on British Race Relations*, London: Oxford University Press, 1969

Rushdie, S. *The Satanic Verses*, London and New York: Viking, 1988

Rushdie, S. *Imaginary Homelands: Essays and Criticism 1981–1991*, London: Granta, 1991

Rushdie, S. *The Wizard of Oz*, London: BFI, 1992

Ruthven, M. *A Satanic Affair: Salman Rushdie and the Rage of Islam*, London: Chatto & Windus, 1990

Safran, W. 'Diasporas in modern societies: myths of homeland and return', *Diaspora*, spring 1991, pp. 83–99

Salkey, A. *Escape to an Autumn Pavement*, London: Hutchinson, 1960

Salkey, A. *The Adventures of Catullus Kelly*, London: Hutchinson, 1969

Samad, Y. 'Book burning and race relations: political mobilisation of Bradford Muslims', *New Community*, 18:4 (1992), pp. 507–19

Scarman, L. *The Scarman Report: The Brixton Disorders 10–12 April 1981*, Harmondsworth: Pelican Books, 1982

Schoene, B. 'Herald of hybridity: the emancipation of difference in Hanif Kureishi's *The Buddha of Suburbia*', *International Journal of Cultural Studies*, 1.1 (1998), pp. 109–27

Selvon, S. 'Finding Piccadilly Circus', *Guardian Weekly*, 1950, in *Foreday Morning: Selected Prose 1946–1986*, Harlow: Longman, 1989, pp. 123–6

Selvon, S. 'A leaf in the wind', *Bim*, 9:19 (1952), pp. 286–7

Selvon, S. *An Island Is a World*, London: Allan Wingate, 1955

Selvon, S. *The Lonely Londoners*, Harlow: Longman, 1956

Selvon, S. *Ways of Sunlight*, Harlow: Longman, 1957

Selvon, S. *The Housing Lark*, London: MacGibbon and Kee, 1965

Selvon, S. 'Little drops of water', *Bim*, 11:44 (1967), pp. 245–52

Selvon, S. 'A special preface by Moses Aloetta Esq.' (1991), in S. Nasta and A. Rutherford (eds.) *Tiger's Triumph: Celebrating Sam Selvon*, Hebden Bridge: Dangeroo Press, 1995

Sibley, D. *Geographies of Exclusion*, London: Routledge, 1995

Silverstone, R (ed.) *Visions of Suburbia*, London: Routledge, 1997

Sinfield, A. 'Diaspora and hybridity: queer identities and the ethnicity model', *Textual Practice*, 10:2 (1996), pp. 271–93

Singh, A. and Singh, R. *Twin Perspectives: Paintings by Amrit and Rabindra KD Kaur Singh*, Liverpool: Twin Studio, 1999

Singh, R. 'Destination Bradford: Bradford's South Asian community', *South Asian Research*, 7:1 (1987), pp. 13–24

Sivanandan, A. *A Different Hunger: Writings on Racism and Resistance*, London: Pluto, 1982

Smith, A. M. *New Right Discourse on Race and Sexuality: Britain 1968–1990*, Cambridge: Cambridge University Press, 1994

Smith, Z. *White Teeth*, London: Penguin, 2000

Spivak, G. 'Diasporas old and new: women in the transnational world', *Textual Practice*, 10:2 (1996), pp. 245–69

Stein, M. 'The black British *Bildungsroman* and the transformation of Britain: connectedness across difference', in B. Korte and K.P. Muller (eds) *Unity and Diversity Revisited? British Literature and Culture in the 1990s*, Tübingen: Günter Narr, 1998, pp. 89–105

Stratton, J. '(Dis)placing the Jews: historicizing the idea of diaspora', *Diaspora*, 6:3 (1997), pp. 301–31

Syal, M. *Anita and Me*, London: Flamingo, 1996

Taylor, T. *A Dream of England: Landscape, Photography and the Tourist's Imagination*, Manchester: Manchester University Press, 1994

Tester, K (ed.) *The Flâneur*, London: Routledge, 1994

Thieme, J. 'The world turn upside down: carnival patterns in *The Lonely Londoners*,

*Toronto South-Asian Review,* 5:1 (1986), pp. 191–204

Thompson, F.M.L. *The Rise of Suburbia,* Leicester: Leicester University Press, 1982

Tiffin, H. 'New concepts of person and place', in P. Nightingale (ed.) *A Sense of Place in the New Literatures in English,* St Lucia: University of Queensland Press, 1986

Tölölyan, K. 'The Nation-state and its others: in lieu of a preface', *Diaspora,* 1:1, spring 1991, pp. 3–8

Urry, J. *The Tourist Gaze: Leisure and Travel in Contemporary Societies,* London: Sage Publications, 1990

Walmsley, A. *The Caribbean Artists Movement, 1966–72: A Literary and Cultural History,* London: New Beacon Books, 1992

Wilson, A. *Finding a Voice: Asian Women in Britain,* London: Virago, 1978

Wright, P. *On Living in an Old Country: The National Past in Contemporary Britain,* London: Verso, 1985

# Index

Note: literary works can be found under authors' names; 'n' after a page reference indicates a note number on that page.

Baudelaire, Charles 76, 96
  see also flâneur
Baugh, Edward 46, 66n50
Bengali Housing Action Group 75
  see also housing
Benjamin, Walter 76, 96
  see also flâneur
Berry, James 31, 101–3
  Bluefoot Traveller 101
Bhabha, H. 2, 12, 18n35, 19n46, 34,
    36, 65n35, 126, 159n31
bildungsroman 126, 158n10
Birbalsingh, Frank 48, 66n57
black
  Audio Film Collective 7
    Handsworth Songs 7, 116
  British cultural studies 10
  conceptual history of 5–6
  destabilisation of 11
  discursive construction of 8–9
  Englishness 2
  essentialism 9, 69, 165
  masculinity 72–4
  popular culture 10
  Power 30, 72, 74, 84, 110, 114
Blackpool 4, 187, 191–4
Bloom, Valerie 95
Blunkett, D. 3, 16n8
Boyce Davis, Carol 18n36
Bradford 3, 4, 12, 16n8, 16n9, 17n15,
    125, 160–3, 167–81, 168,
    194–7

'Bradford 12' 12, 94, 162, 168
Brah, Avtar 12–14, 18n35, 19n45
Braithwaite, Edward 31
Brathwaite, Edward see Brathwaite,
    Kamau
Brathwaite, Kamau 47–9, 65n47, 93–4,
    97, 105
British Black Panthers 72
Brixton riots 78, 81, 91, 106
  see also London, Brixton
Bromley, Roger 124n110, 192, 193–4
Burnley 3, 167

Caribbean Artists Movement (CAM)
    87–8, 93–4
Caribbean Voices (BBC) 93
carnivalesque 191, 193–4
Chadha, G. 187
  Bend it Like Beckham 157n5
  Bhaji on the Beach 187, 191–4,
    200n51
Chaggar, Gurdip 87
Cheyette, B. 18n42
Clifford, J. 12, 19n48, 204
Clinton, Tom 169
commuting 15, 150–4
  see also suburbia
cosmopolitanism 4, 127–8, 129–34, 160
  see also diaspora
Crawford, Robert 2
Critchlow, Frank 82, 88
  see also Mangrove restaurant

Dathorne, O. R. 31
Davies, Hunter 96, 100
De Certeau, M. 76, 97
Deleuze, G. and Guattari, F. 13, 19n45
Derbyshire 182
devolution 2
Dhondy, Farrukh 17n15, 94, 95, 101,
     108–10, 114, 115, 117, 185
   'Iqbal Café' 110–12
diaspora 3, 12–15, 31, 34, 36, 204
   aesthetics of 12, 187
   diasporic vocabularies 4
   dwelling and 12–15
   etymology of 13
   Sikh and Zionist diasporas 15
   *see also* cosmopolitanism;
        travelling theories
*différance* 1
   *see also* black
dub poetry 94, 102, 103, 105
dwelling places 1, 21–68

Emecheta, Buchi 94, 119n9
Eros Statue 1
   *see also* London
ethnicity (white) 128, 147, 161
   *see also* new ethnicity

Fazakerley, G. R. 31
Fishman, Robert 126
*flâneur* 4, 96, 97, 99, 100, 102, 103
   *see also* pedestrian space
*Forward Youth* 92
Foucault, Michel 123n99, 204
Francis, Joshua 107
Frow, John 10

Gilbert, Bart-Moore 151, 159n27
Gilroy, Beryl 94
Gilroy, Paul 1, 2, 5, 6, 8, 10, 12, 27,
     16n10, 17n27, 81, 84, 91–4,
     111–12, 120n33, 125, 145,
     165–6, 172, 204
Glasgow (Sighthill) 3, 187, 189–90
Glass, Ruth 21, 22, 24, 28, 63n5
Green, Renée 34

Griffiths, Peter 25, 26
   *A Question of Colour?* 27
Gutzmore, Cecil 74, 75

Hall, Catherine 16n13
Hall, Stuart 1, 2, 5, 7–8, 10, 12, 47, 69,
     77, 81, 85
   'New Ethnicities' 7–9, 194
   *Policing the Crisis* 81
Handsworth 101, 120n33
   riots 91
Harris, Leroy 107
Hebdige, Dick 70
Hewison, Robert 170
Hinds, D. 21, 63n2
Honeyford, Ray 168
housing 206, 209
   shortages 4
   as site of contestation 75
   sou sou and pardner systems 30
   stairwells 33–6
   refurbishment of 145–9
   *see also* dwelling places
Huxley, Elspeth 28, 96
hybridity 12, 34, 35, 36, 126, 130

identity *see* black; new ethnicity
imagined community 6, 8, 11, 72, 109
Immigration Act (1962) 25;
        Immigration Act (1971) 172
Irish literature 2

Johnson, Linton Kwesi 17n15, 93, 95,
     101, 102–8, 109, 114, 155,
     157
   *Dread Beat and Blood* 106
   influences 105
Julien, I. 9, 17n26, 101, 156, 159n34

Kaplan, C. 18n34
Kay, Jackie 12, 166, 187
   'Sassenachs' 189–91
   *Trumpet* 200n47
Khan-Din, Ayub 166
   *East Is East* 166, 200n50
Khomeini, Ayatollah 168

King, Anthony 126
King, Martin Luther 94
Kitchener *see* Lord Kitchener
Kureishi, Hanif 4, 7, 11, 125, 127, 145,
    158n23, 160–2,
    *The Black Album* 16n9
    *The Buddha of Suburbia* 62, 126–9,
      134–7, 145–57
      and the narration of history
      156–7
    *My Son the Fanatic* 16n9

La Rose, John 93
Laird, Chris 88, 90, 118, 121n57
Lake District 4, 182
Lamming, George 11, 31, 46, 47, 48,
    54, 95, 97
    *The Emigrants* 31–45, 50, 58, 62
    *The Pleasures of Exile* 48–9, 97
Latif, Tariq 187–9, 200n48
Levy, Andrea 186
Lindo, George 95, 103, 104
Liverpool 23, 67n73, 133, 134
London
    Bayswater 54
    Brick Lane 75, 108–17
    Brixton 3, 23, 106, 107, 134
    Bromley 126–7, 147, 149, 155
    Hyde Park 60, 85
    Marble Arch 38, 57, 60
    Notting Hill 3, 72, 83, 84, 85, 86,
      87, 91, 101
    Orators' Corner 60
    Piccadilly Circus 1, 51, 98
    *see also under* Selvon, S.
    Trafalgar Square 56, 60, 99
    *see also* metropolitan
Lord Kitchener 21, 25, 63n1
Low, Gail 16n5

Mangrove (restaurant) 69, 82–8, 90,
    113, 118
Mehmood, Tariq 94, 101
Mercer, Kobena 6, 9, 12, 17n23, 17n26,
    18n35, 72, 92–3, 94, 95, 103,
    116, 129

metropolitan 1, 32, 44, 48, 49, 58, 81,
    127, 128, 160–1
    *see also* London
miscegenation 24, 25, 64n17, 81
Mishra, Vijay 15, 18n36
modernism 9, 10–11
modernity 13
Moughtin, C. 56, 91
Mutabaruka 105

Naipaul, Shiva 31
Naipaul, V.S. 4, 11, 31, 57, 97, 187
    *The Enigma of Arrival* 186
    *The Mimic Men* 31, 57
Nasta, S. 50, 66n50
nationality (politics of) 2, 15
Nationality Act (1948) 5, 22
Nationality Act (1981) 78
nation-state 15
Nazareth, P. 48
New Cross (fire/massacre) 75, 79, 91,
    95, 103
new ethnicity 136–7, 153, 164
nomadology 13
northern riots 16n8, 168
Northern Ireland 3
Notting Hill Carnival 69, 72, 74, 82,
    84, 85, 95, 102, 103
    riots 75, 88, 99

Okri, Ben 11
Oldham 3, 167
Oluwale, David 107
Onuora, Oku 105
Ove, Horace 90
    *Pressure* 92

para-site 14
Patterson, Sheila 23, 24, 25, 27, 28, 30,
    35
Peach, B. 75
pedestrian space 4, 46, 75–8, 85, 91,
    95, 101–3, 153
    rhetorics 4, 44, 46, 96, 100, 103, 118
performance poetry *see* dub poetry
Petithomme, M. 18n30

Pettinger, A. 16n6
Phillips, Caryl 4, 20n56, 184
*Picture Post* 23, 203, 205–7, 209
Pines, J. 5
Piper, Keith 72, 74, 90
Poe, Edgar Allen 96
Pollard, Ingrid 181–6
   *D-Max* 181
   'Pastoral interludes' 182–6
post-colonial 4, 31
   criticism 2
postmodernism 114, 179
Poulantzas, N. 81, 86
Powell, E. 25, 30, 36, 77, 94, 113
   and new racism 172
   and 'Rivers of blood' speech 25–6
Prescod, Marsha 95
Priestley, J. B. 174–5
protest poetry *see* dub poetry

queer 6, 7

*Race Today* 70, 84, 87, 109
Rachmanism 22
racism 6, 8, 25
   imperial racism 171
   new racism 171–2
Railton Road 75, 78, 79, 105–6, 108–9
Ramchand, K. 53
realism 9, 10–11, 92, 94, 103, 105, 109,
      106, 116
   and autobiography 94
Reggae 70–2, 105–6, 122n82
representation, 10–11, 88–96, 103–4,
      107, 109, 111–12, 113–17,
      135–7, 153–7
   access to 80, 110
   burden of 6–9
   as delegation/depiction 9
rhizome 13
Richmond, A. 23
*Riots and Rumours of Riots* 92
Rohlehr, G. 49
Rushdie, Salman 4, 7, 11, 20n54, 184
   *Midnight's Children* 210n8
   'Rushdie Affair' 4, 16n9, 168–9, 172

*The Satanic Verses* 11, 112–18, 155,
     162
*The Wizard of Oz* 117–18
Ruthven, Malise 162–3

Salkey, A. 93, 102
   *The Adventures of Catullus Kelly*
     99–100
   *Escape to an Autumn Pavement* 97–8
Sankofa 7
   *The Passion of Remembrance* 7
*Savacou* 87–8, 93
Scarman, Lord 79–81, 86, 90–2
Scots literature 2
Scotland 181, 187
Selvon, S. 11, 31, 32, 45–62, 96, 98–9,
     100, 102
   'Finding Piccadilly Circus 45, 50–1
   *The Lonely Londoners* 45–62
   *Moses Migrating* 45
   use of dialect 47
shebeen 27–30, 75, 88, 96, 108
Shields, Rob 97, 164, 170, 198n9
Sibley, David 127
Sighthill 3
Silverstone, Roger 126
Singh, Amrit and Rabindra 129–34
   'Indian Summer at Dhigpal Nivas'
     132
   'The Last Supper' 131
Smith, Anne Marie 172
Smith, Michael 105
Smith, Zadie 16n9
South Asian 6, 8, 10, 11, 30, 94, 112,
     114, 126
Southall 3, 75
Soyinka, W. 31, 70, 97
Spaghetti House seige 94
St Andrews 182
stop and search *see* sus laws
suburbia 3, 4, 125–8
sus laws 78, 82, 103, 122n82
Swanzy, H. 93
Syal, Meera 4, 11, 125
   *Anita and Me* 127
   and the narration of history 156–7

syncretism 12

Thatcher, Margaret 79
Thieme, John 50
Tiffin, Helen 31
transnationalism 3, 165
travelling theories 12–13

Urry, John 170, 174, 176

Vagrancy Act (1824) 78
Volosinov, V. N. 8

Wells, H. G. 151
*White Teeth* 16n9
Wiltshire 186
*Windrush* 88, 202, 210n3
    *Windrush–Sea Change* (1998)
Wright, Patrick 170

Zephaniah, Benjamin 95